I'm Still With You:

True Stories of Healing Grief Through

Spirit Communication

First published by O Books, 2008
O Books is an imprint of John Hunt Publishing
Ltd., The Bothy, Deershot Lodge, Park Lane,
Ropley, Hants, SO24 0BE, UK
office1@o-books.net
www.o-books.net

Distribution in:

UK and Europe
Orca Book Services
orders@orcabookservices.co.uk
Tel: 01202 665432 Fax: 01202 666219 Int. code
(44)

USA and Canada
NBN
custserv@nbnbooks.com
Tel: 1 800 462 6420 Fax: 1 800 338 4550

Australia and New Zealand
Brumby Books
sales@brumbybooks.com.au
Tel: 61 3 9761 5535 Fax: 61 3 9761 7095

Far East (offices in Singapore, Thailand, Hong
Kong, Taiwan)
Pansing Distribution Pte Ltd
kemal@pansing.com
Tel: 65 6319 9939 Fax: 65 6462 5761

South Africa
Alternative Books
altbook@peterhyde.co.za
Tel: 021 555 4027 Fax: 021 447 1430

Text copyright Carole J. Obley 2008

Design: Stuart Davies

ISBN: 978 1 84694 107 8

A CIP catalogue record for this book is available
from the British Library.

The transcripts in this book have been minimally
edited for space and clarity.

Printed by Chris Fowler International
www.chrisfowlerinternational.com

O Books operates a distinctive and ethical publishing philosophy in
all areas of its business, from its global network of authors to
production and worldwide distribution.
This book is produced on FSC certified stock, within ISO14001
standards. The printer plants sufficient trees each year through
the Woodland Trust to absorb the level of emitted carbon in
its production.

I'm Still With You:

True Stories of Healing Grief Through
Spirit Communication

Carole J. Obley

BOOKS

Winchester, UK
Washington, USA

CONTENTS

To Dad,
for teaching me the value of integrity and service to others;
and to my beloved Emma,
who taught me to never give up.

ACKNOWLEDGMENTS

The inspiration for and creation of this book came about from communication with souls - both on earth and in spirit –who have touched me very deeply. In recounting these stories with the hope of healing others, I express my heartfelt appreciation to those who have contributed their time, energy and support to the material presented.

Divine Spirit –I acknowledge your brilliant omnipresence in all that I am and do.

Clients who graciously and selflessly shared their stories, sessions and interviews – I pray that your sessions with me have helped, in some way, to ease the pain of your grief and open your mind further to the encompassing truth of the Eternal Spirit.

The souls in spirit who inspired your loved ones through me with evidential messages of your continued survival, offering hope and healing – may your immortal thoughts and words comfort and illuminate others in need of reassurance. The power of love heals all wounds.

My beloved spirit guides and teachers – I am grateful for your gentle wisdom, knowledge, patience and love as my abilities have unfolded. Through difficult times when I wanted to quit, you have never given up on me or on humanity. Together we will touch many.

Alice L. Teeters – your friendship, support and unconditional love are encouraging, priceless and irreplaceable.

My family and friends –I thank you for your dedicated support that has sustained me through challenges and helped shape my life into one of service.

Phil Harris of the Open Mind bookstore – I appreciate your long-time support of my work by sponsoring my message programs and workshops at your facility.

Carol Lee Espy, host of the *Life Lounge* program on KDKA radio, Pittsburgh – I offer a sincere thank-you for the many opportunities you've given me to present mediumship to the public and touch people in need through your enlightening show.

To all who have come for sessions, message programs and workshops – your presence and support mean more to me than you will ever know.

PREFACE

All eyes fixate on me as I stand before a gathering of nearly 300 people in a large conference room at an expo center. Most have come with a fragile heart, an open mind and, above all, a very personal agenda: to hear messages through me – a psychic medium – from their deceased loved ones. As always, I have faith that those in spirit will not disappoint and am confident that profound healing will occur in this very room before the afternoon is over. Silently, I scan the audience and am instantly drawn to a young woman sitting two rows back.

"A man about your age is near you in spirit," I say directly to her. "He is muscular with tattoos on his right arm, and is with a German shepherd. He tells me that you have this dog's food bowl and moved it recently from one place to another. Do you recognize him?"

"Yes, yes I do," the woman responds timidly, tears forming in her eyes. "He's my brother, Ron. That dog was his favorite, and I *did* move the dog's bowl last week."

"He talks about leaving life feeling very confused," I continue. "Ron says that you and your family felt like that, too. You have unanswered questions about his death. As I connect with him, I feel fuzziness in my head, as if he were on drugs. Does this make sense?"

"Yes, it does," she softly sobs. "He died from a heroin overdose. We didn't even know he was using drugs. My mother [pointing to the woman at her left] is devastated by his death, as am I. Does he have anything to say to us?"

I listen with my inner ear for a message. It comes.

"He's sorry for leaving you in the way he did. He gives me the feeling that you and he had words before his death and that you didn't have the chance to heal that. He wants you to forgive him for being so stubborn, as he often was. Again he says he's sorry."

Both women cry and hold hands. The power behind the words is so palpable it touches me as deeply as it does them. Yet I must detach emotionally and move onto other audience members who are awaiting a similarly intimate spiritual dialogue. My attention goes to a dark-haired woman in the back row. I address her by saying, "A woman with white hair and wire-rimmed glasses is coming through with the name of Helen. She died from heart problems. She wants you to know that the child who crossed over on your mother's side of the family is with your mother. Please tell this child's mother that she is safe and whole again."

"Oh, my God!" the woman gasps. "Our family was just talking about my sister's young daughter who died last year. My sister has been in so much grief since Carrie died from a brain tumor. I will definitely pass this message from our Gram along. Thank you so much!"

Spirit* moves me along to the middle section of the audience for another message. "Someone sitting in this area has had three passings, all male, all very close together and from the same cause: a sudden heart attack. The name Joseph is associated with you, as is the state of Ohio," I say to the entire section.

A middle-aged man raises his hand halfway and says nervously, "I think you might be talking to me. My father is Joseph and two of his brothers and my cousin died within the last year from heart attacks. I drove here today for your program from my hometown in Ohio."

The man reaches for a tablet on the floor to take notes. Confident I've reached the right person, I continue.

"Your father comes through and urges you to help his brother's wife who is in need of your support right now. Please tell her she will be fine and to go on with her life. Your uncle is at peace and still with her in spirit."

And so the afternoon goes, with messages of hope and healing coming through me to those who most need them. This is my work, my life, my calling.

What can we learn about life from understanding death? Are

---

* The words "Spirit" and "God" are used interchangeably and refer to the same universal Source of Oneness.

loved ones in spirit able to communicate with us? Is there really a place called heaven and if so, what is it like? How do we come to terms with the grief of losing a loved one? For most of my life I have been fascinated by these metaphysical questions. Never content with superficialities or pat answers, I have always strived to learn about other realms of consciousness. Perhaps you, too, have pondered what will happen when you die and the nature of the afterlife. Maybe you have had dreams of loved ones who have died or experienced unexplainable occurrences or puzzling synchronicities that seem to point to the reality of an existence beyond the physical one. Perhaps you are suffering from grief and are seeking to understand how to come to terms with the loss of someone you've loved. If so, you are not alone; many people seek to know what lies beyond the physicality of life.

For almost a decade, I've had the remarkable experience of communicating with many souls in the spirit world through doing readings in both private and group settings. The sessions I've written about in this book are representative of thousands I've done in which deceased loved ones communicate their continued existence after death, which has provided extraordinary healing for their surviving family members, spouses and friends. My hope in sharing these stories is that more light will be shed on the phenomenon of mediumship and its value in healing grief and transforming people spiritually. I am convinced that the more we know about the process of dying and the spirit world, the less fear we will harbor when we are confronted by death. I also include a chapter on after-death communications that are experienced without assistance from a medium, because many people in my private and group readings have discussed having them. I feel it is important for others who have had similar occurrences to understand that they are not alone in receiving these messages from heaven. Last, but certainly not least, I want to give hope and comfort to those in grief by offering practical tools that I frequently recommend to my clients and teach in workshops. Although I am not a grief therapist, I've found these suggestions to be of great benefit when faced with the loss of a loved one.

When I began to write this book, my main intent was to present spirit communication from a genuine standpoint that would touch readers' hearts and minds. I decided that the most effective way to do this was to show – through transcripts from actual readings and follow-up interviews – how ordinary people who were grieving over the loss of loved ones were positively transformed by hearing from them beyond the veil of death. I also wanted to help people understand the process of spirit communication, which has frequently been misunderstood and maligned, by demystifying and clarifying it through offering insights about how it operates from my perspective as a medium—and to impart to others what I have learned about death and the spirit world through my work. Interestingly, during the course of writing, I had three significant losses in my life: my closest friend's aunt, my dog, Emma and a dear client, Annie, whose story appears in Chapter Two. Perhaps I needed fresh, firsthand reminders about how painful grief is in order to identify more closely with the stories in this book. As is often the case, experience is the best teacher.

I've always believed that the greatest gift we can offer others is that of our own spiritual strength, which frequently comes through hard-earned life experiences. My sincere hope is that the stories in this book give you inspiration and peace of mind on your journey of healing.

C.J.O.

PART ONE
THE CIRCLE OF LIFE

CHAPTER ONE

FROM DARKNESS TO LIGHT:
MY JOURNEY HOME

The flower says, "Well, I must endure the presence of two or three caterpillars if I wish to become acquainted with the butterflies."
-Antoine de Saint-Exupery

From the time I was a very young child, I have incessantly asked the question "Why?" in a never-ending quest to discover what lies just beneath the surface of what can be revealed through my five physical senses. For many years, I've continuously and deter-minedly entertained an unquenchable thirst to explore the boundaries and confines of my rational mind. As I reflect on the pathway that has led me to unlock the mysteries of my own soul, I feel as if I have lived several lifetimes wrapped up in one. I yearn to explore everything from the inside out, and often in direct opposition to the status quo. At times, my zest to understand life from a deeper perspective has worked in my favor by presenting me with new avenues of growth that have been relatively pleasant and joyful. On other occasions, my innate curiosity has led me down pathways of immense physical and emotional pain, as you will see. Paradoxically, the inner strife I experienced contained the seeds for a new and better way to view and live life. That is the beauty of our suffering, our "dark night" – it allows us to commune more deeply and intimately with our soul.

It is my hope that in sharing my story of spiritual awakening that a spark of recognition is ignited within you so you remember who you are and why you are here as a spiritual being with a unique life purpose, despite the pain or confusion you experience.

Long ago, I heard a catchy slogan through twelve-step recovery meetings: "In order to keep it, you have to give it away." Whatever "it" is – hope, gratitude, laughter or love – it multiplies in our life when we share it with others. We need to know we are not alone in our journey of finding our way, our truth and our light through the darkness and oppression of grief, personal turmoil or any of life's challenges. Because we all share a bond as humans and most importantly as divine spirits, we receive insight, encouragement, and inspiration from listening to others' personal stories of their torments and triumphs.

Unlike many psychic mediums who have had paranormal experiences when they were children, I remained unaware of my abilities until I was in my late thirties. I was born into an upper middle class family in the late 50's. My father was a mechanical engineer and my mother, a part-time secretary and homemaker. My only sibling is a brother, three and one half years older. My early home life was stable and loving. Think of the Cleaver family on the *Leave it To Beaver* TV show (even though my mom never wore pearls while she was cooking!) and you've got the picture of my family. Despite growing up in this secure family environment, I felt like a loner much of the time. There were many other children in the neighborhood I lived in and I did mingle with them from time to time. But I often preferred the retreat of my small pink bedroom to the company of other children. There I could read, play with my numerous dolls and listen to music on my small portable record player. I fantasized about beautiful fairies visiting my back yard, leaving gifts of glittering gold jewelry and the most exquisite toys for me to play with. Even though I never actually saw them, I knew in my heart that they were real. In my mind, I imagined myself to be where they were – in a magical land that existed far beyond normal, bleak (to me) reality.

Frequently, I felt like a silent observer of life and the world around me and I always felt somehow *different* from others, especially my peers. For reasons unknown to me at the time, I felt isolated, confused and fearful of expressing my thoughts and emotions. Years later I discovered that these painful emotions originated from the manner in which I viewed life from past life experiences I had not healed. I was uneasy in social situations and therefore had only one close friend who was my next-door neighbor.

The day I entered first grade was traumatic for me because I did not want to leave the safe, familiar world of my childhood fantasies and especially the comforting presence of my mother. I suffered from separation anxiety as I clung to her hand, afraid to go inside the school building. Reluctantly I left her side and trudged up the stairs. The only consolation I had was the silent company of my favorite Barbie doll tucked away in my small red book bag. Little did I know later that day my teacher would take the doll from me and sternly announce, "We don't play with dolls in first grade!" When that happened I felt as if my last vestige of security had been stripped from me. Somehow I made it through that first day of school. I'm sure the knowledge that my mother was coming to pick me up at the end of the day instead of the school bus left me with some sort of security in knowing I would indeed return home.

One of my favorite things to do as a child was to stay with my grandparents on weekends. I loved all four of my grandparents and some of my fondest childhood memories are of spending time with them. I would often take long, leisurely walks with my father's mother, Gram. On one of these outings to a nearby bridge overlooking railroad tracks, Gram and I cut through a cemetery to reach the other side of the road. I was about ten years old. I remember walking through the cemetery, stopping to read the inscriptions on almost every tombstone as we passed. Some of the stones were quite old, dating back to the late 1800's. Others had photos of the deceased, which attracted me. Letting go of my grandmother's hand, I walked closer to study the photos and dates of each person's birth and death. I recall curiously wondering about what this individual must have been like. *Where did he grow up? What was his life like? How did he die? Where was he now? Did he know I was standing here looking at his grave?* Some of the engravings indicated that the deceased was a child at the time of death. This made me sad to think that someone would die so young. It seemed very unfair. *How could God allow such a thing to happen?*

Even then, I longed to know what happens when we pass over. *Do we go to heaven as I had been taught in Sunday school? Would we be reunited with our families after we passed? Do we play harps and sit on clouds with the angels like the TV shows I had seen?* Curious as I was about death and the afterlife, I harbored a fear surrounding the entire subject. I dreaded going to funeral homes when a family member died, often having nightmares after viewing the body. Alone in my room, I would sometimes sleep with the small bedside lamp on, too afraid to imagine what I might see if the room was completely dark.

Death wasn't the only thing I feared as a child. I was also anxious and uncertain about school most of the time. Even though I excelled academically throughout most of my school years, I seemed to always be filled with fear. Of what I was not sure, although social situations seemed to accentuate it. On Sundays, I attended a Protestant church with my family, going to Sunday school and sometimes the regular services. Even though I hated getting up early to attend, I really enjoyed Sunday school because I yearned to know more about God. I also wanted to know more about how to *respect* God since He seemed to be capable of inflicting all sorts of terrible things if He was displeased with humans. All of my young life, I held an image of Him as a tall man who lived in the sky with a long gray beard wearing a robe, holding lightning bolts. If he became angry with us, he could make us sick, take away our money or worse – make us die. After all, I kept hearing from others that such and such was God's "will."

Miss Johnson, my Sunday school teacher required us to memorize the books of the Bible in order, both Old and New Testament. I remember reciting them at home, knowing that we would be quizzed on them the following Sunday. We were also required to learn the 23rd psalm and the Lord's Prayer because we recited them each week before class began. I loved the 23rd psalm because it gave me a sense of security and peacefulness. Miss

Johnson was a schoolteacher during the week and ran her Sunday classes much like a regular schoolroom. We sat in rows and were strongly discouraged from engaging in chatter during class. She prepared us for confirmation, a serious commitment to church membership that entailed the adult responsibility of under-standing and serving God primarily from the knowledge given in the Bible and taught in the church.

During the years spent with Miss Johnson, I learned many things about the Bible, religious teachings, and the life of Jesus. I made new friends and attended the church social events that were offered. Yet I remember feeling lost, spiritually unfulfilled, and unable to really *feel* God. I thought I must have been missing something, especially since I tried so hard to connect with Him through the Bible and the church. It was as if I left God behind in the Sunday school classroom each week when I physically left the church building. At the same time, I was increasingly aware of feeling different and isolated from my school peers, no matter how hard I tried to fit in. I seemed to look at the world differently than they, even in the simplest of matters. Every question I asked about the lessons I was taught in Sunday school and the public school classroom prompted ten more questions in my mind. Fitting into established systems of thought or belief were the most difficult. *But why does it have to be that way?* I would ask, somehow knowing that no one could ever satisfy me with an answer, no matter how profound. Unwittingly and unconsciously, I was setting the stage for the journey towards knowing God through *my* own truth, however it may unfold.

During this time, I had an unquenchable thirst to investigate the paranormal—particularly ghosts and after-death phenomenon. UFOs intrigued me to the point that I read any book or watched any movie I could find on the subject. *The Twilight Zone* and *Star Trek* TV shows were favorites. No one else I knew in my small circle of friends seemed to share my fascination with the unexplained, which intensified my feelings of uniqueness and loneliness. I just couldn't relate to most people around me, despite my efforts. Music and books provided the much-needed solace I lacked from my social interactions. The singers of the top forty songs on the radio and the characters in my books seemed to know and understand my feelings. I longed to be anywhere but in the reality I was in. Everyday life bored me compared to the fascination I found in exploring other realms of existence. I craved the magical and the unusual in everything. I became even more determined to find it.

Feelings of Loneliness

By my teen years, the feelings of loneliness and separation were intertwined with intense feelings of low self-esteem. At the age of 15, I began to seek escape in recreational drug use. A boyfriend in high school introduced me to marijuana. It and I became best friends. Under the influence of the drug, I could reach and tune into the expanded states of consciousness that I had merely read about in books or imagined as a child. I believed smoking it gave me the insights I so craved, especially about what exists beyond the physical realm. It also enabled me to feel "cool" and part of the "in" crowd, which I desperately longed to be included in.

By this time, my taste in music had changed to include more rebellious musical groups that reflected my inner angst that I was convinced no one but I had ever felt. I became a "partier," seeking relief from feelings of alienation and low self-esteem in substances, people, and things, which offered me a temporary remedy from my everyday malaise. Yet I never felt so alone. I don't know how I managed to get inducted into my high school's honor society and became co-editor of the school newspaper. The latter I did with some reserve because of my inclination to want to go far beyond the basic facts that most journalism presents. Editorials were my favorite pieces to write because they allowed me to articulate a more personal perspective and to inject a little creativity into the process. They also gave me the opportunity to present new ideas and a fresh outlook on timely topics of interest to the student body. Privately, I harbored a strong desire to criticize the established rules and regulations of the school and society in general. I knew the sponsor of the paper would never tolerate this so I resigned myself to sticking to the mundane mainstream reporting of school events. If I had been more introspective and less self-pitying, I would have realized that writing offered me a productive outlet for my intrigue with extraordinary reality. Instead, I chose to continue on the pathway of comfortable confusion that I had become accustomed to.

Upon entering college, I made the decision to major in English. I had always loved to read and it seemed like a natural subject for me to pursue. I decided to take education classes so I could teach it. I changed my mind after having a discouraging experience student teaching at a local secondary school. The curriculum didn't incorporate enough room for creativity or personal expression. I felt hemmed in by others' expectations. Nonetheless, I decided to continue in English as my major.

Despite maintaining excellent grades, I had immense trouble in my personal life. It was not easy to make friends on campus, and it really didn't interest me much to join school organizations. I spent time in the record stores and pubs that served the student population. Just prior to high school graduation, I had discovered the warm, anesthetizing effects of alcohol and the long-sought feelings of self- worth and confidence it seemed to give me. In college, I attended many campus parties where I would seek refuge in this familiar comfort that drinking offered and in the company of the most "on the edge" and extreme people I could find. *They understand me*, I thought. All I wanted was someone to share my thoughts and feelings. That "someone" never appeared because I wasn't emotionally open enough to welcome anyone into my life. I began to blame others for my despair because I was unwilling to take an honest look at myself. I projected the burden of my feelings onto others in my life and the world in general. I wondered why life was so difficult, empty and unfulfilling. I was filled to the brim with self-pity.

Regardless of my personal turmoil, I graduated with honors. Although I had a degree in English, I had absolutely no idea what I was going to do with my life. This was mainly due to the fact that I remained oblivious to the spiritual purpose of my life. Over and over, I asked myself the same questions: *Why am I here? What do I have to offer the world? Where do I fit in?* I felt as if I was sleepwalking through life. It seemed as if everyone else had life figured out but me.

Age of Reckoning

After graduation, I continued to seek comfort in alcohol. At the age of 22, it was my constant companion, and I allowed my feelings of isolation to control my outlook on life. *No one understands me*, I would moan to anyone who would listen. I had few friends as I continued to wallow in feelings of self-pity and anger. Exactly who I was angry with I was not sure, but certainly it was somebody's fault that I felt alienated. My life felt meaningless and out of control. I had no conscious recognition of a spiritual awareness or identity. Instead, I sought to stretch every boundary I had grown up with, been taught about, or previously respected. I lost a lot of sleep, most of my self- respect, and all common sense. By the age of 25, I had hit bottom.

I realized I couldn't continue living the way I had and sought private therapy and attended 12-step programs. With the help of therapists and many others in recovery, I was able to stop drinking. Three to four times a week, I attended meetings where I heard others tell their personal recovery stories. Some of the stories were quite fascinating and I made many new supportive friends. But the most intriguing part for me was at the beginning of each meeting when the 12 steps were read. They seemed to call out to me and invite me to embark on the wondrous journey of under-standing myself for the first time. I began to diligently "work" the steps and speak at meetings – give "leads" in the lingo of 12-step language – about my life and the feelings that I tried to escape through drinking and using drugs. As I look back today on this period of my life, I realize with a definite sense of gratitude that I chose to discover my spiritual identity through the challenges that addiction and recovery offered. Truly, if I had not endured the pain of nearly losing myself completely in the quagmire of addictions and the unconditional love and support of the 12-step groups in recovery, I probably would not be serving Spirit through my work as a medium today.

I was well on the road to recovery when I landed my first job in years, a presser at a dry-cleaning plant. As part of my continuing recovery, I read and studied books about women's issues, self-empowerment and healing. I knew that I had to change from the inside out because what I was doing before in my life simply wasn't working. Period. Even though I had expressed my feelings and experiences at 12-step groups, I still desired to reach and explore deeper levels of my core identity (such as my awakening spiritual awareness,) with others who would recognize and validate my perceptions. I desperately needed to believe I had a purpose in life and was lovable, yet I didn't actually believe these things myself. I remember thinking that I wanted to be *someone*. I longed to fit in and be like everyone else in my life, yet I sensed that people would not accept me as I was. Or rather I *believed* they would not.

My Own Business
Over the course of ten years, I gradually developed greater self-esteem and a sense of personal power from attendance at recovery meetings, self-help books, and introspection. I read and studied metaphysical books to satisfy my hunger to learn about alternate concepts of reality. I noticed that my feelings of separation and isolation lessened in direct proportion to the amount of time I spent listening to and sharing with others of like-mind in recovery. I realized I was not alone and never had been. What I had felt and thought for many years was an illusion that I had allowed to nearly destroy me. My self-identity slowly evolved from being the loner who was emotionally unfulfilled to one who was connected to others and in control of life. This, I thought, was a miracle.

In my mid-thirties, I was offered the chance to own and operate a local laundromat and dry cleaning establishment, which had not done well under the previous owners in recent years. I had accumulated experience in the business of fabric care from working in several different positions in the dry cleaning plant. I jumped at the offer, mostly because I saw it as an opportunity to take charge of my own destiny. I was up for the challenge. Regardless of my emotional turmoil, I have always been true to the characteristics of my astrological sun sign of Capricorn, fiercely determined to succeed and largely perfectionistic. My own business would be the perfect outlet for my need to feel successful, in control, and financially secure. My business partner, Kathy, and I signed the lease for the building and began the job of cleaning the place.

Things went reasonably well for a year or so as Kathy and I rebuilt the business. The prior owners had allowed the place to sink into disarray and had employed less than reputable business practices. This was the reputation we had to overcome, which was no small feat. In addition to having the daily maintenance of the equipment and machinery we used for operation, we had all of the regular duties of attending to customers, pressing clothes, and running commercial laundry accounts. Most days I put in 12 hours, falling into bed exhausted each night. My social life was non-existent. A vacation was out of the question because of the constant attention required by the business. I had no real identity outside of the business and I felt spiritually disconnected. I *became* the business. I started to question whether this was what life was about – working, eating, and sleeping. As I calculated each day's monetary intake of the business, I silently set my expectations on the next day, hoping things would get better. They didn't. In fact, they got worse.

Kathy and I struggled to keep our heads above water with the many financial demands of building a business. The utility bills alone were staggering, as were the costs of rent and repairing the equipment. It was all we could do to make a small profit by the end of each month, despite both of us spending numerous hours working every day. We tried many avenues to manage financially, including cutting costs and taking on larger commercial accounts. It was still not enough to pull the business out of debt. At the age of 35, I once again grappled with feeling that life was essentially meaningless. I was merely existing, not living. I was working my life away, with very little to show for it. And then everything changed overnight with a phone call.

A Phone Call That Changed My Life

At about three years into running the business, I had grown accustomed to the routine of working 12-hour days. Sometimes I worked even longer, depending upon how quickly we finished the commercial accounts. We were still struggling financially and seriously considered taking out a business loan to repay some of the debt we had accumulated from the high utility bills. I was frustrated and disillusioned. I have always been a person with large reserves of determination. At this point, however, I found my fortitude was running precariously low.

One night in March of 1995 I came home from work, relaxed, and went to bed as usual. Around 4:00 a.m. I awoke to the sound of the telephone. A feeling of alarm went through me as I jolted out of bed and ran into the other room to answer it. On the other end was Rick, my business landlord. "Carole, you'd better come quickly. The building is on fire! The fire department is already down there. I'll see you there," he said and hung up. Shock waves pulsed through my mind and body as I threw on the nearest clothes and shoes I could find. I ran to my car and drove to the building, which was only two miles away.

I prayed that the damage would not be extensive. I must have thought of a dozen things at the same time that morning; it is amazing how many thoughts can bombard our consciousness in a few minutes in an emergency. I thought about the start-up money I borrowed from my brother and how I hadn't yet paid it back. I thought about the fish aquarium in the building and whether the fish would survive the fire. I silently calculated the amount of customers' clothing we had in the store. Most of all, I let my mind go back to the prior evening and particularly the condition of the building when I left it. *What had gone wrong? Did I forget to turn off something? Had a customer left a cigarette burning that had ignited the place? Why hadn't I checked everything more closely?* I felt guilty without even knowing the cause of the fire. Then I thought *it's probably just a little fire that started a short time ago and will be quickly put out.* My heart sank as I rounded the bend and saw the scene, which included about three fire trucks and two emergency vehicles, all actively engaged in extinguishing the fire.

It took about an hour to completely put out the flames. As I walked through the debris, it was hard to tell that it was the same neat, tidy place that I had spent many hours in each day. All but the equipment was a pile of rubble. The TV set was a melted ball of plastic. Most of the customer's clothing and the commercial accounts were extensively smoke and water damaged. There was no way we could remain open for business. It would take months to rebuild. I was devastated. In an attempt to retain our customers and the commercial accounts, we worked out of a nearby plant that graciously allowed us to temporarily use their facilities. Slowly we picked up the pieces. I felt angry, confused and totally defeated. Little did I realize at the time that I stood at a major crossroads in my life, one that led to the pathway of my life's true purpose.

Phoenix Rising From the Ashes

After the fire, it became apparent that Kathy and I had to decide whether to rebuild the business or move on. To complicate matters, there was a dispute concerning the cause of and the liability for the fire. We were able to settle the customers' claims for their damaged goods, but received little compensation for our lost wages. Additionally, I had been unable to repay my original start-up costs. It just did not seem feasible to rebuild. All things considered, we decided that it was time to move on.

For several months I wallowed in self-pity, feeling depressed and useless. I hadn't a clue as to which way to turn in my life or what type of employment to seek. Once again, life seemed meaningless and dull. Because I had worked so many hours in the business with practically no social life, I found myself without the support of friends in my time of crisis. I began to say vague prayers for guidance, not really expecting any answers, yet asking nonetheless. I went on a few job interviews. Still nothing happened. For six months, I wrestled with which direction my life should take. At one point I remember thinking angrily that I wish someone would assign me a job- any job- so I could cease struggling with the question of what to do with my life. I resigned myself to working on the commercial accounts from the now defunct business. I was unhappy, nearly broke, and – to borrow a phrase from 12-step programs – spiritually bankrupt.

One day, a friend I had not seen in quite some time called to see how I was doing. After pouring out my heart to her, she casually told me about a metaphysical healing center she'd recently visited in a nearby town. I asked her the name of it. "The Universal Life Healing Center," she replied. I listened with some interest as she described the center's Sunday services, healing sanctuary, and supportive fellowship. Then she invited me to come along the following Sunday. I took down the directions, all the while not really planning on attending. By next Sunday, however, I changed my mind and decided to give the center a try. What did I have to lose? Things could not possibly be worse in my life.

I found Universal Life intriguing. Started several years earlier by three female ministers, it was housed in a former Baptist church building. According to the statement of beliefs contained in the hymnal, it was founded to promote the concepts of universal brotherhood and healing. Classes on metaphysical topics, book study groups and private sessions for healing and spiritual readings were offered on a regular basis. There were about 25 members who attended weekly. Most of what I experienced that day during the hour long service was mysteriously familiar to me. Although I had always been interested in spiritual metaphysics, I had never taken the opportunity to take classes in it. The Sunday service consisted of a guided meditation, a presentation on the metaphysical meaning of healing, several songs with a universal spiritual theme, then a voluntary hands-on healing segment. Although I found the rest of the service appealing, I felt incredibly drawn to the healing part of the service. We were encouraged to go to the healer of our choice. I chose the minister who happened to be standing nearest to me.

During the five-minute healing, I felt indescribable warmth, tingling and most of all, love. After the healing, the minister said quietly, "In your heart chakra, I sense a beautiful red rose just about to bloom. It represents all the love you have inside to offer the world." Upon receiving this message, I felt more strongly connected to God than ever before. I began to sense a purpose for my life and a desire to find out what it was. When I sat down, I felt like a different person who was somehow fuller, happier, and loved unconditionally. I decided to stay for fellowship after the service.

The Acceleration of My Pathway

Soon after going to that first service, I began to attend the center regularly. One Sunday, I decided to nose around the center's library, which contained many books on metaphysical topics such as healing, reincarnation and karma, the chakras, and life after death. Each week, I checked out a few books and borrowed guided meditation tapes so that I could learn how to reach more expanded states of consciousness for healing. Perfectionist that I am, I felt that I was not "doing" meditation correctly. I even asked one of the ministers about what I was supposed to feel and see during meditation. She put her arm around my shoulders and quietly said with a smile, "Carole, it's not possible to fail meditation." Obviously I was unaware just how conditioned my left-brain thinking had become. Since those early days, it has become an inside joke at the center that if "Carole could open her right brain enough to become a healer and medium, anybody can!" Years later, I have come to appreciate the value of my rational side much more than before. In many ways, this logical side of me enables me to be a more effective teacher for people who take my psychic-intuitive development seminars. The best teachers serve by power of example.

During the first several years I attended the center, I was absolutely determined to learn everything I could about mediumship, the journey of the soul through eternity, and metaphysical healing. I longed to do something more meaningful than my current job of managing the commercial laundry accounts, but still wasn't sure what that might be. In an effort to find out, I took many classes that were offered at the center. I felt an increasing desire to facilitate the spiritual healing that took place in the center's healing sanctuary – the same type of healing I'd experienced during my first visit there. I had already taken the necessary training to become attuned to Reiki, a Japanese healing modality in which the healer channels universal life-force energy. I performed Reiki every chance I got, especially distance treatments, which involve the use of special symbols to focus the healing energy. But I didn't want to stop there. I wanted to be one of the healers who stood up front every Sunday, serving Spirit by being a healing channel. So, in the typically intense way that I approach life, I set my sights on training to begin my apprenticeship as a spiritual healer.

Magically, every time I set my intent on taking a class to intensify my training, the funds to do so suddenly appeared. Sometimes, it was amazing how quickly this happened. For example, when I made the decision to study Reiki, the money for the class was gifted to me within two days by my grandfather. When I later took intensive mediumship training at Delphi University in Atlanta, I was able to pay for the entire tuition from funds that were given to me from a friend. Many people who have come to me for readings have shared similar stories of how their finances miraculously supported their spiritual pathways. I firmly believe that when we meet with our divine purpose, the very sky will open up to help us move more quickly along the intended pathway for our soul's growth. This is what I call "divine acceleration," a phenomenon that we all can experience when we remove our personal resistances of doubt and fear and begin the healing process.

Two years after my initial visit to Universal Life, I was doing spiritual healing there on a regular basis in the healing sanctuary. I had completed all of the preliminary training and was now an apprentice to a more experienced healer. I loved doing the healings, which consisted of a 20-minute laying-on-of hands for people who came to the sanctuary. During this time my reluctance to do anything halfway reared its head again and I began to feel as if I was inept as a healer. Since spiritual healing is mostly an intuitive process, the healer often relies on spirit healers to give psychic impressions of the client's energy field. I felt as if I was not receiving detailed enough psychic impressions of the individual's energy field. On top of that, my healing spirit guides were not being clear enough with me about the placement of my hands. I felt as if I was not receiving these impressions at all. In frustration, I asked them why they were not giving me enough information. Their reply came through one of the other healers who told me to be patient and let the process develop naturally. My left-brain was once again working overtime; I persisted in doubting my intuitive ability. Finally one of the ministers told me in a curt tone to stop asking so many questions and simply trust the process. I tried to defend myself, although I was genuinely concerned that I would never be able to do this work that required me to give up so much control of my own thinking. I was wrong.

Delphi

Soon after beginning work in the healing sanctuary, I decided to further my spiritual training by attending intensive mediumship classes at Delphi University near Atlanta. All of the ministers at the center had attended and gave it favorable reviews. The classes for the first level in mediumship training lasted one week. I immediately made the decision to go because I had such a strong desire to develop and expand my abilities. My discovery of Delphi is a perfect example of synchronicity. Had I not been attending the center, I probably wouldn't have known about Delphi. I believe we are miraculously ushered to the people, places, and situations that help us to transform our lives according to our individual divine blueprint. When we act in complete faith that everything in our lives happens according to this plan, we orchestrate our lives with much less resistance than if we try to run the whole show with our egos as the conductors.

I left for Delphi six weeks after hearing about it. I had an uneasy but welcome feeling that my entire life was about to change. I shared a room in the campus housing with my friend Wendy whom I had met in Lilydale, New York, a spiritualist community where we had both taken classes. It was reassuring to know someone in a strange place. I hadn't been away from home for an extended period of time since college, and I could feel my anxiety begin to rise the minute the plane departed from Pittsburgh. In an undefined way, I felt as if I was leaving behind everything that was familiar to me. As the coming week would prove, indeed I was. I had no idea how transforming my experience at Delphi would be, although one thing was certain: I went with a compelling desire to stretch my personal boundaries to communicate more clearly and deeply with Spirit. My spiritual memory banks were about to be activated in a profound way. I knew this was something I *must* do.

The week consisted of intensive training in the recognition and development of mediumship skills. We began each morning with a group meditation, followed by breakfast. We then had morning and afternoon classes with lunch in between. After dinner, we finished the day with a three-hour evening class. Experiential in nature, the classes were designed to build trust in receiving and interpreting the inner voice of Spirit. We worked in small group settings, which allowed for individual attention. Many of the exercises were designed to break down self-imposed barriers that prevent us from connecting with the inner voice of the Divine. Tears of joy and relief welled up each time I felt an emotional breakthrough. At times, I became defensive and wanted to quit when a classmate "pushed my buttons." *I can do this,* I thought. *It's only a week.*

At mid-week, we were given half a day off to explore the beautiful mountain setting around the school. I gathered natural crystals from the wooded areas on the ground as souvenirs to share back home. As I walked, I thought about where my life was headed and why I felt so compelled to study spiritual mediumship and healing. *Have I done this before in a past-life? Is that why I'm so drawn to it?* I wondered why I felt inexplicably guided to follow this pathway beyond the familiarity of rational reasoning and break through the boundaries of fear that had kept me in place for so many years. I resolved to find the answers that would unlock the mystery of this calling.

That week, I became keenly aware of the presence of my spiritual guides and teachers. They gently introduced themselves to me in stages so I would not be startled by them. Earlier in the week our class meditated to connect with a guide who comes to us with unconditional love. During the experience, I sensed a beautiful, loving woman who handed me a large red heart. I was overwhelmed with peace and joy as she gently reached out her hand to welcome me home. She communicated to me that I needed to trust more and remove the shield in front of my heart to allow love to flow. Although I still don't know her name, I recognize her loving presence with me even now. Later in the week, we took what are called "trips" – one-on-one sessions with an instructor, that are designed to build trust in the process of intuitive development. This is where I met Ra, a magnificent lion animal guide. During the session, he revealed himself to me in my mind's eye by standing directly in front of me. At first I thought I was imagining him, because it seemed so improbable that I had a lion as a spiritual guide. My instructor encouraged me to trust what I saw. Since that first meeting, I have seen Ra many times, especially when I am in need of courage during challenging times. Other guides have introduced themselves to me over the last several years. One of these has been Rolf, my joy guide, whom I describe in Chapter Three. During dark periods of doubt and fear, I have found his presence to be comforting, reassuring and uplifting.

On the last day of class, each student was expected to give two mini-readings for volunteers who come to the school from neighboring areas. I was afraid of not being able to do the readings, but realized that I was once again allowing fear to control my thinking. It was a pattern that I desperately wished to release. By the time I was finally alone in a small reading room with two complete strangers, I was determined to prove to myself that I could apply all I'd learned that week, especially the need to trust in the validity of the information I received from Spirit. I decided to walk directly through the fear and summoned my spirit guides to help me. I greeted my first "client" nervously but cheerfully and began the reading.

To this day, I have no fixed ideas about how mediumship actually works. From the time I did that first formal reading, I have been astounded by the amount of accurate information, guidance and healing that Spirit imparts to others through me. The first person I ever read, an older woman with a friendly demeanor and a broad smile, confirmed almost everything I said. It was the most magnificent, exhilarating and magical feeling I have ever experienced in my life. Intuitively, I was given many specific details that I couldn't have logically known about this woman. The most baffling aspect of the whole thing was the experience of starting a sentence and somehow finishing it without any forethought on my part. This has happened to me many times since in readings, and it never ceases to amaze me. I begin to speak, not knowing exactly what I'm going to say and what comes out is invariably accurate and applies to the topic or person at hand. This is what is possible when we are able to release the judgment of our left or rational brain and go with the flow through our inner senses. Spirit is then able to speak to us through our intuition, which is a function of our right or feeling brain.

The best way I know how to describe the reception of this information is by using an analogy: Suppose that you are standing in front of a painting covered with a dark cloth that you have never viewed before. Imagine that someone removes the cloth, as you continue to stand in front of the painting. What is your "gut" response to the painting? What feelings does it evoke in you? What is your overall impression of it? Does it elicit memories of your life? The sensations and thoughts that I receive in a reading come through in much the same way as the experience of viewing the painting for the first time. The impressions I receive are interpretations of clients' or spirit loved ones' energetic "canvas" as they are revealed to me through attunement to their soul. I will discuss this process more fully in Chapter Two.

The last night at Delphi was one of pure elation and joy. I felt a great sense of accomplishment and a renewed sense of connection with my purpose. Most of all, I felt fully *alive* as if I belonged with the family of humanity, possibly for the first time in my life. Feelings of alienation had evaporated from the warmth of the new light that filtered through my previously closed and dark being. I packed my bags, said goodbye to Wendy and flew home. A new day was dawning.

Getting Out There

Upon my return from Delphi, I posted a sign-up sheet for readings at Universal Life. More than ten people immediately signed up. At graduation, the instructors told us we needed to give five readings at home in order to receive our certificate of mediumship. I ended up doing 15 readings. I sent in the forms and received an official gold seal for my graduation certificate from Delphi.

As I continued to do readings, I began to feel an incredible sense of unconditional love and peace. I felt more aware, alive, strong, and connected to life. There was definitely more going on here than met the eye; I still had no idea where I was going with all of this newfound awareness. I loved being in the space between the physical and spirit worlds, acting as a translator and mirror for clients and their loved ones in spirit. I began to get a good reputation for being accurate. People started to come to me by personal reference. The depth and scope of the readings continued to expand. Up until this time, I had not charged money for my readings because I felt they were still part of my apprenticeship. However, I soon discovered that some people attach little value to free services. I felt emotionally drained and questioned whether I needed to seek a steady job that offered the certainty of a regular paycheck. I asked my guides for help.

Soon after, I was offered an opportunity to read professionally at a metaphysical bookstore in Pittsburgh. Although I jumped at the chance, I still had doubts about my abilities. *What if I was wrong about some of the information I gave people? What if I unintentionally hurt someone by giving incorrect guidance?* Perhaps I had just been lucky up until now and the people I had read for were just being kind in verifying the information I had imparted. Again fear began to eat away at me.

Today, as I look back on these and other feelings of doubt I had, I am grateful to have experienced them. They have enabled me to get in touch with the lack of trust many people feel when they begin to open their intuitive senses. I completely understand the sense of disbelief many of my students of psychic development experience when they begin to receive their initial intuitive impressions during the developmental exercises we do in class. As one who has walked the path, I try to allay their misgivings with reassurance and loving support that is so necessary to validate the inner voice of intuition. I have found that without trust, it is nearly impossible to learn to do mediumship. When I was starting out, I put undue emphasis on attempting to prove the accuracy of my readings. I now know that any information that I receive, no matter how insignificant it seems to me, is meaningful in some way to clients. Even though they may not be able to validate it at the time, I often receive confirmation of the information's accuracy from them later. After countless readings, I've learned to trust that there are no accidents as far as what comes through.

I began to read at the bookstore one day a week and kept two other part-time jobs to pay the bills. I wasn't able to trust *that* much! But before long I had weekly appointments at the store – sometimes as many as four readings in one afternoon. Despite my doubts about attracting clientele, Spirit was certainly providing. Each reading I did provided me with a renewed sense of confidence in my abilities and enabled me to open to a deeper level of trust. When I received feedback from clients on the positive effects of the experience, I felt incredible satisfaction that I helped someone grow spiritually. I hoped to make mediumship my full time profession.

A few months later, I returned to Delphi to take further training in mediumship and spiritual healing. After completion of all of these classes, I became ordained as a metaphysical minister, a step that was beneficial in starting my own practice of counseling and healing. The second trip to Delphi was not as pleasurable as the first; I was sick the entire time with the flu and was barely able to attend all of the classes on past life regression, hypnosis, and healing modalities. Determined to make it through the curriculum, I forced myself to go to all but one of the classes. During that time, I recognized that being ill was due to two inter-related causes: fear of going to a deeper level of commitment with my work and to getting in touch with a past life experience in an Egyptian prison that had adversely influenced me for lifetimes. I had been a prophet who was unjustly persecuted for empowering others with spiritual information. I intuitively realized that this unhealed experience was one of the root causes of the feelings of isolation and sadness I had felt most of my life. This awareness enabled me to begin to heal by peeling away more layers of fear.

About 18 months after becoming certified, I was offered an opportunity to give readings on a local radio station with a huge listening audience. It was near Halloween when all mediums become more in demand. The show aired very early in the morning and I had to drive to the station at 4:00a.m. The night before, I was extremely nervous about what questions I would be asked by the DJs and what would happen during the readings. I had done phone sessions for clients and found that the voice vibration of the individual on the other end transmitted a wealth of information. I could read just as clearly over the phone as in person; it seemed to make no difference. Yet I was concerned about doing this on the radio, with thousands of people listening. The head DJ assured me that he and his partner would not judge what I did. That put my mind at ease, although I was still unsure about what was going to happen on the phone lines.

The show went well, actually better than I expected. I was connected with three callers, interviewed between calls, and was out of the station before I knew it. Friends had taped the show for me and applauded me when I walked into the house. The most powerful reading I did that day was one in which a woman desired to hear from her grandmother in spirit who came through very clearly, announcing (for validation) that her birthday had just passed and that she was trying to help family members resolve a dispute over money. The call ended on a positive note with me relaying the message that a lot of heart energy and unselfishness was needed to resolve this situation. I was pleased to deliver such confirmation from the world of spirit to help someone. I was also happy that I had conquered new territory, breaking through my fear of going in the public eye with my mediumship. I would continue to shatter more previously held self-limitations in the coming year.

The Media

Soon after, I was offered the chance to do more local radio and TV shows. The segments usually consisted of a short introduction by the host, a brief interview on mediumship and psychic phenomena, followed by on-air readings. Every time I was on a show, I felt entirely blessed to be doing the work publicly, but also quite relieved when it was over. I discovered that media appearances can be incredibly pressure-filled experiences. I liked the spontaneity of not knowing what callers were going to ask, but I was intensely aware of being scrutinized by the radio DJs and the public. In all fairness, not a single soul was unkind or disrespectful to me; it was merely my fear of ridicule and exposure that was causing my unease. Over time, I came to a deep realization that this mindset needed to be released. How could I expect others to value and take the work seriously if I played host to so much fear?

Today I am entirely comfortable with being in the media and I welcome each appearance as an opportunity to share my work with those who need the healing it brings. I love the challenge of doing on-air readings that require me to tune in very quickly to callers because they give me the chance to hone my skills. Each time I've been on a radio show, I am uncomfortably aware of the large number of people who are suffering from unresolved emotional pain or grief due to life circumstances. At first, I carried this awareness as a heavy burden because I knew I could not possibly help each person in need on an individual basis. I relinquished this feeling when I realized that the best way to help many people at one time is through sharing my work through writing books.

From the time I began professional mediumship work, I have sought to establish and maintain honesty and integrity within its scope. The true groundbreakers in modern mediumship – John Edward, James Van Praagh, Rosemary Altea, George Anderson and others – have succeeded in presenting the concept of spirit communication in a genuine light to the masses through mainstream media and books. Because of their efforts, public opinion of mediumship has changed dramatically and favorably in the past decade. In addition, the media and their financial sponsors must be credited with lending their vehicles and support to bring mediumship to the attention of the public. As a result, more people today are shifting their beliefs to include the possi-bility of non-physical communication with not only departed loved ones, but spirit guides and angels as well. I believe those of us who are called to do this work must lend our voices and talents to sustain even more credibility to the reality of mediumship and its undisputed value in creating healing for those who seek it.

I am grateful for the experiences I have in the media because I consider it a privilege to reach people I normally couldn't without its benefit. When I think about the experiences I have had in demonstrating the reality of spirit communication and other metaphysical topics through the media, I am profoundly aware that we, in our current consciousness, have touched only the tip of the iceberg, so to speak. There is so much yet to discover that will benefit the spiritual evolution of our planet.

Your Journey Out of Darkness

I am sharing my story with you with the intent of illustrating how you, like me, can overcome any pain or trauma in life, heal and transform from the darkness of grief and in the process, connect more fully with your purpose in life. You may not yet be consciously aware of how this will happen for you or the exact pathway that leads to your healing, yet you are most assuredly doing it when you ask to see the light, the way, in your darkness. The smallest particle of light diminishes the blanket of darkness it infiltrates. In reading the narration and stories in this book, you will realize that hope, healing and love exist beyond life's challenges and hardships. During the toughest times of our lives, if we have the mere willingness to ask for healing, we are somehow miraculously led back onto the pathway that is our unique divine blueprint, contained within the overall cosmic scheme. Our intuition, the voice of the Divine within us, is our internal navigation system that guides us along the way. That is why trust in our own intuition is indispensable in the course of our life's journey. My experiences have shown me that in sharing these intuitive experiences with others, we recognize and validate the light of God within them, which in turn, intensifies and magnifies our own.

At various times in my life, I take the opportunity to rigorously examine what spiritual wisdom I can gather from my life experiences. I ponder choices I've made and their implications for my growth. If given the chance to change or erase the painful and difficult pathway I've chosen in the past, I would undoubtedly decline because each step has brought me into full and perfect alignment with where I am today as an instrument for Spirit. My personal journey is invaluable since it has gifted me with a heightened sensitivity to help others on their pathways and serve as an example of spiritual transformation. Simply stated, what were once weaknesses are now strengths. I've come to understand that contained within each moment is the decision we have, as divine beings with free will, to either live in love or fall into the trappings of fear. In reflection, each time I've made a choice from the standpoint of love and with the service of others in mind, it has undeniably connected me more completely with my life purpose.

As you reach beyond life's disappointments, hardships and pain by reconnecting with the source of spiritual strength that lies within you, you spiral closer to the true nature of who you really are – the expression of Spirit in the physical plane. Your healing begins in this moment.

CHAPTER TWO

IN THE MIND OF THE MEDIUM

From delusion lead me to truth.
From darkness lead me to light.
From death lead me to eternal life.
-Hindu prayer from the Sanskrit Universal Prayer

The loud knock on my front door startled me as I swallowed the last bites of my lunch. My first client for the day, Annie*, an attractive woman in her mid-thirties with long, brown hair, had arrived early for her appointment. She promptly stepped into my dining room and extended her hand to greet me.

"I've never done this sort of thing before," she announced nervously, as if making a confession. "I'm a little scared."

Over the years, I've gotten used to people being on edge when they come to work with me. Despite my assurance to them that my work is healing-based and not scary, people are not quite sure what to expect during a first-time session with a psychic medium. Nor are they prepared to see a normal looking woman (without a gypsy costume and crystal ball) answer the door when they arrive. Except for a few genuine portrayals of mediumship on TV like John Edward's *Crossing Over,* most people know little about how spirit communication actually works. Part of my job, in addition to reuniting people with their loved ones, is to educate them about how mediumship operates, heals grief and dispels the fear of death. In a nutshell, I instruct them on how to receive their loved ones' messages so they can benefit from the session.

I made a quick assessment of Annie's demeanor. She seemed anxious for the session to begin yet politely reserved in her attitude

---

*All client names in this book have been changed.

towards me. People in grief often wall themselves off emotionally for self-protection. I realized I might have to do some preliminary work to help her relax so the spirit world could come through in the session. Good readings depend partly on the emotional openness of clients, since they are an indispensable part of the communication process. Spirit beings want to be heard but can't get through strongly enough if we're carrying heavy emotions, such as anger or extreme sadness, that block our awareness of their messages.

After I ushered Annie into my reading room, I asked her to take several deep breaths and relax by focusing for a few minutes on her breath. I explained that the spirit world communicates with me by impressing their thoughts and feelings on my mind – a form of mental telepathy – then I interpret what I am sensing for the client (also called the sitter.) I told her that the process of mediumship is not perfect; sometimes, there are misinterpretations on the part of the medium whose frame of reference and life experiences are used by the communicating spirit. I advised her to be open to everything that was said, even if it didn't make immediate sense. Since the reading would be taped, she could listen to it later and validate things she initially missed.

Unlike most of the sessions I do, I knew who Annie wanted to hear from in spirit. Several weeks earlier, when she called for her appointment, she told me that someone had referred her to me and (before I could stop her) that she wanted to make contact with her recently deceased husband. As a rule, I want to know as little as possible about clients—in particular, *who* they want to connect with in spirit. Seldom do I know their last names. With no prior knowledge, I can come from a pure space and the integrity of the spirit communication process is preserved. In Annie's case, it was too late; she had already revealed what she wanted.

"I can't guarantee your husband will come through," I told her before starting the session. "Those in spirit have free will, just as we do, and they can choose to communicate or not. I can't make them come through."

Annie nodded silently and her agitation subsided as she settled into the comfortable rocking chair in front of me. I took a deep breath and rubbed my hands together before holding Annie's hands to recite the prayer that I use to begin every session. In my legs and around my head, I could feel energy from the spirit world start to flow as I focused on whom and what I perceived around Annie with my inner senses. After a minute or so, I was strongly impressed with the presence of a man in spirit directly to Annie's right side. I knew he must be from Annie's generation, since I always ask spirit beings to "come in" and appear in the appropriate place according to their relationship to the sitter. I adopted this system of identification years earlier to help with the recognition of those in spirit. In this case, I knew he was around her age since he stood next to her.

"A man has stepped in from spirit and stands right beside you," I began. "Since he is right next to you, he must be around your same age. He says his name is Jim. Does that make sense to you?" I asked.

Annie's eyes grew big, as she leaned forward in her chair and excitedly said, "Yes, yes, that's him! That's my husband! I can't believe you said his name!"

"He's describing how he died," I continued. "It was very sudden and unexpected. When I connect with Jim, I feel as if I lost consciousness very quickly and I exited my body in a hurry. He's not telling me the exact cause of his death, just that it was very quick."

Annie began to cry softly. "Yes, he died very suddenly," she confirmed in a whispered voice. "It was a massive heart attack and I was the one who found him. Thank God that Amie, my five-year-old daughter, wasn't home at the time. I didn't want her to see him like that."

In no uncertain terms, Jim began to impress me with thoughts about his life on earth. My link with him was strong and palpable. He communicated his love of family, friends and even the specific type of music he listened to. He was an effective communicator, unlike some spirits who don't understand how to reach my mind. It was clear to me that it was easy for him to come through because he was connected to his wife by a deep love that had assuredly survived death. In many readings I've done, this heart bond strengthens the communication process and brings healing to those in grief.

"He says he liked country rock music and especially the Charlie Daniels Band. You have some of his CDs and were thinking of giving them to a few of his close friends as a keepsake the other day. He is saying the name Denny and somehow there is a connection to the police force with his friends."

In my mind's eye, Jim showed me a large group of people who came to his funeral. "He says to say hello to all of the people who knew him and came to his funeral."

"Yes, yes! Jim loved country music and Denny is a friend of his on the police force. Many friends came to his funeral." Astonished by the specificity of the information, Annie moved to the edge of her seat as the reading continued.

I became aware of Jim's surroundings in the spirit world. He appeared to be in a large, peaceful field near a wooded area.

"He is standing in an outdoor area that is very serene. It gives me the feeling that he loved nature and it was very important to him to be outdoors a lot. He wants you to know that's where he is in spirit," I said.

"He loved to be outside," Annie answered, her voice cracking with emotion. "He had a really strong bond with trees and animals."

I sensed a picture in my mind of carvings with a heart surrounding them that looked like initials in a tree.

"I'm not sure what this means," I said, "but did he carve both of your initials in a tree near your house? He also shows me rabbits in your backyard that are near this tree."

Without hesitating, Annie replied, "Yes, he did carve our initials in the tree in our backyard many years ago. He always said we were soul mates and were meant for each other ever since we started going together in high school. And the rabbits, well, I see them all the time in our yard and just today one came all the way up to the back door."

Another impression was forming in my mind, this time of a cassette tape being rewound and then played. Although unclear (as many impressions are during a reading), I tried to put into words what I was seeing. I knew it could be an important evidential piece of information—those seemingly inconsequential spirit messages that turn into irrefutable proof of life after death. Since I consider myself to be an evidential medium, I constantly ask the spirit world to communicate these bits of information for their loved ones during readings.

"He shows me a cassette tape, one that is being rewound and played. Is this something you've done recently or did he give you one before he passed?"

Annie thought for a moment. Suddenly, she gasped, "Oh, my! Yes! Just last week, I had to run to the store. When I got into my car, I decided to listen to some music. I turned on the radio but nothing was on that I liked, so I pushed in a cassette tape I hadn't listened to in months. I tried to rewind it a few times, but it would only go so far and then begin to play. Well, the song it kept stopping at was Jim's and my favorite song. I didn't want to listen to it because I didn't want to become upset. I've been in such pain since he died. I tried again to fast-forward the tape and when it came back on it was in exactly the same place, playing our song— the one we had danced to for years. That time I listened. Wow! It really *was* Jim trying to tell me he's still around!"

I was pleased that Annie was receiving the confirmation she so desperately needed that her husband was still very much alive in spirit. During the reading, her mood shifted considerably. Even though I've done thousands of readings, I never lose my sense of joy and wonder when spirit beings communicate specific information that brings healing and comfort to their loved ones. To be a part of someone's healing journey brings me deep satisfaction and makes my work worthwhile.

At this point, I could feel Jim begin to withdraw from the session. The communication began to ebb. It requires much energy for those in spirit to communicate to a medium because they must lower their thought vibration to reach mine. At the same time, I have to maintain my focus to sustain the connection for any length of time. If either of us loses the link, the communication becomes weak.

"He's pulling back, Annie, but he leaves me with the distinct impression that he wants you to know he's always with you. Oh, and he says to not speak of him as if he were dead, because he's not. He says his life is a bit different than what he experienced on earth but he's still very much alive in spirit. He stresses that he wants you to carry on and live your life happily."

Annie lowered her head as her eyes filled with tears.

"I have not wanted to go on without him," she said. "My life has been turned upside down since Jim died. We were so close and his death was such a terrible shock for Amie and me, especially since he was so young. He understood me like no one else. Until today, I couldn't bear the thought of living without him. Nothing's the same since he died. I lost my soul mate and best friend. Truthfully, I guess I worried more about him than myself, where he was and how he was doing after his passing. Do you think I'll be with him again when I cross over?"

I assured her that Jim was fine where he was in the spirit world and repeated the message he had communicated to her in the reading.

"Remember that he wants you and Amie to continue with your lives. You have work here on earth to finish. It's not yet your time to return to spirit. He'll be with you, giving you signs of his presence like the cassette tape incident. It's important that you take care of yourself and Amie."

Annie seemed receptive to this advice. "Yes, I know that is what I need to do now. I feel so much better knowing he's still with me and watching over us. I can't thank you enough. I am blown away by how clearly Jim came through in the reading. There's no way you could have known any of the stuff that came through."

I advised her to do positive things each day to nurture herself and her daughter while they worked through their grief. On her way out of the reading room, still caught up in the excitement of the session, Annie mistakenly opened the closet door, right next to the exit door into the hallway.

"See how blown away I am?" she laughed. "I can't even find the door!"

I followed her to the front door and hugged her goodbye. Turning to me, she said, "How soon before I can come back to see you again?"

"You need to work through your grief some more. Give the reading some time to settle," I answered. "You know, you can communicate with Jim on your own. Just think of him and send him love. He'll feel it and come through to you. It's not good to become dependent on a medium or anyone else, for that matter. And look into getting some grief counseling when it feels right," I suggested.

I couldn't help but notice how much Annie's mood had changed in less than an hour. While outwardly excited, she seemed internally calm. As she opened the door to leave, she turned to me and said, "You know, I never believed in this kind of stuff at all. A year ago, I would have never been open to the idea of seeing a medium. On the way here, I thought I might as well take the money for this session and throw it out the window. Well, you have certainly made a believer out of me."

"It's not me," I shrugged. "I am simply a messenger for the spirit world. Thank your spiritual guides and Jim for helping you to see the light."

Like other clients, I knew that Annie was embarking on a journey of spiritual awakening because of Jim's passing. I also knew that the communication she received during her reading would help her to understand that the relationship she had with him continued in spirit and that as a result of this understanding, her heart would begin to heal. I am not suggesting that a reading will magically alleviate or replace the necessary emotional grief work that follows a loved one's passing; it won't. However, after doing many readings, I've seen people transform and benefit enormously from the reassurance that death doesn't part us from those we love.

After Jim's passing, Annie was diagnosed with and treated for bipolar disorder, which was complicated by a dependence on drugs and alcohol that helped her numb the pain of grief. She felt as if she was on an emotional roller coaster due to the combination of the illness, addictions and grief. Because I knew her substance abuse would prevent her from dealing with grief, I strongly advised her to seek help through 12-step recovery meetings. It was more than a year after Jim's passing before she decided to stop using substances to cope with her feelings. Once she did, she fully realized that she had been hiding behind them to avoid feeling the emotional pain of losing Jim.

In addition to that first reading, I saw Annie for periodic spiritual counseling sessions to help heal her grief. Along with assisting her in confronting painful emotions, I delivered messages from Jim in which he told Annie that he was still with her and Amie, whom Annie was especially concerned about. Through these discussions, Annie discovered that part of her purpose in life was to be the best mother she could. Knowing this strengthened her resolve to carry on despite her intense grief. She felt Jim wanted her to realize that they were still a family and he was parenting Amie from spirit through love and inspiration.

Besides coming through in readings, Jim sent Annie messages by ringing the telephone and making Annie's own number appear on the caller ID box (by all accounts an impossible occurrence.) He also periodically made the hallway light flicker near Annie's bedroom. She thought she was imagining these manifestations until I explained to her that these types of communications are ways that loved ones let us know they're still around.

After Jim's passing, feeling unsafe and alone, Annie had moved from her home into her parent's and began counseling with a psychotherapist. During our professional relationship, she thanked me many times for helping her to grow beyond Jim's death. Through counseling, she became clean from drugs and alcohol. Several months later, she wrote and told me she and Amie had returned to the home they had shared with Jim.

One hot summer morning, I received a disturbing phone call

from Annie's best friend Erica that Annie had passed away in her sleep the previous night. I was shocked and stunned. Annie was only 40 years old! Ironically, she had emailed me the prior week and made an appointment for the following Thursday to connect with her mother who had passed from cancer just six months earlier. Instead, I would now be going to see Annie in a funeral home.

The cause of death was unclear. Intuitively I felt her heart collapsed from the combination of stress from grief, a fluctuating weight condition from psychiatric medications and years of hard living. Her body was simply not strong enough to recover. I also sensed she was overjoyed to be reunited with her beloved Jim in spirit. My thoughts went to Amie, just nine years old, who had lost both of her parents within a few years of one another. I prayed for her to have the strength to get through the trauma of her mother's sudden passing and to realize she was not alone because of the love of her extended family and friends. When I went to the funeral home several days later, I gave Amie a gift, a cuddly stuffed dog to hug when she felt alone or afraid. I quietly assured her that both of her parents would be watching over her as she grew up. Her granddad, Annie's father, told me she was going to live with Annie's brother and his family in Germany where he was stationed in the military.

As I viewed Annie's body lying in the casket, I silently thanked her for her presence in my life. She had given me the priceless gift of confirmation that my work as a medium was indeed helping people in grief to heal. Our sessions together left an indelible imprint of love on my heart. Despite all of the difficult times she endured in life, I sensed her shining radiantly in spirit.

Life is Not the Same After Someone Close to Us Dies
I chose Annie's story to begin this book because it's a good illustration of how the death of a loved one – in this case, a spouse – changes life in the most fundamental of ways. This reading shows how spirit communication serves as a powerful healing force in the grieving process by demonstrating the continuation of life. If we

realize that life indeed goes on in spirit, we feel more at peace with the loss of loved ones, especially if we know they are safe, happy and still with us. Annie's story also shows how loved ones in spirit communicate by sending us signs confirming their existence from beyond the veil of death, helping us to move through grief with the reassurance that they survive.

When someone we love dies, we often feel that a part of us has died, too. Our world is turned upside down as we grieve. Nothing is as it was. As human beings, we will all eventually share the inevitable pain of losing someone we love. It is perhaps the greatest common denominator among us, besides our own death. When we mourn, we are filled with many emotions in an effort to readjust to life without our loved one. Life isn't the same, nor should we expect it to be. In time and with perspective, we will comprehend the spiritual meaning of the relationship with our loved one and how we have grown through it. This often involves taking an honest look at the role we play in our relationships and the feelings we have about the person we're grieving. For example, if we have regrets or resentments, we need to heal these feelings through forgiveness. In Part Three, "Living Beyond Grief," I discuss specific feelings that we're all likely to have following the death of a loved one. When we lose someone unexpectedly as in Annie's case, the pain seems to magnify because we feel paralyzed, even victimized, by our loved one's death. In tragic instances like suicide or accidental death, our hearts seem to almost explode with the pain of loss. Even when we have time to prepare for a loved one's passing, we still experience many changes in our lives that we must adapt to. It's important to realize that death is a transition for both our loved ones and us. We must adequately mourn the person who has passed if we ever hope to move forward and continue living. Despite the darkness of grief, death can and does act as a positive catalyst in our emotional and spiritual maturity by providing us with opportunities to grow beyond the pain of our loss. Miraculously, we become stronger and more spiritually centered in the process. As you will see in some of the stories throughout this book, we may even become beacons of light for others in their journeys through grief or tragedy.

Understanding That We Don't Die Brings Healing

By doing many readings, I've gained amazing insights about the soul's incarnation, journey through earthly life and its return to spirit. Spirit beings have communicated what it's like in the spirit world and how they continue to evolve after death. I've delivered information that is sound evidence for the continuity of the soul after death. I've seen clients' past lives and how they affect their current day situations. I've witnessed people leaving a session feeling emotionally lighter because they opened up to receive guidance, confirmation and healing from the spirit world. Above all else, I've learned how love between people transcends death.

The value of communicating with the spirit world is its ability to dissolve fear and promote healing and closure after death. Fear prevents us from experiencing love and peace. If we allow it to dictate our life choices, we undermine the strength of our innate connection to God. If we fear dying because we don't understand who or what waits for us on the other side, our transition into spirit is unnecessarily difficult and takes longer. Inviting compassion, trust and love into our lives alleviates fear and brings spiritual healing. Understanding and accepting that death is a natural transition for us when our spiritual lessons on earth are finished eases our passage into the spirit world. Knowing that our spirit continues to evolve in other realms of consciousness gives us reassurance that life is eternal.

Fear blocks communication from the spirit world and must be eliminated as much as possible before a session begins. When this occurs, I ask clients to take a few deep breaths to relax. I also tell them that I won't give them scary information and that my work is healing based. In my experience, people fear mediumship due to lack of understanding, as well as social and religious conditioning. I feel an obligation in my work to dispel the myths and stereotypes about it so it can be understood as the healing tool that it is.

After readings, many people comment on how much more

peaceful they feel. I believe this is because spirit communication connects us directly to our souls, which exist beyond the domain of the physical senses. We remember our divine nature, which is love. We realize that we're not alone in navigating the challenging journey of life and are comforted to realize that death doesn't separate us from loved ones. These understandings give us hope and help us to heal more quickly. In addition, when spirit beings communicate about challenges they've faced on earth, they give their loved ones invaluable guidance from a higher perspective in dealing with similar situations.

As a medium, I am sensitive to people's emotions and although I detach during readings, I am still aware of clients' feelings. It's never easy to deliver information about the circumstances of a child's death to a grieving parent, for example, yet I've seen how this information can assist in the overall acceptance of the passing by providing emotional comfort and closure. If a person is nervous, anxious or depressed, I can feel this before the reading begins and advise them to relax and be as open as they can to whom and what is coming through.

My work connects me with many kinds of people with varying religious backgrounds, careers, ages and ethnic origins. Unique as each one is, the one characteristic they share is the desire to seek information from sources beyond the physical. Even people who aren't certain whether they believe in mediumship admit they are curious about the spirit world and what happens after we die. On the other hand, it's amazing how far some people will go to try to discredit and deny the information that comes through. Halfway through one reading I once did, the client announced that he believed I went on the Internet to research background information on people before they came to see me. After I flatly denied doing so, he then asserted that I "seemed very intelligent and well spoken," so I could be making things up as I went along. Needless to say, I was relieved when this session ended. This "prove-it-to-me" attitude is very effective in blocking people from receiving the gifts of healing and insight that come from the spirit world. Experiencing spirit communication is certainly not a cure-all for a die-hard skeptic yet I believe it nonetheless serves a purpose by opening these people to realms of belief to which they wouldn't ordinarily have been receptive.

The Mechanics of Mediumship

Because it's important to understand how spirit beings communicate through our inner senses, I would like to share with you how this process works for me. When I first started doing readings, I had a hard time distinguishing between my thoughts and those of spirit beings. Years later, I am accustomed to comfortably shifting back and forth between my physical (outer) and inner senses. You too, can become adept at listening and interpreting spirits' messages with practice through meditation and listening to your intuition. It is important to understand that you, as a spiritual being, have a direct line to the spirit world and can receive and interpret its messages to you through diligent and patient practice.

The process of spirit communication is called mediumship because it refers to the ability of those in spirit and those on earth to meet mid-way and communicate through the facilitation of an individual who is sensitive to the spirit world. Mediums must raise their awareness above the threshold of normal, waking consciousness to receive messages, and spirit beings who exist in higher realms of consciousness must lower the vibration of their thoughts to communicate. For a message to be transmitted and received, spirit beings must energetically connect with the aura and mind of the medium, as well as the client. If this link is complete, the connection to the spirit world will be strong; if it's not, messages come across as scattered, fuzzy or chaotic. Every reading is a unique experiment because of the variables of the medium's abilities, the strength of the communicating spirit and receptivity of the sitter. Because of this, I (or any medium, for that matter) cannot ever guarantee the outcome of a reading.

People often ask me how I receive information from the spirit world. The answer is through what I call the three C's: clairvoyance (seeing), clairaudience (hearing) and clairsentience (feeling). *Clair* is a French word that means "clear." These inner senses connect us to our intuition and the perception of higher (than the earth) worlds of spirit, or divine consciousness. When I do readings, I focus on the subtle information that I receive through these inner senses. Although we all have inner senses, it takes time and practice to fine-tune them enough to separate our own thinking from spirits'. Daily meditation and group development circles are indispensable to building trust in the process. The inner senses are like muscles; the more they're exercised, the more they strengthen. If we do something enough, we grow to understand and trust the experience.

Prior to doing private or group sessions, I fill my mind with feelings of unconditional love, harmony and peace through meditation and prayer; this lifts, purifies and focuses my thoughts. Preparing this way helps me to release expectations about the session and improves my ability to facilitate healing for clients. I call on my spirit guides (souls who have agreed to assist me with my work as a medium) to help with the communication process from the spirit world. (See Chapter Three for more information on spirit guides.) Since some spirits don't know how to communicate because they are new to the process, I silently ask them to be as clear and specific as possible in the thoughts they send me so their loved ones will be able to identify and recognize them.

Although spirit beings come through with many different types of messages, most present enough validation to prove their identity and existence – including names, months associated with birthdays or passings, illnesses they passed from, their personality, occupations and many other facts supporting their identity. Commonly, spirits will come through with memories of their lives on earth such as shared experiences with clients, where they lived and what activities they engaged in. I often feel their personalities – if they were fun loving, serious or sad. I then relay this information to clients as soon as I receive it so nothing is lost.

During sessions, I glean information through my inner senses in several ways, the most common being telepathy or thought transference from someone in the spirit world. When this happens, I hear a thought in my head and tell the client what it is.

I also feel and sense mild impressions in my body. An example of this is when spirit beings communicate how they passed. If it was from an illness such as heart disease, I'll feel a sensation around my heart. In cases of death by car accident with head injuries, I'll feel an impression in my head. Because I tell spirit beings not to overwhelm me with these sensations, I never have lingering physical symptoms after sessions. Spirits beings also show me pictures of their thoughts on the screen of my inner eye. These can be anything they want to communicate to their loved ones–including objects that belonged to them, familiar places on earth and what their home in the spirit world looks like. My inner senses frequently operate together to form a full, rich link to those on the other side.

The communication process is three-way between the spirit world, clients and me. If any part is off balance or disconnected, the reading is misconstrued. Because I strive to remain as emotionally and physically balanced as I can, the quality of a reading largely depends on the communication strength of those in spirit and the receptivity of clients. For example, if a client is fearful or extremely skeptical – both relatively dense energies – it interferes with the psychic energy that is being transmitted. I am not claiming that I never have off days; it happens occasionally, especially if I am tired or nervous. All sides of the triangular link must be solid for the process to work well. Some spirits are better "talkers" than others, just like people on earth. If a person is reserved and shy before passing, he'll be the same in spirit because we retain our personalities for a while after death until we move into higher realms of consciousness.

I once did a reading for a couple, Frank and Jan, who wished to hear from Frank's father, Joe, who passed several years earlier. Although other relatives and even pets came through in the reading, Frank's father didn't. With 10 minutes remaining in the session, Frank asked why his father hadn't spoken when that's who both of them really wanted to connect with. I sensed that Joe was present during the reading but was standing back, allowing others to come through because his nature was soft-spoken, a man of few words. When I asked Frank to confirm this impression, he did. I explained to them that Joe was just being himself: the strong, silent type.

Misinterpretations can and do happen on my part. An example of this is when I hear names clairaudiently that sound similar, like Mary and Maria or Frank and Francis. In addition, since spirit beings use my frame of reference during readings to get their messages through, I might misinterpret an image that's being shown. To eliminate this as much as possible, I describe what I'm seeing to clients so they can make sense of it from their own experience. Another area for possible confusion happens when related spirit beings' thoughts intermingle and come through to me as one thought. For example, if three members of a client's father's side are being acknowledged during a reading, their thoughts sometimes mesh and I have a difficult time distinguishing which thought or fact goes with a particular spirit. In these cases, I simply make clients aware of what is being communicated and ask to which of the spirits this information applies.

To help me identify spirits more easily, I ask them to come through and "stand" in a place relative to the client that indicates what relationship the two of them shared. This system also reveals how many generations the spirits are removed from the clients. For example, if a spirit comes in and stands beside a client, he is from the same generation–a brother, husband, cousin or friend. If he stands just behind the client, he is a father, uncle or someone from one generation back. Grandparents stand further back than parents. Children come through in different ways: by themselves with no particular placement, in the arms of an older family member or with a friend in their generation who has also passed. The maternal side of a person's relatives will often appear to me on their right side and their paternal, on the left. When spirits give me a name, it often makes reference to which side of the family it connects to.

Generally, the most persistent and talkative spirits are the ones who come through clearly in readings. This is especially noticeable in group settings when some spirits are so insistent on grabbing my attention that they jump up and down beside their loved ones or continually whisper their names and other information in my ear until I say it aloud to the group. Being in front of a group delivering messages is like being in a crowded room where everyone is trying to get my attention by speaking at the same time. Given this, it's easy to understand how miscommunications can happen. Because those in spirit know that a medium will hear them, any spirits who are even remotely connected to sitters in a session can attempt to get their messages delivered. In most readings, "unexpected" spirits do come through, often with the intent of bringing healing to another family member, friend or simply an acquaintance who desperately needs it. In fact, it is quite common for spirits to send a message to someone not present at the session.

Gary, Meg and their two adult children came to my home for a group reading to connect with Gary's father, John. Before John came through, I clearly heard the name Paul. When I asked Gary about the relevance, he immediately identified Paul as a man he worked with whose son had died unexpectedly in the past year. Because of their working relationship, Paul's son wanted Gary to tell his father he was fine and to let go of any guilt he was carrying about the death. Gary confirmed that Paul had indeed been extremely distraught following his son's death because he felt guilty about a recent misunderstanding they'd had. A month later, Gary called to tell me he had delivered the message to Paul, who felt a welcome sense of relief from hearing it.

There are reasons why spirits don't come through in readings. These include a lack of readiness to communicate, such as not understanding how the communication process works or needing a rest period in the spirit world (this can happen if the reading takes place too soon after death). Some spirits are engaged in study or other pursuits and don't want to be interrupted. In other instances, the timing of the reading from a spiritual standpoint may be off, perhaps because of either side's inability to receive the healing that needs to take place. Karma (unfinished spiritual and emotional energy) may be a factor in readings with spirits who have been murdered, in that communicated information is not to be revealed in the timeframe of the reading. In the case of suicide, spirits must work through heavy, unresolved emotions before clear communication can take place. As a medium, I've learned to detach from the disappointment clients feel when loved ones don't come through. I encourage them to connect with loved ones in spirit by sending prayers, which helps with the orientation process in the spirit world. No matter what the circumstances of one's passing, love is never destroyed by death.

Before clients come for sessions, I suggest that they make an appointment with the spirit world by sending love to the person they want to hear from and also by writing questions. I recommend they come with as few expectations as possible about what will be said during the reading. I've discovered that the best dialogue occurs when clients are open channels with no strict agenda, such as wanting proof of a spirit's identity by a secret password, phrase or nickname. Spirit beings relay what they want to and it usually serves no purpose to impose our demands on them. In fact, it often blocks the process.

Because mediumship speaks to our intuitive senses, which are part of our subconscious minds, questions that people have are frequently answered in the course of the reading without being verbalized. This often occurs through symbolism, another a common way the spirit world communicates, in addition to evidential information. Symbols that appear during readings reflect situations, concerns and issues of the client and are a concise way of getting across an important message.

Karen, a woman in her late fifties, came for a reading and both of her parents who had passed from cancer came through. A month earlier, Karen herself had undergone surgery to remove ovarian cancer. When I saw her mother in spirit during the reading, she was sitting in a rocking chair, a favorite resting place of hers when she was on earth. When I described this to Karen, I added that the chair was symbolic of Karen's need to relax and take it easy while recovering from her surgery. Her mother's advice made perfect sense to her, as she admitted feeling very drained by both the illness and other stressful situations in her family.

Another example of symbolism is from a reading I did with Beth. During the reading, Beth's mother – wearing a bright, yellow hat and dress, sitting on a bench bathed in sunlight – came through and mentioned the name Tom. When I relayed all of this to Beth, she said that Tom was a man with whom she had recently ended a long-term relationship, which left her feeling very depressed. Through the symbolism of the color yellow, I felt strongly that her mother was telling her to keep her chin up— sunnier days were ahead. Beth confirmed that her sister told her about a dream in which their mother appeared wearing the same outfit. I assured her that her mother was relating that she was aware of Beth's emotional pain from her break-up and was trying to cheer her by sending these images.

Often, a seemingly mundane message can provide much needed reassurance for those in grief. Here's an example.:

In a group session, a woman stood up and asked a question. As she did, I noticed a woman in spirit standing close to her right side.

"There's a lady here who comes in on your mother's side of the family," I said. In the next instant, I clairvoyantly saw several beautifully painted, antique teapots.

"She is showing me teapots. There's a connection between you and her with these. Do you have someone's teapot collection?"

Tearfully, the woman acknowledged that she owned her mother's prized antique teapot collection. "I knew it was her as soon as you mentioned the teapots," she said, smiling through tears. "Mom told me shortly before she died, less than a year ago, that she wanted me to have them. Coming here today, I had really prayed to hear from her. Thanks for the message."

People ask me why those in spirit don't communicate more dramatic, revealing information such as whom or what God is, or the meaning of life, for example. A common misconception is that death brings immediate enlightenment while the truth is that we leave life with the amount of spiritual growth we've accumulated while alive. Spirits communicate from their level of understanding and in ways that those who knew them on earth will be able to recognize. We take the consciousness we developed on earth into the spirit world and continue to evolve.

When I am finished doing readings, I am able to "turn off" the spirit world and go about my normal, day-to-day living. Many people have asked me if I am constantly bombarded with thoughts from spirit beings who are trying to get my attention. A woman in one of my group mediumship programs wanted to know if I was able to go to the grocery store without being bothered by spirits! This is not the case because I've learned to set boundaries and close the door to the other side when I have to. It would take a mighty strong spirit to get my attention when I am not working. When I do readings, I open the door again to receive information. Occasionally, I do hear from spirits before a session, when I am meditating. They are usually anxious to come through to family members scheduled for a session and have no sense of time since it doesn't exist in their realm. I ask my guides to bring them through when the session begins.

Sometimes spirit beings will communicate future events for clients. I've done readings in which spirits talk about an impending family reunion or wedding. The spirit world, which exists as a realm of thought as opposed to matter, vibrates at a higher level than earth and events "register" there before they happen here. Souls who exist in spirit are aware of these thoughts and can communicate them to us. It's important to remember that we have free will and can change our thoughts at any time. Therefore, all prophecy relayed in a session is subject to change depending upon the exertion of our free will.

As you can see, when it comes to getting their messages across, spirit beings are quite determined and ingenious. Just as we need to be acknowledged by our family and friends, those on the other side desire to be recognized and remembered by those who loved and knew them on earth. Some of the strongest messages they want us to know concern their continued existence after death and their strong bond with family and friends. In many readings, spirits impress me with names of loved ones who are with them or still on earth. Although a message is sometimes given with the name, many times it serves as a simple acknowledgement for that individual, as if they are claiming the relationship. Other times, spirits mention names as a way of saying thanks to individuals for taking care of them before passing or honoring them in some way, as with a donation or special church service. Whatever the case, names provide important evidential information and add another dimension of authenticity for clients.

In addition to reuniting clients with loved ones, I also teach people how they can recognize and communicate with spirit guides and teachers (without a medium) to receive insights that improve the quality of their lives. When we know we're not separate from, but one with, other realms of consciousness, we are more fully aware of our purpose and potential as human beings. Knowing that we're not limited to our physical bodies and that our souls are immortal, we experience life from an entirely different perspective: one of harmony, fulfillment and peace.

The greatest obstacle I've had to surmount in my work is my own lack of trust in the information coming through. Through the years and after many validations from clients, I've learned to give a message regardless of whether it can immediately be validated or not. When I first started doing readings, I doubted the accuracy of messages because I had little experience with how the process works. If clients didn't confirm messages, I assumed I was wrong. Years later, I've learned that messages may not be immediately identified because the events haven't happened yet or clients don't remember or aren't aware of the given circumstances. Time and again, clients later validate information from sessions after they've had a chance to confirm details through older living family members. I've discovered that a message may not make sense to me as the interpreter but can be full of meaning for the client. My job is to pass it along, no matter how insignificant it may seem to me.

Skepticism

Despite, or perhaps because of, the attention that has been given to mediumship in the last decade, especially on national TV, skepticism about the process is alive and well. Among other things, critics charge mediums with the exploitation of people in grief, denouncing them as money grabbing charlatans who fool people into believing they are really connecting with their loved ones in spirit. Mediums such as John Edward, James Van Praagh and Rosemary Altea, who have demonstrated their talents on national TV, have been favorite targets of skeptics' scathing reviews. Because I share the profession, I feel a kinship with mediums who have been attacked unfairly by people who understand little about the process, and an obligation to stand up for the truth. The fact is that there are frauds and greedy people in any field. Do we not find what we are looking for, if we look long and hard enough? Should we disregard and ignore all of the good work that mediums do to help grieving people simply because skeptics say mediumship cannot be proven according to their standards?

Spirit communication is vulnerable to criticism because the process is not normally measured by the five physical senses, which are routinely used in analytical, scientific thinking. Psychic communication is received through the right hemisphere of the receiver's brain–the feeling, creative, imaginative center through which spiritual and mystical experiences are also perceived. If one is not familiar with right-brain processes and how they function, it may feel as if the information is being made up. For this reason, mediumship presents challenges to the belief system of people who adhere to rational thinking. Thankfully, this is changing as more mediums come forward to be tested by scientific methods. For example, *The After-Life Experiments: Breakthrough Scientific Evidence of Life after Death* (G. Schwartz and W. Simon, Pocket Books, 2002) documents many examples and results of tests conducted with mediums who scored high accuracy ratings using accepted scientific methods that measured their skills. Research on mediumship continues to grow as institutions and universities create and maintain special departments dedicated to the exploration of mediumship and the question of what happens to us when we die. One example is the University of Arizona's VERITAS program, created to test the hypothesis that a person's consciousness survives death. This division of the university's psychology department regularly tests mediums and records the results. (To learn more about these studies, see the resource section of this book).

In my practice, I discourage skeptical clients from wasting my time and their money on testing me. These are always no-win situations and I have no interest in attempting to convert someone's beliefs. While making appointments over the phone, I can usually feel if the caller's motive is to discredit me or what I do. In my entire career, this has happened only a few times, although these have been enough to last me a lifetime. I have also received a few emails denouncing what I do as morally wrong from people who claim to be religious. I suppose they consider it their duty to inform me that I've got a one-way ticket to hell reserved in my name. Although it is psychologically and emotionally draining to have my credibility and integrity challenged, I learned in these instances to stand my ground quietly and not engage in arguments. The practice of mediumship is one of few professions that exist in which practitioners routinely have to prove their reputation and credibility. At the core of this skepticism towards mediumship is fear and ignorance of the higher reality of God and the soul's true identity as a divine, limitless entity that never dies. With this understanding, I choose to disengage from debating with a skeptic by ending the session (if it is private) or simply moving on to another person (if it is within a group). Trying to deliver messages to someone who is closed feels like hitting my head against a brick wall. Skeptics are much more likely to emerge in group settings or come to events like psychic fairs where readings are often given for reduced rates, rather than to private readings. Some people will always doubt the validity of anything they can't detect or validate through their physical senses.

Can life after death ever really be proven beyond a shadow of a doubt? I believe that we are now living in times in which matters of faith and belief are increasingly being supported by scientific research, which makes people more accepting of communication from the spirit world. In addition, more people are having their own subjective experiences and are coming forth to talk about them. As human consciousness continues to evolve, we will fully realize the indestructibility and divine essence of our souls and that our spiritual progression is the result of everything we think and do.

How to Find a Reputable Medium

When seeking services from a medium, I suggest that you first ask friends, family or work associates for recommendations of mediums they have visited. You should also ask how well the medium connected with their loved ones in spirit–including the amount and specificity of evidential information that came through in the reading. Of all the forms of advertising I've done, by far the best for me, as far as return, has been word-of-mouth from satisfied clients. Most people who come for sessions with me do so on the recommendation from family and friends. I stopped doing paid advertising when I discovered that my work was speaking for itself.

Another important consideration is the effect the reading has on clients. In other words, how do you feel after receiving it? I've personally received readings in which I felt worse afterwards because the medium was reading from an ego perspective, without a genuine connection to the higher mind of Spirit. A good reading should be uplifting and provide guidance and offer options for your life challenges, as well as present evidence of life after death. Please note the word "options"; you should not be given immediate answers or commands about what you *must* do. Spirit works with infinite possibilities and will *never* insist that only one way or answer is the right one. If you go to a medium or psychic who imparts such information, end the session and don't go back. Remember that the ultimate purpose of a reading is to empower you and remind you of the divinity of your soul.

Anyone who claims to have all the answers probably is not reading from an elevated spiritual level with your best interest in mind.

Although prophecy is often given in readings, a better gauge of the quality of a reading is the spiritual nature of it. In addition to foretelling events, a good reading offers you the philosophy of harmonious, balanced living and recognizes the sanctity of your free will.

I suggest that when looking for a medium, let your own intuition guide you. If possible, read the person's website or printed brochure and tune into what you are feeling, especially if photos are available. Is the fee reasonable as far as the medium's expertise and training? When making an appointment, are you asked to give your last name or other personal details? (As little as possible about you should be revealed before the session to preserve its integrity.) Finally, ask Spirit to guide you to the best person and then pay attention to signs you receive through others, articles and books or the Internet. This is your intuition's way of guiding you on your pathway. Loved ones will often inspire us to be in the right place at the right time to make the contact we need with them. Listen!

CHAPTER THREE

DEATH: A BEGINNING

*I am standing upon the seashore. A ship at my side spreads her
white sails to the morning breeze and starts for the blue ocean.
She is an object of beauty and strength. I stand and watch her
until at length she hangs like a speck of white cloud just where
the sea and sky come to mingle with each other. Then someone at
my side says, "There, she is gone." "Gone where?" Gone from my
sight. That is all. She is just as large in mast and hull and spar
as she was when she left my side, and she is just as able to bear
her load of living freight to her destined port. Her diminished size
is in me, not in her. And just at the moment when someone at my
side says, "There, she is gone!" there are other eyes watching her
coming, and there are other voices ready to take up the glad
shout, "Here she comes!" And that is dying.*
– Henry Van Dyke

What happens when we die? Where do we go and what awaits us?
Since the beginning of time, humans have sought answers to these
questions through religious teachings, philosophy and the arts.
Throughout history, mankind has explored the meaning of life and
death from a spiritual perspective and strived to comprehend the
nature of God. Western religions teach about the soul's survival
after life and its rewards or punishments bestowed by God, who is
thought to exist outside of and independently from humans. Yet
relatively little is taught about the process of dying, the journey of
the soul after death and the concept of God residing within each
individual. Unfortunately, many people fear death because of this
lack of knowledge and fail to understand that it is a natural
transition to our home in the spirit world (also called the astral
world or plane), similar to other stages we go through in life. In

fact, dying is the movement from one state of consciousness to another, a temporary end to physical life and the beginning of the soul's return to its spiritual existence. From the moment of separation from the body, the soul embarks on its new life in the world of spirit–a realm of consciousness that is quite expansive compared to the one we know on earth.

Through my work as a medium, I have discovered that the more we know about the process of dying and where we go afterwards, the less likely we are to fear death. We are also more inclined to have an easier transition into spirit when the time comes and adjust to the spirit world more quickly if we know what to expect when we get there. When loved ones die, understanding where they go helps us move more easily through the grieving process by providing us with peace of mind. To help you better understand what happens when we die, I have divided this chapter into sections about what the other side is like and what one is likely to encounter there. This information has been revealed to me through thousands of readings, from my spirit teachers and from years of metaphysical studies. Please note that it applies to *most* souls, although there are exceptions, some of which I will discuss.

Departure

At the moment of death, the soul exits the physical body for the final time, usually through the top of the head (crown.) If an individual has been ill enough to be in a coma, the soul often exits and travels to the spirit world several times before it releases all contact with the body. A silvery-blue energy cord, also called the etheric cord, which connected the soul to the body before birth, breaks away because it is no longer needed. Within three days, this cord dissolves completely.

After the soul exits, it floats away from the body and usually becomes aware of a bright light leading into a tunnel which connects the earthly dimension to the astral world. Spirits coming through in readings have told me how exhilarating it is to be free from the density of their bodies, especially if there has been pain or illness. There is a feeling of freedom and wonder at being able to move about without attachment to the body. People who have had near-death experiences describe the sensation of floating above their bodies and being able to view the entire area surrounding them. Deceased family members, friends, pets and sometimes spirit guides joyfully greet souls and assist them in moving through the bright tunnel into the spirit world. Souls I've communicated with in readings describe these reunions as overwhelmingly happy and of great assistance in helping them to feel welcome in their new life on the other side. These "welcoming committees" serve much the same purpose as family and friends who care for newborn babies coming into earthly existence in that they are temporary caretakers for souls during a period of adjustment and orientation.

Dying people are often aware of the spirit world and deceased family members a short time before passing. Many people have told me that while sitting with dying loved ones, they call out names or make reference to others in spirit. No matter how long deceased family members and friends may have been in spirit, they usually look the same as they did in life so souls can easily recognize them. In addition to escorting newly transitioned souls through the tunnel, these familiar souls help by making them feel comfortable with new surroundings.

Personally, I have never spoken to a spirit who has wanted to linger for long after leaving the body. Although most view their bodies after leaving them, they are beckoned on by the prospect of experiencing the all-encompassing peace of the other side. Souls can choose to attend their own funerals or wakes (many do and give evidence of that during readings), but most are very anxious to move on. Spirits who linger for extended periods of time, such as in haunted places, either don't know they are deceased (in traumatic accidents or murders) or don't have the belief that their consciousness survives death, so they hover closely to their bodies, believing they are still attached to it. Other reasons for earthbound spirits are emotional attachments to earthly conditions, desires and addictions. These must be worked out in the astral plane which, like earth, exists for the spiritual evolution of all souls in their eventual return to unity with God. In the vast majority of cases, souls cannot wait to return home and the transition is smooth. Because free will is the right of all souls, it applies to all choices made by us both on earth and in spirit. That is, we choose when we want to move on; no one can decide for us.

Entry into the Spirit World

Upon entering the spirit world, a newly crossed soul is taken to a place of orientation where it is urged to rest and acclimate to its new environment. Relatives and friends may remain to help in this process. If a soul has left earth from an illness or condition that was especially long or entailed much suffering – such as certain cancers, AIDS or Alzheimer's disease – it may go to a spirit hospital or other place of healing. Here it is given care by trained healers who remove stressful thought patterns and bathe the soul in frequencies of light to restore balance. For those souls who are in need of it, special counselors who help with the acclimation process are available and souls are encouraged to see them. During orientation, souls adjust to living without a physical body with all of its requirements, like eating, sleeping and exercising. Walking is no longer necessary since souls can be at a particular destination by merely thinking about it.

The amount of time required for this adjustment phase is individual and based on the newly crossed spirit's expectations, beliefs and level of spiritual development. More highly advanced souls adjust more quickly and are anxious to get on with their work in the spirit world. Less advanced souls must learn to release emotional attachments to the earthly life they just left before they can move on. For example, I have done readings in which spirits talk about their challenges in letting go of the need to eat. Usually these are people who had strong attachments to food and must accept that it is no longer necessary in their new life. Other spirits have to deal with their addiction to substances like drugs or alcohol through counseling, much like they would on earth. All of our thoughts and feelings, good and bad, are taken into the spirit world when we die.

Panoramic Vision

Based on a soul's readiness, it can review its completed life at any time after making entry. Most souls choose to see this spiritual "movie" soon after making transition with the assistance and support of their guides, counselors and teachers. I call it a movie because it is a vision of the newly completed lifetime that is three-dimensional and alive with action and feeling. Through this movie, souls relive every second of their previous life with the experience of feeling and knowing the repercussions of all of their thoughts, words, choices and actions, as well as their life purpose and mission. They are also shown how they could have made different choices in terms of spiritual development. An entire lifetime on earth can be viewed in the equivalent of a few seconds in the spirit world. Past lives, which are normally blocked from conscious memory before birth, can also be viewed and considered at this time to compare and contrast lifetimes of spiritual development.

Egoic defenses for self-protection do not apply in the spirit world. In other words, what you see is what you get, as far as spiritual growth is concerned. For example, if we harmed others on earth, we will see and feel this when we have our life review. It would not be possible to deny it. If we lived a decent life and helped others along the way, we will likewise recognize the resulting growth from doing so. Ultimately, we are the judges of our own lives. No one, including the ascended masters, saints or angels can do this for us because of our free will.

Decisions to continue certain lessons in the spirit world are made after the life review. Spirit counselors assist in giving support and encouragement for souls in making a determination of continued spiritual development, which is directly influenced by the level of spiritual consciousness attained during the previous life.

Choice, Blueprints and the Wheel of Life

During a life review, we become fully aware of the plans we made before coming to earth and how good of a job we did in fulfilling them. Imagine that a soul (who incarnates as a man) sets the goal of learning about forgiveness before being born. Further, say this man has a son who is murdered and as a result, the man becomes full of anger, bitterness and emotional pain. If he does not work through these feelings and begin the process of forgiveness, when he dies he will need to continue this lesson on the other side. He may also choose to come back and have the same experience or a similar one to fully learn the lesson of forgiveness.

Before we are born, we know what lessons we will learn on earth and we make plans that support this purpose. Some people call these karmic contracts, but I prefer to call them blueprints because they are more open-ended than a contract in that we can determine the circumstances involved in learning these spiritual lessons. Simply put, blueprints serve as frameworks for our life lessons and are the primary reasons we come to earth. Subconsciously, on a soul level, we know what this framework is, although we are seldom aware of it on a conscious level until we encounter various reminders – wake-up calls, so to speak – throughout life. At any given time in life, we are presented with options for carrying out our missions. For example, imagine that you, as a soul, have chosen to work on developing compassion. At various points in your life, you are presented with different opportunities to learn this, such as caring for a sick child, working in a nursing home with elderly people or volunteering for an organization that rescues abused animals. Each of these circumstances is unique, but all offer the chance to learn how to be compassionate. You can freely choose how to fulfill your blueprint.

The signposts that point to our blueprints are events and circumstances that create a turning point in our lives' directions. Examples of "negative" wake-up calls are physical or emotional illness, relationship and work-related problems, addictions and dissatisfaction with life. Although these wake-up calls can be devastating, ultimately they serve as points of transition in helping us become aware of our life lessons and purpose. In my life, the   fire that destroyed my business was a huge wake-up call that ultimately led to finding my life's calling in mediumship. Pleasurable circumstances, such as the birth of a child, a harmonious love relationship or self-fulfillment through a career can also activate and reinforce our memory of blueprints.

What happens if we ignore lessons and refuse to learn them? In the long run, we are only hurting ourselves by short-circuiting our own growth. We can choose to learn now or later, but we *will* learn, since spiritual growth is continuous. We can spend many lifetimes learning a single quality, such as unconditional love. Time is immaterial to the immortal soul, since it has no concept of it.

Meeting our karma means that we are responsible for our thoughts and actions, both good and bad. We return to earth in successive lifetimes to balance karma, which is created through our thoughts and actions. To understand the concept of karma, imagine life as a constantly revolving wheel. Each lifetime on earth is a spoke in the wheel and the hub represents the soul, which is stable and unchangeable. The rotating motion of the wheel can be compared to the circular nature of life with birth and death continually taking place until we are one with God.

The key to releasing karma is to live in love, kindness and forgiveness. The cleaner we can keep our slate, the better off we will be. Great masters like Jesus, Buddha and Krishna have demonstrated to mankind through the examples of their lives how to live in unconditional love and harmony with God. Each day, we are given precious life energy to use in whatever way we choose under the direction of our free will. These choices directly determine our karma and ultimately where we will go in the spirit world after we die. Souls who are like-minded will be with us in the level that matches our consciousness. For example, if we chose to use our life energy in service to others, we will spend time on the other side with souls who also did this or a similar activity. On the other hand, if we lived in hate, greed and exploitation of others, we will be with other souls who chose to live this way. Soul groups, both small and large, are made up of souls who possess similar or identical levels of spiritual development. Members of soul groups are in the spirit world and on earth at any given time. Recognition of fellow soul group members on earth usually happens through the common experience of a deep emotional or spiritual connection with spouses, friends, acquaintances or co-workers. Our earthly family members may or may not be a part of our soul group, depending on their spiritual consciousness. In the spirit world, we seldom leave a soul group until we are ready to move onto another, nor do we intermingle with other soul groups.

Think of spiritual growth as a spiral that moves upward and outward simultaneously. Because the soul is eternal and indestructible, it does not know suffering as we perceive it; it knows only growth. No matter what the circumstances, the soul does not stagnate. It continually seeks expression to remember and reinforce its innate connection to God.

The Spirit World Has Many Levels

When comforting his disciples about his impending death, Jesus said, "In my Father's house are many mansions." (John 14:2.) Metaphysically, this can be interpreted as meaning that heaven is made up of various levels that are each different depending upon their spiritual vibration. This is reflected in the amount of light that is present in each level. The levels closer to earth are densest in vibration and darker than the higher ones, which are continually lit by a soothing, warm glow. Lower levels are occupied by souls who have engaged in criminal or other self-serving behaviors on earth. These souls harbor feelings of hate, jealousy and greed that keep them confined to these levels—which most people commonly refer to as hell. But no soul is banished to this place by a punishing god who wields fire and brimstone. Rather, souls who make choices on earth to engage in activities that are self-serving and harmful to others earn their new home in these dark, lower levels that are much like prisons on earth. The difference is that in the spirit world, the bars and chains that confine souls are comprised of their own malicious thoughts. When these souls begin to see the folly of their ways through their own suffering in the darkness of the lower levels, specially trained rescuing spirits, some of whom are counselors, take them to a different place on a higher level.

The majority of souls who cross over go to the mid-levels, which are surprisingly similar to earth, while those who have attained a higher degree of spiritual consciousness reside in the upper ones. We can visit different levels accompanied by spirit guides but rarely spend time in them unless it serves a purpose in our development or that of others. An example of this is the rescuing spirit who works to assist those in lower levels who express the desire to move beyond the limitations of their own thinking into a higher level. Spirits who do this type of work have been apprentices to others who have also rescued souls and are highly compassionate.

People have asked me if houses or other dwellings exist on the other side. The answer is definitely yes–if we desire them. Some spirits construct houses of thought that are replicas of ones they had on earth. The longer souls are in spirit, the less likely they are to model their existence after earthly life. This is due to detachment from physical needs and desires. Just about anything that exists here on earth has a counterpart on the astral plane, with one crucial difference: places are built from thought, not from material substances. There are churches for worship, schools, ornate libraries and temples of healing. I have seen viewing ports where souls can look in on earth and others through which they can consider future lives prior to incarnation. Hills, gardens, valleys, ponds, streams and mountains abound.

The spirit world is extremely expansive compared to earth and the experience of containment in a physical body. In readings, some spirits make reference to this when they communicate how relieved they are to be out of the confines of the body, how unbounded and free they feel in the bliss of the spirit world.

There is no time or space in spirit. What seems like a few moments on the other side may actually be 50 years on earth. The closest comparison to this is how time seems to stand still when we are dreaming, meditating or deeply engrossed in an activity. This is because the rational left-brain, which perceives events from a linear perspective, is not as active during these states where the subconscious mind, which has no reference of time, takes over. Spiritual existence is similar in that the concept of "now" is all that is realized. This is why it is fruitless to ask spirits to come through to you at a certain time when they have no reference of it. Spirit connects with us through feeling and desire rather than the artificial construct of time.

Two of the most striking differences, visually speaking, between earth and the astral world are the brilliancy of its colors and its topographic fluidity. Colors in the spirit world are so bright, they seem to vibrate with their intensity. This has been especially apparent to me when spirits come through in readings in outdoor settings like gardens or meadows with bright, green grass and vibrantly colored flowers. These beautiful surroundings are common in the spirit world and exist for souls' peace and enjoyment. Often, they are places of healing where souls can quietly reflect and bask in the perfection of God's creations. People who gardened or enjoyed the outdoors on earth can do so in spirit.

Because the other side is much lighter in density than earth, it appears fluid-like. A good comparison is the blending of colors in a watercolor painting, with no rough or distinct edges or bound-aries. One of the most accurate depictions of what the spirit world is like is the movie *What Dreams May Come*, starring Robin Williams. The vivid colors and rolling, water-like scenery portrayed in the movie are truly reflective of the astral plane.

Another difference between earth and the spirit world is the absence of illness. Many spirits who were sick prior to crossing are excited to show their loved ones who come for readings that they are whole and well again. Illness is a vehicle we use to learn lessons on earth and is therefore not necessary in spirit. When we release the physical body, we also release the need for illness. In the orientation phase, souls who have had an extended illness must realize that they are no longer sick and are free to move about without their prior physical limitations.

What do we do on the other side? Souls carry on with their growth in whatever method will best advance it. Again, this is dependent on the age or spiritual advancement of the soul. For a time after crossing, souls can choose to engage in activities that were familiar to them on earth. I have seen spirits come through in readings who are fishing, boating or hiking. Since there is no time, they can enjoy limitless freedom. However, most souls ultimately move on to other activities geared to their spiritual development, such as learning in classrooms and libraries, performing apprenticeships or assisting other souls in various ways. In a reading I did for a woman who had lost her son from a drug overdose, the young man said he was helping others who had crossed in the same way. Although this reading was quite emotional for his mother, it helped her to understand that her son's death had not been in vain because he was continuing to grow through service to others in spirit.

Children and Infants

When children and infants die, they are greeted and taken care of by older members of their families in spirit. In many readings I've done, a close family member like a grandmother, parent, aunt or uncle will bring them through. If no one from the family is available when these souls cross, spirit guides and angels assist them with their transition. No soul is ever abandoned and help is readily given to those who need it. Parents who have lost children can take great solace in knowing that their little ones are loved and cared for in spirit just as they were on earth.

It's important to understand that our chronological age on earth doesn't necessarily translate to the age of our soul, which is measured by spiritual development. It is often the case that more spiritually advanced children come into life to teach their less advanced parents important lessons, such as nurturing, kindness and unconditional love. In addition, some children and infants who die are relatively older souls who have chosen to come to earth to advance medical science in some way through a particular illness that needs to be researched in hopes of a cure. Because the soul does not know suffering in a physical sense, any illness or condition that is experienced is temporary and used as a means to grow spiritually. When these lessons are complete, these brave spirits return home with the wisdom they obtained from life. When parents and other family members die, they will be reunited with their children and become aware of what lessons they came to teach them.

Miscarriages are different from souls that have fully incarnated in that they do not completely link with a physical body. In these cases, souls decide to remain in the spirit world for one of several reasons. Timing may not be optimal for incarnation. Souls may decide on another set of circumstances other than the ones originally chosen. In other instances, physical defects of the fetus may not be conducive to what souls need to advance spiritually. In the case of stillbirths, a soul exits the body before birth for many of the same reasons it does in the case of a miscarriage.

In my experience, parents who endure the death of a child are inevitably changed by the experience. Despite carrying a heavy burden of grief or perhaps because of it, many parents and families of these children are transformed spiritually by their deaths. (For specific examples, see Chapter Four, "Forever Young.")

What About Suicide?

It is indeed tragic when people are in so much emotional or mental anguish that they take their own lives. I can honestly say that in my experience as a medium, I have never communicated with a soul who has been happy about his choice to commit suicide. Most suffered some kind of mental or emotional imbalance that caused them to think unclearly and self-destructively. In linking with these spirits' minds, I find that most are reluctant to reconnect with the overwhelming and dense feelings of hopelessness, depression and confusion with which they left earth making the communication strained during these sessions. Some spirits who commit suicide are surprised and dismayed to discover that unresolved problems and emotions they experienced before death must be worked through in the astral world and that ending their physical life has created far more problems than it solved. That lifetime's previous karma is now layered with the new karma of ending life unnaturally. Add to this the devastating grief that family and friends feel as a direct result of the act and it's easy to see that no good can come from taking one's life.

Souls who die by suicide must eventually deal with the thoughts and beliefs that caused them to do so. Mental and emotional illnesses must be healed before further growth is possible. In my experience, most suicides spend time healing in the spirit world. Spirit counselors lend support in this process, which may take the equivalent of many years. I have seen no evidence that they immediately incarnate to finish what they left behind, although there are always exceptions. Souls who commit suicide are not banished to spend eternity in hell as some religions teach. No soul is ever lost or denied God's love. If help is desired, it is always available. After a time, some suicides choose to work with others who crossed in the same way and others train as spirit apprentices who help people on earth suffering from the same emotional problems. When the time is right, these souls choose to come to earth again.

Where Do Animals Go When They Die?
Animals, birds and insects co-exist with souls on the other side. A beloved pet on earth can rejoin us in spirit. In the majority of readings I've done, pets come through with people they once knew and loved. Animals can also spend time with other members of their species, sharing with them what they learned on earth, which is then absorbed by the group mind of the species. Peaceful forests and other outdoor places are filled with spirits of animals we knew on earth. As with human souls, there are caretakers in spirit who help to nurse animals who've passed from debilitating conditions or abuse. These animal hospitals are situated in places that resemble lush meadows on earth with grass, trees and wildlife. In the spirit world, all of God's creatures are loved and

cared for.

The Role of Spirit Guides Before and After Death

When we choose to be born, we have advisors or guides who help us determine our lessons during that lifetime. These wise souls know us well through their association with us from other lifetimes and are usually members of our soul group. Also, teaching guides help us with particular areas of spiritual growth or inspire us with their expertise in special subjects. For example, I have several guides who help me with my work as a medium. One of them was a medium on earth in her last incarnation and the others act as gatekeepers to usher communicating spirits through during readings. All of them help with the communication process from the spirit world.

Many guides have apprentices who work closely with them to learn the responsibilities and duties of their role. They understand the trials and tribulations of human life because they have also been on earth. Their role is to offer direction that supports our spiritual purpose and individual blueprint we made before birth. Deceased relatives are rarely guides, although they may take on that role in an earthly sense when they are alive.

Guides are very diverse in their manner and methods of helping us, depending upon our needs and their personalities. Some guides are extremely nurturing and give us emotional support when we falter. Others take more of a hands-off approach and allow us to learn lessons, offering support in a minimal way so we can spread our wings. Still others come to us through humor to help ease our cares and concerns.

One of my main guides is Rolf, who was Austrian in his last incarnation. I was first introduced to him through an energy-based therapy I received. While resting on the table after the healing, I suddenly got a clairvoyant image of his name written in script and underlined. I had no idea who he was or what role he had in my spiritual development until a few years later. In the following months, he came to me several times in meditation and during other quiet moments. Rolf looks like Santa Claus minus the red suit. He has a potbelly, a white beard and smokes a pipe. A former Austrian mountain dweller, he wears green shorts with suspenders and a pointed, felt hat with a feather on the side. Shortly after I became aware of him, he told me that he had been alive during World War II and lost some of his family in the battle, although he had escaped into the hills of Austria. Humor became a coping mechanism for him to live with the atrocity of war. For the first several years when I did group message programs, I was keenly aware of his presence when I stood in front of the crowd. Although Rolf can be somewhat of an egoist (he loves to be acknowledged in front of groups), his personality is warm, loving and refreshingly humorous. He's taught me to laugh at myself and not take life as seriously as I have a tendency to do. He is like a grandfather in spirit who knows me well and loves me unconditionally.

While guides give us support and direction in meeting our life lessons, they are not permitted to learn these lessons for us but instead act as our coaches in the game of life. Nor are they allowed to interfere with the karma we are solely responsible for. Depending on what lessons we have chosen, we will attract corresponding guides who are versed in those particular areas of assistance. The length of time that guides stay with us depends on our individual growth, which is determined by the life choices we make. When we graduate from a certain level of development, we attract new guides. The exception to this is a master guide who oversees our divine life plan and stays with us throughout life.

When I teach spiritual development, I tell students to think of their guides and themselves as a team. The object of the game is to grow spiritually through learning to love oneself and others unconditionally. People make the mistake of putting guides on a pedestal instead of viewing them as equals. I learned this from my own guides when they intuitively told me they understood my disappointments and celebrated my accomplishments with me. I've come to think of them as friends in spirit who know me as well as my friends on earth.

When we die, guides will either greet us on the other end of the tunnel or when we are preparing to go through the orientation process. They are almost always present when we have a life review and provide insight, support and guidance in assessing the completed life's lessons. Like good friends, they encourage us in moving forward with our development in the astral world and assist in the reunion with our soul group. During the time we spend in the spirit world, guides continue to work with us in the progression of our lessons. They will also prompt us when the time comes to return to earth and help us in the selection of the appropriate lifetime.

Leaving the Spirit World

The length of time spent in the spirit world between incarnations is dependent on souls' individual needs. Some souls spend the equivalent of many years in spirit before deciding to return to earth, especially if they've lived a long life on earth. Others choose to return much sooner to further develop on the earth plane. Generally, the determining factors in rebirth depend on our unique spiritual evolution and the perfect circumstances that will support it. Nowadays, the time spent in spirit is shorter due to acceleration in human consciousness. Since September 11, 2001, the day of the attacks on the Twin Towers in New York City, many more souls are choosing to return to earth to balance karma. In a spiritual sense, that day was a huge wake-up call for collective humanity to hold unhealed parts of itself to the light of God for examination. Because of this, I believe we are becoming increasingly aware of the need to help one another, heal the planet and move beyond our fears. We continue on this pathway today.

When our lessons are temporarily completed in the spirit world, we intuitively sense it is time once again to return to physical form. People often ask me if a current lifetime is the last they will have and whether or not they'll come back. My response is to ask them if they feel equal in their spiritual wisdom to a saint. Of course, most deny this, saying that they are disappointed to know they will probably be back. Why would we want to leave the tranquility, blissfulness and unity of the spirit world to come into the harsh reality and duality of earth? Because we are aware that coming into physical form gives us many opportunities for growth that being in spirit doesn't. Time, space, density and a body are effective tools in teaching us indispensable lessons. None of these exist in spirit, so we must incarnate to experience them.

When the decision is made to come back, souls begin to make plans for a new life, which includes devising a blueprint. An intriguing part of this phase involves the viewing and consider-ation of possible future lives on earth. Before you think this is too far out to be taken seriously, let me explain.

With the knowledge of uncompleted lessons in mind, souls go to an area in the astral world, similar to a library, where they contemplate future lives by watching them on a viewing screen. The projection of these lives in the spirit world is possible because linear time doesn't exist. All aspects of the life, such as genetic influences, parents, time and place of birth and economic circum-stances are considered before making a decision. Souls can view hundreds of lifetimes before finding the perfect one that is suited to their exact needs. They may also consult with spirit guides about which life will best afford the opportunities to support the blueprint that has been written. Because most of us incarnate with people who share our karma, this must also be considered in the selection of a new life. In most cases, we have karma with our parents and vice-versa. Before we are conceived, a soul agreement is made between us regarding the roles of parent and child. This is true even if other parents adopt us after birth.

After a life is selected, preparation is made for taking physical form. Souls are instructed on the process of entering and connecting with their new infant body prior to birth. From the moment conception takes place, newly incarnating souls form an energetic bond with their parents, especially the mother. During the nine months of pregnancy, souls will go in and out of the developing fetus many times, entering and exiting through the crown. They will spend time in the spirit world between visits to earth. Just prior to birth, souls form a complete link with their new bodies through the etheric cord.

Before coming into physical life, we go through a process that temporarily blocks all conscious memory of past lives and spirit world experiences. This serves to allow us to focus attention on the new life. These blocked memories, which are stored in the subconscious mind, are sometimes recalled in the dream state and through certain procedures like hypnosis and past life regressions. They can also be acted out in behavior patterns that have no basis in people's current lives. From birth, we once again make adjustments to being contained within a physical body with all of its requirements, and life goes on.

The Circle of Life

We are eternal souls whose spiritual growth is endless in the quest to become one with God. With each turn of the wheel of life, we become more aware of the light of God within us and how we can use it to help others evolve. Each lifetime is a chance to move closer to the realization that living in love and harmony to the best of our ability means that we're doing our part to uplift humanity. Every earthly trip gives us a chance to peel away layers of karma and learn to love more fully. We come into life with unique abilities that can be used in service to others and, in the process, heal our karma. Ironically, a physical body and the earth are necessary for us to learn about our divine identity. Death, our return to spirit, is the natural shifting of our consciousness back to the full awareness of the immortality of our souls. Through it, we remember who we really are as immortal spirits. Much like the seasons of nature, the circle of life assures that we are continually renewed and reborn through God's love. When we die, we are filled with the recognition of our individual contribution to the entire universal plan. At the same time, we become aware of the deeper meaning of relationships and events in our lives. The expansiveness of this spiritual vision reveals to us the beauty and unity of all of life, in which every soul is equally precious in the mind of God.

PART TWO
TRANSITIONS

CHAPTER FOUR

FOREVER YOUNG

For what is it to die, but to stand in the sun and melt
into the wind?
And when the earth has claimed our limbs, then we
shall truly dance.
-Kahlil Gibran

The most emotionally challenging readings I have done are for parents who have lost children. The pain of grief is especially devastating in these cases because people normally don't expect to outlive their children. Shattered hopes and dreams for the future, lack of emotional closure and a sense of helplessness and guilt often compound the grieving process. Parents and families for whom I've done sessions have told me how hard it is to go on with their lives in the aftermath of such pain and loss. It is difficult for us to comprehend that our souls make the choice to leave the earth after completing spiritual lessons we've agreed upon before birth. The amount of time this takes can range from hours to 100 years or more, depending on our soul's unique calling. Until we cross back into spirit, we may not fully under-stand the implications of our choices. Some children are intuitively aware that they have come to earth for a relatively short length of time and verbalize this to family or friends. Yet the death of a young person is always a shock that seems incomprehensible.

Parents have shared with me how a piece of them died with their child and how difficult it is for them to feel happiness or joy again. Some lose all trust in life after enduring such a tragedy. On the other hand, some have shared with me how their child's death has made them emotionally stronger and able to handle whatever life may bring. In my experience as a medium, losing a child deeply transforms parents spiritually by acting as a catalyst in awakening them to probe their purpose in life and help others who've had similar tragedies. Despite the enormity of pain involved when a young person passes, I've seen people become comforted and healed by receiving communication from their children during readings. During these sessions, the gift of peace that mediumship provides is priceless. In these situations, I feel especially blessed to be able to deliver messages that bring understanding and reassurance to alleviate others' suffering.

The sessions I've included in this chapter share the common thread of the tragic and untimely loss of a son. Interestingly, all of the stories involve alcohol or substance abuse. I believe Spirit sent these families to me for understanding and healing because of my own journey through addiction and recovery. As is often the case, we best teach what we have most needed to learn.

On the Beach

The first transcript is taken from a session I did with a family that was coping with the unexpected loss of Bryan, who sent his family many signs that he was still around them. Among other things, this session illustrates that we must work through unresolved earthly emotions by facing and attempting to heal unfinished business created in the life we left. One way this is done is by helping others in need who have experienced the same pain as us.

Katy and John, an attractive, professional couple in their fifties, came to see me with hopes of hearing from their son, Bryan, 23, who died the previous year. Their daughter, Krista, accompanied them and took notes during our session. Their other son, Thomas, was unable to attend because he was at college. I had previously met Katy and Krista at a group session in which Bryan came through; however, I didn't remember his name or any details of that earlier reading. Once they were settled in my reading room and I said the opening prayer, I began by telling them information that I'd received before they had arrived.

"Just before tonight's session I felt your son was here because the name Chad kept coming to me. Is that your son?"

Katy's eyes lit up as she looked at me and smiled. "No, his name is Bryan but that's very interesting because his best friend's name is Chad."

"He's asking you to say hello to Chad," I said.

In my mind's eye, I saw a young man in his twenties standing on a beach wearing long, brightly colored shorts. I described this to the family.

"That's him! That's Bryan!" Katy exclaimed. "He wore those types of shorts a lot."

"What's the connection with Hawaii? I asked.

"We had a vacation there."

"He tells me the family's going back there, although you may not know it yet. I feel it's also symbolic that he's coming through standing on a beach, surrounded by tranquil water. He's communicating that he's at peace in spirit. He says he looks exactly as you remember him."

I continued interpreting the images and feelings that Bryan was sending.

"I feel your son's personality to be one of innocence, at least that's the way he comes through to me. There's also a lot of creativity with this young man–a tremendous amount, as a matter of fact. He speaks of drawing, painting and having a strong connection with music. He says you have some of his CDs," I said, turning to Krista.

"Yes, I do, but I don't listen to them," Krista responded.

"Well, there's a heart connection that's there and he wanted to let you know that he's aware of your having them. One of the ways he communicates with the family is through music and the association of certain songs with him that go from his heart to your heart."

Bryan impressed me with thoughts about his death and how both he and his family were healing from his tragic passing from a drug overdose. "He's saying that you're doing a good job of healing from his death and he's also healing in spirit. This makes him most happy. He says this is the number one message he wanted to get through to you. He is showing me a picture. I think it's a painting he did of a scene with him by the water. Does this make sense to you?"

Katy thought for a moment. "We have no painting, just a pencil sketch of his and a photograph of him on the beach that we cherish."

I realized that I'd misinterpreted the image that Bryan was sending me.

"Oh, yes, yes. I see now. It *is* a photo and he tells me you look at it a lot and think of him. He gives me the impression that this is the way he wants you to remember him, because it's telling of his true nature."

Bryan seemed to want to communicate his personality so his family could understand him better and why he had used drugs.

"Your son could be kind of introspective, quiet at times. This was the side of him that was perhaps the most challenging for you to understand and reach. He wants you to know he's gotten in deeper touch with this part of himself, the part that felt isolated and a little different from others. His spirit guides and counselors on the other side have helped him do this. He tells me he's had to work through unfinished emotional business he left earth with, and it has nothing to do with you, so please don't hold any guilt. He says that when he was here, music helped him to get in touch with feelings he couldn't communicate. It made him feel more connected to others."

The family looked at one another and nodded in agreement.

"He says that he is like you, Katy. Both of you are creative. He shows me drawing, painting and interior design. Have you been thinking of doing some redecorating this spring? Does this make sense to you?"

Katy replied, "Yes, we are. We spoke of this just recently."

"That's why he's bringing it through. Loved ones want us to realize they know about details in our lives. He says he'll inspire you with color schemes and such. Bryan wants you to know who he's with on the other side. John, he says he's with the older male on your dad's side of the family, a man who acts as his mentor. Is this your dad?"

John, previously silent, sat up in his seat. "Yes, Dad crossed a while ago. You know, that's very interesting because Katy's sister who is psychic told us the same thing, that she saw Bryan with my dad."

"Well, thank you for validating that because Bryan wants you to know that his grandfather has helped him by being a mentor to him. He's helped Bryan with some of the confusion he felt prior to crossing. Your dad, John, had the patience of Job."

John smiled. "Yes, this is true."

Bryan continued impressing me with the healing he had experienced in spirit.

"He says he had to face the repercussions of what he did here, his drug use and the way he left life. He says he saw how it also affected all of you after he crossed. He's very sorry for that."

Katy, John and Krista were silent. I noticed tears forming in Katy's eyes. In my mind's eye, I saw Bryan in a sailboat gliding on clear, blue water. Sensing the image was partly symbolic, I shared it with his family.

"He's sailing. I get the feeling this was a favorite activity of his, but it's deeper than that. He makes me feel as if he's overcome the stormy waters he experienced on earth. His emotions, symbolized by the water, are clearer. He's free of the drugs and it's smooth sailing now."

Katy replied, "Yes, he did enjoy sailing. We're so glad to know he's okay."

Suddenly, I got an image of Bryan with another male around his same age. "There's another young man with him, around his age, and he tells me his name starts with a 'J.' I feel he's from Bryan's paternal side. Who would this be?" I asked.

John thought for a moment before answering, "Oh, my! That must be my sister's son, Joseph, who passed! They were from the same generation–cousins."

"There's also a dog with him, a mid-sized one with long hair and floppy ears that turn down half-way. Sound familiar? I asked.

"Absolutely! That's our dog Tupper, a sheltie we had some years ago," Katy replied. "Does he happen to mention a cat by any chance?"

"Yes, I saw him with one earlier, a gray one. He says he is taking care of both the cat and the dog. He thought you'd like to know that."

Krista spoke up. "That was his favorite animal ever! She died not too long ago. Ooh, I'm so glad she's with him!"

Bryan showed me a large photo of himself sitting by a computer. "Do you have photos of him right next to your computer?" I asked. "He says he feels it when you look at these and think of him."

"Yes, we have several," Katy answered.

"He says he spends time in his old room every so often. He says he is able to move things on his dresser and that you've noticed this."

Krista exclaimed, "Yeah, we've noticed that things get moved around. We couldn't figure that out, although we thought it was him!"

I sensed it was important to Bryan that his family understood he was around them because the next image he showed me was a bright, yellow tulip.

"This yellow tulip I'm seeing, is it growing in a place you hadn't expected it to grow?" I asked. "Bryan is showing me it is growing by a tree."

Katy's eyes grew large as she said, "Why yes! We noticed it the other day and for some reason, felt compelled to cut it and put it on his grave. Was this a sign from him?"

"Yes, he says that it was. He also says he knows about Dad fertilizing the grass the other day."

"John just did that!" Katy said with excitement.

After a few more messages that validated his existence in spirit, I said, "You have done remarkably well in healing grief after Bryan's passing. I feel it has to do with the strength of your spiritual beliefs."

There was peace in Katy's voice as she spoke. "I hadn't felt before we lost him that my beliefs were that strong but Bryan made it so obvious through the signs he sent us that there is life after death and that what I wanted and believed to be true, he proved to be true."

I said, "You know, I feel very strongly that you and John are going to speak in front of groups about how you dealt with losing a child under tragic circumstances. There are a lot of people who could really benefit from hearing you. I feel there will be opportunities coming that Bryan will have a hand in from the other side."

Katy seemed surprised. "Us? Speak?"

"Yes, and don't be afraid to talk about the after-death communication you've received from Bryan through readings and on your own. People need to hear that since many others have had similar experiences."

Katy replied, "Oh, I'm not afraid of telling people that. I'm just shy about getting up in front of a group."

I laughed. "Well, I guess that proves that people fear public speaking more than death! Seriously though, you would be a shining example of a family who's survived an emotionally devastating event and reached out to help others. Part of your spiritual mission now is to share your healing. Bryan's memory will live on through your courage and generosity."

The family looked at one another as they considered the possibility. Katy said, "Well, alright. When the opportunity comes, we'll see. It does sound like a good idea, I guess."

"Bryan seems to think so," I answered, ending the session on this positive note.

When I spoke with this family more than a year after Bryan's death, I was amazed at the spiritual transformation they had undergone.

"I was never really certain that there was life after death," Katy said. "I wanted to believe it but I had no proof. My religion taught about an afterlife but I still had doubts. When Bryan died, he proved to me that it's true. I know my son is dead (in the physical sense) but I don't feel it because I know in my heart he's alive in spirit. I know that where we are now (on the earth) is just a temporary place to be, that there's something much larger," she said. "I feel that my mission now is to help other people understand they can connect with loved ones who have crossed. The reading with you gave me strong validation of Bryan's existence. You knew nothing about my son but gave me definite confirmation about his life. I am confident in helping others to accept that life goes on; to support that, I've built and maintained a website dedicated to Bryan that many people have visited."

Interestingly, John validated his son's compelling message addressing his parents' need to help others avoid a similar fate with drugs. He said, "I like to think that Bryan died for a reason, that drugs and his addiction put him in a position that he had no choice but to move on. We know he really loved us yet the drugs he used caused him to steal from us to support his habit. It was an intolerable situation for all of us. I believe he's trying to get me, from the other side, to help other kids avoid the problems he had. I don't know whether I'll be able to fulfill that desire, but I certainly do feel him inspiring me. Shortly after his passing, I began to take notes about what I was hearing from Bryan. In some of these, he advised me to put together a talk to give to parents and students about the danger of drugs. Recently, our local public school system sent me a letter to meet with them in an open forum to discuss ways to prevent drug abuse in our community. Before Bryan's death, I wouldn't have gotten involved with such a project but now I feel the need to do so and have already attended a few meetings."

Prior to their loss, the family rarely attended church, although they had gone years earlier. The week after Bryan passed, they went and have been going regularly since.

Krista said, "I now realize that when someone dies, the relationship lives on. The bonds are everlasting and I am no longer afraid to lose loved ones in my life. The fear of death is gone."

The Strong Survive
Imagine the immense grief of losing a son and a spouse within six months. The next story is one of courage, hope and transformation in such a situation. It shows the incredible spiritual strength we access in times of need and the resulting growth we experience as

a result of surviving extremely challenging circumstances.

Susan, a soft-spoken woman in her fifties, and her daughter, Beth, 33, entered my reading room and sat quietly as I said my opening prayer. For some reason, I felt the need to call upon extra healing energy from the angels and Divine Mother to help with this session. I soon discovered why.

"There's a woman standing next to you on your mother's side, two generations back from you, Susan," I began. "She is bringing through a child, someone definitely younger than you. It's not clear who he belongs to or how old he was when he passed but she is clearly bringing him through to you. Can you place him or does this make sense to you?"

Susan said softly, "Yes, it does. It's my son, Mark."

"She is saying that there has been a tremendous amount of healing that's taken place for you in the past several months through some sort of counseling you've both been doing. She is saying she is the one who inspired you to seek it. She urges you to continue because she indicates that you were considering not going back."

Both women nodded in agreement.

"I don't know who you want to contact in spirit, but in addition to the child, there is a man who stands right beside you, Susan, This means he is in your generation, a brother or spouse. He stands very close by your side. Has your brother crossed?"

Susan perked up and answered excitedly, "Yes!"

"He's here to support you," I said.

Suddenly I felt a sharp sensation in my head. "Your son is talking about the way he crossed. He impresses me with a severe injury to his head."

Susan began to sob. I reached out and took her hands in mine as I continued the reading.

"Your son gives me the impression he passed very quickly in a car accident."

"Well, yes, it was an all-terrain vehicle," Susan said tearfully.

"Oh, okay," I said. "It is the impact I was feeling. He wants you to know the momentary pain he suffered when he passed is over.

He's at peace now."

Susan sighed as Beth stroked her mother's arm.

Mark continued to impress me with details surrounding his death. As he connected with me, I felt as if he was a young man – 25, at the most – with a somewhat dare-devilish personality.

"He says he didn't have his helmet on and that was very stupid of him. He hit a rock in the trail and that's what threw the vehicle off balance. There was a prior accident, he says. That one he obviously survived."

"Yes, yes!" Susan blurted out.

"This communication has the feeling of being relatively recent because he's having some trouble understanding how this process works and getting his thoughts through to me. How long ago did this happen?"

"Just two months ago," Susan said.

"Oh, no wonder then. He shows me some sort of tribute done for him. It looks like a poem that someone in the family wrote for him. He says it's about his life and was read at the funeral. He appreciated that. Did you do this, Mom?" I asked Susan.

After a few moments, Susan answered, "Yes, it took me a few minutes to remember but yes, I did."

"He also is acknowledging a collage of photos you put together for his funeral. He liked the ones when he was young that you chose. And he was amazed at how many of his friends came to the funeral."

Mark then showed me an image of himself lying on the ground after his death.

"He wants you to know how easy it was to exit his body. He says he floated out of it and then hovered above it. He says, 'It was really neat, Mom. I could see everything that was going on around me and I went in and out of my body before I finally left it.' He mentions some concern on your part about the rescue efforts, — that that they weren't done right or fast enough. There's a message about the need for you to release that blame and guilt about not enough being done to save him."

Susan said, "Yes, it's true. We did feel that way, that more could have been done to save his life."

It seemed to be important to Mark to emphasize to his mother and sister what he felt physically before he passed into spirit. Sensing our concern with how much pain or suffering they might have felt, spirits who have passed in violent or accidental ways often want family members to know they are now at peace.

"He blacked out and never fully regained consciousness. He wants me to stress to you that he didn't really feel any pain because of this. He was out of his body before any pain registered. He is appearing to me to be physically fit, much like you remember him. Hopefully this eases your mind."

Both Beth and Susan looked relieved.

"He says he had a large music collection, some of it country music and that the two of you recently went through it. He talks of writing, performing and publishing music. Did you give some of his recordings to his friends?"

"Yes, we did," Susan answered.

"Well, he's happy that what he wrote is being shared with others. He wants me to tell you that he is playing music and spending time with children in spirit. This brings him joy.

"Mark is acknowledging a younger male, younger than him, in his family on earth. Who would this be?" I continued.

Susan and Beth looked at one another as they thought.

"It might be my son," Beth said.

"I don't know how old your son is but Mark tells me your son can see him. Children under the age of seven are usually tuned into the spirit world much more than adults," I said.

"He's three," Beth answered.

"Speaking of children, Mark says that there will be another child coming into the family here. He doesn't say when this will happen but that it will because he's seen the child in spirit."

Beth and Susan seemed a little surprised, yet happy with this news.

Suddenly another man in spirit stepped into the reading and stood next to Susan.

"There's a man who stands next to you and tells me he had

diabetes. Do you recognize him?" I asked.

"That must be Jim – Mark's father – my first husband!" Susan exclaimed.

"Mark impresses me that the month of July is important for some reason. What is the significance?"

Susan began to cry as she answered, "That's when Mark moved back home with the family. He had been estranged from us for a while because of his addiction to drugs and alcohol."

"I see. He is saying that he regrets that and urges you to tell others in the family to not be stubborn and do the same thing as he did. This is part of the healing that needs to go on for your family. There is no time like the present to make amends," I said.

Susan and Beth shook their heads in agreement with this message.

"Who is Jeffrey?" I then asked.

Susan let out a loud sob and answered, "Oh my God, that's my brother!"

"Mark is acknowledging him and also wants you to say hello to the rest of the family for him. It's important to him that they know he's not still upset with them. I don't know if they believe in mediumship but I'll pass the message along anyway so you can tell them."

The older woman who had appeared earlier, two generations back removed from Susan, suddenly stepped back into the reading.

"An older woman, seems like a grandmother to you, is coming through and talking about someone in your family who has been having routine blood tests done lately. She says the condition fluctuates with this person; sometimes he feels good, sometimes not. Does this make sense to you?"

Susan replied, "Yes! That's my husband, Frank. He's had to have these sorts of tests for a while now."

"She is also telling me he has a condition related to the bone marrow."

"Yes, that is true. He's ill with cancer as well as diabetes."

"She is saying there might be an improvement in his health

soon but to keep on praying because it works."

At this point, I could feel the energy from the spirit world begin to dissipate. In the span of less than an hour, Susan and Beth had received significant validation that Mark and other family members were with them in spirit. Both women's moods were noticeably lighter than when they had arrived. Susan especially seemed deeply moved by the session.

"Please know that your son, brother and other family members are with you in spirit. It was difficult for Mark to come through so soon after his passing but he desperately wanted you to know he's fine. He is saying he will communicate with you in dreams. He loves you very much," I finished.

Six months after Mark's death, Susan's husband, Frank, passed. A short time later, Susan and her family came to a group session in which Mark brought Frank (his stepfather) through and told the family he had come to get him when he passed. One amazingly specific thing that Frank communicated during the reading (Susan later validated it) was that she had recently moved his wristwatch from her dresser to a desk downstairs, right next to his photo. As many spirits do, he thanked her for taking care of him for seven years when he was sick. He also expressed his wishes for Susan to find love again.

Due to the tremendous void Susan felt after her son's passing, she suffered from insomnia and depression. Because of Frank's illness, Susan quit her job to take care of him fulltime. Awake for most of the night, Susan, who had never really sewn before, began to make beautiful pieces she never imagined she could create. She had no idea where this ability had suddenly come from. As she sat sewing one night, she heard Mark's voice say from spirit, "Mom, this is a gift from God for all of your pain and suffering. Use it." Susan slowly started to feel a renewed sense of purpose. Grateful for something to focus on, Susan gave the items she made as gifts and before long, people offered to buy them.

When Frank died, Susan was still grieving Mark. With both her husband and son gone, she felt devastated and alone. In addition to traditional therapy, she continued to sew, which was also therapeutic. Within a year, Susan had made enough items to open a gift shop in her home and planned a grand opening celebration.

In a recent phone call, Susan said she felt a strong drive to continue sewing and running her shop. "I feel inspired to do this and that is something I pay attention to nowadays–the intuitive guidance I receive. When my husband died, I was so relieved that he wasn't suffering anymore but when Mark died, I can't even begin to describe the pain I felt," she said. "He and I were very close. Even though he was in his early thirties when he died, I felt as if he was still a child because he had so many problems that he needed my help with. Despite his addictions or maybe because of them, I felt as if I needed to take care of him and his death was so hard for me to accept. My spiritual beliefs have deepened since Mark died, after which I started to read all the metaphysical books I could to bring me understanding and comfort. The more I read, the more I believed he was not dead and that he was still with me. I wanted to know how I could still have contact with him. That is why I sought help from you, Carole. My readings with you brought me great comfort because they confirmed many things for me, things that you could have never known. Mark showed me through you that life is not over when we die. I feel peaceful knowing I'll be with my husband and son again when I pass into spirit."

Here's a Rainbow for You, Mom

The following session demonstrates how loved ones in spirit remind us to live in the moment and release the past, including events surrounding their deaths. In some readings I've done, spirits refuse to connect with the physical or emotional pain associated with their passing because they realize, from a spiritual perspective, that it prevents them and loved ones from moving on. Some, such as suicides, simply don't want to re-experience the trauma of their death. Many communicate the desire to be remembered in a more uplifting way, such as happy memories they share with family and friends. After crossing over, spirits become aware that their mission on earth is temporarily completed and it's time to return home to rest, review the completed lifetime and make plans for further spiritual growth.

Pam, 45, sought my help to reconnect with her son, Tyler, who had come through briefly in one of my group sessions. He had passed in a car accident, the cause of which was never fully clear. Pam had many questions about Tyler's death. She hoped he would come through more strongly in our private session and provide answers to give her emotional closure.

"What I most want to know is, was it really Tyler's time to die or was his life cut short?" she asked, her voice full of anticipation. "I want to know who or what caused him to run off the road. Was there anyone else involved?"

An image of a piece of paper with writing on it formed in my mind. "Your son is showing me some kind of a written report concerning the accident. I feel this is something you either have now or will have in the near future. It feels to me as if it is a police report. Is this something you already have?" I asked.

"I have the coroner's report and it says there was intoxication at the time of the accident, but it doesn't describe how the accident happened. I need to know if someone else was involved."

"I feel it was an accident and no one else was involved but him. He impresses to me that he was visually impaired, perhaps because of the weather. Tyler wants you to go on with your life, to lay these things to rest so you can experience joy again. Many spirits come through with this message. He had completed what he came here to do. It was time for him to move on. That doesn't mean he intentionally caused his death, do you understand? By your stressing the accident, it keeps you locked in to grief. He wants you to move beyond that. Have you looked into group counseling?"

"Yes, I am in a small group at my church."

"He tells me that he inspired you to do that so you could get help. Please understand that moving on from his death does not mean you don't love him anymore. He doesn't want to talk about the accident because he is detached from it. He wants you to understand that what's really important is your happiness. He says that you still have work here to do."

With frustration in her voice, Pam asked, "How am I supposed to make these life changes? What am I supposed to do?"

"Release the past through forgiveness. This has to do with other family issues besides his death. Where is his father?"

"He's in town but we are divorced."

"Your son urges both of you to forgive one another," I advised her. "Cleanse your heart of any bitterness you have. He also comes to his dad and inspires him to do the same. Interestingly enough, he acts like a teacher and a healer, a "way shower" to both of you. He's reversed the roles of parent and child."

As he drew nearer to me, I sensed Tyler's personality.

"Your son was a free spirit. He expressed himself best through creative vehicles like writing poetry and music. He communicated many of his feelings in this way. I get the sense of his being very sensitive emotionally, yet very genuine and warm. He was a deep thinker. He says his brother here on earth is very much like him and that he comes around him."

"Yes, yes, that's so true. His younger brother, Tom, is very creative and intuitive. He has told me he feels when Tyler comes around him." Then Pam validated a puzzling message that Tyler had given about Tom in the earlier group session I had facilitated about Tom giving him an embroidered necklace in the shape of a guitar.

"At the time, I couldn't think of what he meant by the necklace. When I asked Tom about it, he immediately recognized it as a reference to the macramé necklace he made for him," she said. Pam paused for a moment before asking, "What was Tyler's lesson on earth?"

"He says that he was a teacher of sorts, and still is. He is working with autistic children on the other side. By the way, he gives me the feeling that there was no generation gap between the two of you. The two of you were more buddies than parent and child. You learned a lot from him."

"Yes, that is true," Pam answered. "I'd like to know what I'm supposed to have learned from his death."

"His death taught you many things. You will help others who have lost children. I also get the impression that you'll be speaking and writing articles to help other people cope with grief because one of your missions in life is communication. He wants you and others to understand what it's like in the spirit world so he'll inspire you with this when you're writing and speaking. He says he will help Tom write and publish music someday. Tom will also be involved in teaching."

"Yes, I don't doubt that I'm to share what I've learned with others and it's true that Tom is going to school for art education," Pam said.

Like many people I've read for, Pam had doubts about whether Tyler was happy in the spirit world. In response to her question about this, Tyler sent me a striking image.

"He's showing me a large, yellow smiley face, the kind that was popular in the seventies," I said.

"That is so perfect!" Pam said, with pure delight in her voice. "Tyler loved that symbol! I remember the time he borrowed his brother's smiley face necktie to wear!"

We both laughed. It was an excellent validation that we were indeed talking with Tyler.

"I do have one final question," she said, aware that the session was almost over. "How do I reach Tyler in spirit? I mean, how can I easily communicate with him?"

It's a question I've been asked many times. "Use a photograph of him and send love to him while looking at it," I suggested. "He will also visit you in your dreams and will come to you through music. When you get the hunch to turn on the radio or tune into a particular station, there will be a song playing that will remind you of him. It's called synchronicity and it's a common way spirit communicates with us. You can also ask him to come to you in a way that's easily recognizable. Inspirationally speaking, he says he'll help you to finish the poem or song you started after his death. Do you know what this means?"

Pam replied, "Yes, I did start to write a song and never finished it. Wow! I didn't know he would know about that!"

"He will work with you to complete it," I reiterated.

Tyler then delivered a final message about who he was with in the spirit world.

"He shows me an older male at least two generations back from him. He says the two of them spend a lot of time talking over there. This man used to smoke a pipe and says that you once gifted him with something that had to do with smoking. Can you place him?"

Pam thought for a moment before saying, "Hmmm, that sounds like my ex-husband's father, Pap. I gave him a beautiful pipe. It's nice to know he's with Tyler."

As the session drew to a close, Pam's anxiousness about having her questions answered had subsided. I felt satisfied in knowing that Tyler had delivered some powerful evidentiary messages to validate his existence in spirit. He had also provided valuable insights that would help his mother gain closure with his death, despite not having all the answers about it.

Up until Tyler's passing, Pam was reasonably satisfied with the amount of spiritual growth she had experienced through reading metaphysical books, meditating and praying. After Tyler's death, however, the inner peace she had worked so hard to achieve was replaced with anger and bitterness as she was forced to cope with her tremendous loss. Realizing she couldn't remain immersed in these self-defeating feelings for long, Pam made a decision that ultimately changed her life.

"I knew I needed to connect with Tyler on a level beyond the anger I felt about his untimely death," she said. "In addition to being mother and son, Tyler and I shared a special bond, one of deep understanding, support and friendship. After his death, I began to ask myself how I could connect with him in a way that I hadn't when he was alive. My brother told me, 'Pam, I know this is the worst that could happen to you but if there's anyone I know who can make lemonade out of lemons, it's you.' I had believed in life after death but Tyler's passing gave me the motivation to really test that belief. I began to tune into his spirit and notice what signs he might be sending me."

Since Tyler's passing, Pam has been blessed to receive many signs that he's still with her. The most powerful of these has been the appearance of rainbows when she is feeling especially sad. On one such day, as she was driving to work, Pam silently asked Tyler to send her a rainbow if he could hear her. A few minutes later, she looked up at the cloudy sky and a beautiful one appeared out of nowhere.

"I started to laugh because I knew it was a direct message from Tyler. He had sent me rainbows before when I was missing him. It's his way of letting me know he's happy and that I need to be, too. Instead of worrying about petty issues in life, I now search for the deeper meaning and lessons behind everything that happens to me. I used to spend time focusing on what *I* lost when Tyler died. I've since learned to focus on what is best for *him*. Although I miss him terribly, I now know I love him enough to let him go.

"The days when I begin to question the 'whys' and 'ifs' of his death are the days I try to focus the hardest on reaching my son through love, which elevates my mood," she continued. "In the beginning, I felt as if many mornings I didn't want to get out of bed because Tyler was gone. Now I understand that I can connect with him in a totally different way than I had before when he was here with me. My reading with you, Carole, showed me that it is possible to connect with those in spirit. It was so clear to me that the messages were from Tyler because they were so specific. It was emotionally uplifting because it helped me to release blame and guilt about his death. The reading provided me with the realization that despite his young age, his mission here was finished. That gave me peace. Most parents are concerned with the whereabouts and well being of their children. When Tyler died, I wanted to know where he was, if he was safe and happy. The reading gave me the reassurance I needed. At first, I wanted to come back to you again and again to receive this communication I so desperately wanted. But I realized I needed to establish my own connection with him. I now have the confidence to do this.

"I've developed a closer relationship with my spiritual guides since Tyler's death. Even though I've always considered myself to be a spiritual person, I never really asked for much guidance from God. Losing a child initially made me lose trust that life was going to happen the way I wanted it to happen. Now I feel I'm able to trust that when I ask for guidance, I will definitely receive it. I believe and accept that Tyler's death has meaning and that he can touch and help people through his death."

It's Really Me, Mom and Dad!

Rick, his wife, Nancy, both in their fifties, and their daughter, Jenny, came for two sessions in which they wished to be reunited with their son, Rick Jr., 23, who passed in a car accident two years earlier. I was particularly touched by Rick Sr.'s emotional sensitivity and grief concerning his son's passing when several times during the sessions, he broke down in tears as Jr. came through and offered indisputable proof of his continued existence in spirit. Nancy and Jenny had also been extremely traumatized by Jr.'s sudden passing and wanted answers to understand how and why this tragedy had happened. I knew this family was in desperate need of the reassurance and healing spirit communication offers. My readings with them contain strong evidentiary validation of life after death, including a strange physical manifestation that occurred during our second meeting.

After explaining the process of mediumship to them and saying my prayer, I perceived that a spirit woman was standing between Rick and Nancy, indicating she knew both of them, although she seemed to be closer to Nancy. She conveyed her personality as a talkative and somewhat stern, no-nonsense woman whose duty was to look after the family's health and well being.

"This woman acknowledges a diabetic connection that's related to her and also the family," I said. "She is concerned about your mom's health, Nancy, and is directing healing energy to her legs and feet. She also is telling you to make sure you exercise so your diabetes is kept under control."

Nancy shook her head in agreement and matter-of-factly said, "That's my grandmother."

As the reading progressed with other confirmations of relatives who had passed, I saw a young man standing back from the other spirits. He seemed reserved and hesitant to speak.

"I feel your son is here but he is standing back and letting the others speak first. He impresses me that he was like that in life. There were parts of him, especially his emotions, that he didn't show everyone. As I connect with him, I feel as if there may have been a slight chemical imbalance in the brain. Not huge but definitely there. That's part of why he had trouble relating to people on an emotional level. But he also impresses me as being a bit of a jokester, a tease. He especially liked to kid you, Jenny."

"Yes, that's true. He was always doing that," Jenny responded.

The family listened with interest as I continued describing what Jr. was telling me.

"He talks of his passing in a car accident and the impact to his head. There is also a message about a lot of shattered glass lying around him after the accident. But please know there was no suffering. I feel as if this was very quick, that he was out of here," I said, snapping my fingers.

"I get the feeling Jr. could be a bit of a daredevil because he's showing me himself riding on the back of a motorcycle with a friend. That's part of what contributed to his accident – his being a daredevil, that is."

"Oh, yeah!" Nancy exclaimed in agreement.

"He shows me an accident investigation being done and the police reports – especially conflicting ones – that showed different accounts of the incident.

Jenny gasped, "Oh, my gosh!"

Rick said quietly, "Yes, we know about the different reports. We weren't sure *what* happened."

I knew the delivery of this specific information (things I would have no way of knowing) was important to validate Jr.'s continued survival in spirit.

"There was a discrepancy between the reports with the timing and cause of the accident. He shows me the police measuring the skid marks on the road."

"Yes, yes, that's true!" Rick replied, his voice getting somewhat louder.

I sensed the smell of alcohol. "There seems to be a connection here with drinking. I don't know if your son used it on a regular basis," I said, hoping I wasn't delivering a message about their son that was too hard for Rick and Nancy to digest.

The couple shook their heads silently before saying with some resignation, "Yes, we knew that."

"Jr. is whispering the name 'Mark.' Who is he?" I asked.

"Oh, my gosh!" the family shouted in unison.

Jenny replied, "Okay, Mark is a guy I work with. He is the one who came across my brother right after the accident. He had his hand on my brother's heart when he died."

"Jr. says he watched the whole scene from hovering above his body," I relayed. "He says he stayed at the scene because he wanted someone to find his body. He shows me the area where it happened, near an embankment, by a large tree. There is a memorial wreath that someone placed there after it happened."

"Yes, that's true! Someone did place a wreath in that spot!" Rick said.

Nancy asked, "Is he pleased with Mark?"

"Yes, I feel as if there's an acknowledgement for him. Jr. wants to thank him for being there. Will you please pass that along?"

"Yes, I will," Jenny agreed.

I felt the link with Jr. grow stronger as he continued to bring through detailed information that would erase any lingering doubt in his family's minds that it was him.

"The other name he gives me is Ron," I said.

Again the family gasped as Jenny announced, "That's one of his best friends."

"He says to tell him hello," I said.

The next thing Jr. said brought tears to everyone's eyes, including mine.

"He says he wants you to move beyond his death, to see how it has changed you and made you understand yourselves better spiritually. He wants you to learn and grow from his death, to not let it be in vain. He says you'll help other parents who have lost children by sharing your story with them. Down the road – when you're stronger –you'll do this. He wished he could have opened up more emotionally when he was here. That was part of his mission, to get in touch with himself on a deeper level. He says he is doing that now over there."

After a few moments of silence, Rick, his voice filled choked with emotion, asked, "Does he know how much he is loved?"

"Yes, he does, even though he did not express it to you when he was here. That was hard for him to do. But he does know it and says that his coming through to you tonight and also in your thoughts is his way of giving back to you the love you gave to him. He knew he wasn't going to be on earth for a long period of time and he told you that, didn't he?" I asked.

"Yes, that's true. He told Dad a few months before he died that he wouldn't live to see 25," Jenny replied.

"Each of us contracts for certain lessons and the approximate length of time it takes to learn those before we are born. We choose our parents and they agree to have us as children," I explained. "When our lessons are complete, we return to our home in the spirit world. I know that may not make sense to you, but it is the way our souls operate."

A moment passed before Rick spoke up, "I just want him to know he can come to me at any time, and tell him if he's going to come around me to make it clear it's him so I don't miss it!"

"He does come to you and he will," I responded. "That radio you have in the basement – the one by the workbench – he'll make it change channels when you're down there working. He'll come to you in many, many ways. Please understand that your son is free and happy in spirit. He wants you to be happy too," I said, as the session drew to a close.

Six months later when I met with the family, I was strongly impressed by my spirit guides before the session began to help them examine their emotions about Jr.'s death. Rick, especially, had struggled after Jr.'s passing. I knew this would not be an easy session to conduct but one that was vital.

"It's time to look at the anger, guilt and grief you are feeling about Jr.'s passing. There is a feeling I sense with him that you are angry about what he did – the senseless way he died, especially with the alcohol involved in the accident. He says he has some guilt about leaving the way he did and he is concerned about your welfare. He says he wants you to feel better, to not be mad or sad anymore. He speaks about his lack of self-esteem, something he really didn't get in touch with when he was alive. Jr. was and is a teacher for you to heal these issues in yourselves."

Nancy was upset by this message. "It makes me feel bad that Jr. thinks we're mad at him! We are not really mad at *him* but at the stupid thing he did that caused him to lose control in the accident," she said.

"Your son says that alcoholism is present on both sides of the family," I commented, looking at Nancy and Rick. "Even though neither of you drink, there are inherited behavior patterns of alcoholism that are passed down to other generations. It's important in gaining closure with Jr.'s death that all of you get in touch with how these patterns have affected you. He says that he's discovered that he tried to make himself feel good with things outside of himself. Part of his healing, and yours, is learning about feeling good from the inside out."

"Yes, it's true about the drinking," Rick admitted. "My father had a problem. But does Jr. hold back from communicating with us because he thinks we're mad at him?" he asked, with hurt in his voice. "Because if it's true, please tell him no matter how mad we may have been about his death, we always love him and want to hear from him. I just want to make sure he knows that."

I responded, "You can tell him that on your own. You don't need a medium to say that because you have a strong heart connection with your son. Loved ones in spirit are around us constantly and can hear our thoughts and feel our emotions."

All of a sudden, a strange thing happened. As the family watched in amazement, a large wisp of smoke rose from the incense burner on the altar behind me. I had extinguished the incense 45 minutes earlier and no smoke had been present since then. Yet there it was, clearly burning as I turned around to look at what the family was pointing at.

"Wow! It wasn't doing that before!" exclaimed Nancy. "I saw that a minute or so ago, but I thought it was just my imagination because I saw you put it out when we came in!"

"That is bizarre," I said in a low voice, shaking my head in astonishment. This strange occurrence had not happened before in any of my sessions. I was amazed by Jr.'s ability to produce such a manifestation.

"I think it's great!" said Rick. "He's letting us know he's here."

"Well, we've certainly had a manifestation here today that proves Jr. is around," I said. "He'll give you others, one of which will be through your TV. So, if it hasn't happened yet, it will. Please remember that the most important thing for all of you to do now is face and deal with your emotions. People get stuck in grief when they stuff their feelings. I recommend you try counseling to deal with this."

Nancy quickly responded, "We tried that. It only made things worse because we constantly talked about his death. But I know I have a lot of anger to deal with–that I admit."

"The key to moving beyond this tragic event is to use it for your growth. That's what Jr. wants you to do. Talk about your feelings. You must begin to pick up the pieces and move on," I advised.

Although the session had been difficult emotionally, the family left feeling pleased with the validation and messages they received from Jr. I knew they were still coming to terms with the fact that their son and brother was not coming back, even though he was still very much connected to them in spirit. Their spiritual awakening had just begun.

When I spoke with Nancy and Rick three years after Jr.'s passing, they were still dealing with their grief about his death. Both talked candidly with me about their feelings.

"I don't get the enjoyment out of doing things that I used to," Rick said. "Some days it is an effort to just get out of bed. Although I still get things done, it seems to take me longer.

Sometimes, I think about Jr. and I'm fine; other times, I just lose it and break down. It's really unpredictable. For example, the other night I saw something on TV that reminded me of him and I became sad."

Nancy also found it difficult to carry on. "I have tremendous anger that I have a hard time dealing with. It's not anger towards Jr. or God; it's anger at the situation that took him from us. I put so much effort into being a 24/7 mother; I did what I did because I loved him so much, and now he's gone. However, I do believe there was divine intervention in Jr.'s death because he didn't suffer when he died. It was as if God wanted him to go quickly in the accident and he did. Years before it happened, I dreamed that Jr. had been killed in an accident, so I think I was being prepared in a way. I feel that my spiritual beliefs have intensified, especially when Jr. lets us know through signs that he's around."

Rick added, "As you told us in the session, we believe Mark, his friend, was meant to come across Jr. that night so he wouldn't be alone when he died. What's been really hard for me is constantly wondering if what everyone tells me about seeing loved ones again on the other side is actually true. I hope it is because I want to see Jr. again. Will he still recognize me as his dad?" Rick asked me, choking back tears.

"Absolutely," I answered. "When we die, we are reunited with many people we've known and loved on earth."

The couple agreed that their sessions with me had given them a stronger connection with their son.

Nancy said, "You're the link with the spirit world we needed. I feel closer to Jr. because of you."

"We've met people who don't believe in this," Rick added. "I don't push my beliefs on them but instead smile inwardly knowing the peace of mind this type of communication has given us. It gives me a great sense of security to know that you, as a medium, can hear what Jr. is saying and that you can answer our questions."

Jr. has sent his parents many indications that he's around, the most recent occurring on the third anniversary of his passing.

When Rick came home from work that day, the answering machine's outgoing message played twice spontaneously. Later that evening, it came on again. The couple felt it was Jr. announcing his anniversary in spirit (validated by the machine playing three times, once for each year) and giving them comfort. Rick examined the machine, which was relatively new, and found nothing wrong with it. "We were feeling down that day and he knew it," said Rick.

Another incident that they believe involved Jr. had been mentioned in the second reading I did for them. "The surround-sound on our TV set hadn't worked for over a year," Nancy said. "The night we had our reading with you, I was up late thinking about the session. I put the dogs outside and on my way through the living room, I heard talking. Startled, I looked up and noticed the screen of the TV I had shut off was lit with a blue background and snow on it. When I pushed the power button on, the set came on. When I pushed it off, the screen returned to the way it was, with the blue background and snow. I decided to leave it that way for the night. The next day, I told Rick to check out the set but didn't tell him about my experience from the night before. When he turned it on, the surround-sound that hadn't been working came on. After I explained to Rick what had happened the night before, I said, 'Well, I guess our son fixed the TV set for us!' These things seem to happen when we are feeling our bluest. I've kept track of the timing of these incidents and that's when they happen."

"I know he does it to bring us comfort," Rick agreed. "No matter what he does to let us know he's around, we always say, 'Thanks, Jr. We're glad you're here'."

CHAPTER FIVE

A PARENT'S LOVE NEVER DIES

Life is eternal and love is immortal; and death is only a horizon,
and a horizon is nothing save the limit of our sight.
—Rossiter W. Raymond

In August 2003, my mother quietly passed after suffering from Parkinson's Disease for eight years. Because she clearly stated in her living will that she wanted no extraordinary means of life support at the end, when she lost the ability to swallow (a common symptom of the illness), my family and I made preparations for her death. For a week, we visited her in the nursing home where she'd resided since breaking her hip nine months earlier. Her written wishes dictated that we give her means of comfort only, such as morphine for pain and mouth swabs to relieve dryness. I held her hand and told her I loved her. Until she became unconscious, she answered me in a whispery voice, saying she loved me, too. We played soft music in her room to comfort her and I brought a small, plush dog for her to hold as she lay motionless. Each night during that week, I prayed for her easy transition into spirit and asked my spirit guides to give me the emotional strength to cope with her death. I was terribly concerned about what my mom was feeling physically, with the complete absence of food and water in her system. Due to her illness, she had already lost many pounds and her body was frail. The thought of her suffering during the dying process was intolerable. When I looked at her lying in bed, she seemed so vulnerable, so helpless, her small frame nearly disappearing under the blankets.

Despite my years of work with reconnecting clients with deceased loved ones, I felt alone and afraid. My mom was dying and I wasn't sure how to cope with it. I began to question some of my long-held spiritual beliefs. *Is this stuff about the afterlife really true?* Maybe I, as a medium, was merely reading people's minds and honing in on their memories of loved ones. *Was Mom really going to die?* Never mind that two weeks before we knew of her inability to swallow, her side of the family in spirit appeared to me in meditation and said, "If there's anything that needs to be said to your mother, now is the time." I had sloughed off the message as my imagination since Mom was stable at the time. *I made that up,* I thought. *She'll probably live another two or three years.* When it became evident that my relatives on the other side were indeed right about Mom's passing, I began to wonder if she would communicate with me after she passed. Maybe she would be angry that we, her family, didn't at least try to save her despite her wishes.

One night as I lay awake, I received a message that I will never forget. A voice in my head said, "Carole, look beyond the physical. Don't get wrapped up in what you're seeing happen to your mom's body. The soul does not know suffering. When you visit your mom tomorrow, see the immortality of her soul instead of the wasting of her body." Amazed and overwhelmed by the clarity and the power of the message, my eyes filled with tears. It seemed simple enough, but would I be able to do it?

The next day, my perception had noticeably shifted. When I walked into her room, I focused on the beauty of Mom's spirit, not the hollowness of her physical form. I became aware of the grace and dignity of her dying and felt relieved that she was going home after a good, satisfying life. Mom's death transformed me in many ways, not the least of which has been a deepened sense of compassion for clients whose grief I can now empathize with. I've had several dreams in which Mom appeared to me, letting me know she is alive and well in spirit and I've often felt her presence. At times, I hear her voice in my head, offering advice as only a mother can, with particular situations I've struggled with. I know beyond any doubt that I will see her again when my life on earth is finished.

No matter where we go in life, the physical, emotional, mental and karmic bonds we share with our parents influence our lives deeply and significantly. Even in the absence of a direct relationship, such as estrangement or adoption, we still carry the genetic blueprints of our mother and father, which affect our biological make-up, tendencies and choices. For many of us, in addition to being primary nurturers during childhood, parents are role models, mentors, protectors, confidants and teachers. When a parent passes, the child inside of us mourns. We may feel orphaned, even if one parent survives. Our family as we knew it in childhood is changed forever. No matter how much we may have idolized them as children, when parents die, we realize they are mortal. During the grieving process, we need to know they are safe and still watching over us. Since loving relationships are eternal, they are never destroyed by death.

The stories in this chapter are representative of many readings I've done in which mothers, fathers and other earthly guardians communicate their existence in spirit with messages of love, hope, forgiveness and sometimes, humor. If you have experienced the passing of your parent(s) and are grieving, my hope is that reading about these sessions brings you comfort and healing.

The first story is about a woman who sought my help in gaining reassurance that her mother's existence was continuing in spirit. The session was particularly memorable for me because in addition to providing specific evidence of this mother's life on earth, it offered validation – by means of an astounding physical manifestation – that proved she was still very much alive in spirit.

Dimes from Heaven

Gail, a strikingly pretty, well-dressed woman in her early fifties, came for a session shortly after Thanksgiving one year. Unbeknownst to me, she had lost her mother two-and-a-half years ago and was still in grief over her passing. After opening with a prayer, I immediately sensed the presence of a strong female spirit on Gail's right side, indicating that she was from the maternal side of Gail's family. I soon discovered that this spirit was one of those who are so overjoyed by the process of reconnection with their family that their thoughts come through fast and furious—sometimes too quickly for me to interpret correctly. When this happens, I calmly tell them to slow down so nothing is lost in translation.

"The female who stands on the mother's side of your family is coming through very strongly. She seems to want to emphasize that she is very much with you all the time. She is very excited to talk with you and says she's been waiting to come through to you in this way—she knew you were coming to see a medium. I'm going to have to ask her to slow down her thoughts because I'm having some difficulty keeping up with her."

Gail's face lit up with a large smile, even though she said nothing.

"She feels like a motherly figure to me," I continued. "Again she impresses me with the thought that she is with you 100 percent. She wants you to know that she has been sending healing energy to your shoulders. She makes me feel as if you've been experiencing some kind of stress lately."

Gail nodded her head in agreement, her eyes becoming misty. "Yes, I know, it's my mother."

"She wants you to know that the dream communication you've had is indeed her. It's not your imagination, in other words. She says she told you she would be visiting you in your dreams and to not doubt that it's really her coming through to you in this way."

"Yes, I have had many dreams of her," Gail said.

Suddenly, I sensed the smell of roses in my mind. "She also comes through to you with the scent of roses from time to time. She is handing you a pink rose, which is symbolic of her softness, her gentleness. She tells me the rose matches the color that is in your aura, which means you have a gentle and heart-centered way about you."

I next became aware of a mild pressure in my chest area. "Your mom tells me there was something wrong with her heart or lung area. I feel pressure and shortness of breath right here," I said, placing my hand over my chest. "Is this what she passed from?"

"Yes, she had both heart and lung problems."

"She says she is with her mother, your grandmother, whose name sounds like Mary or Margaret. And there is a woman, Ruth, who makes her presence known to you also."

"Those are both of my grandmothers' names!" Gail exclaimed. "Margaret is my mom's mother."

Gail's mom showed me the number 10 for some reason; I knew it had to be of significance. "Why does she show me the number 10? Either there's a connection with the tenth of the month or the tenth month, which is October."

Gail looked puzzled and said, "Wow, I don't know."

I am used to the fact that people may not be able to immediately claim information that comes through in a session. That's why I tape-record the spirit communication whenever possible. I advised Gail to simply store the message for possible future validation.

Images of a shiny ring and other pieces of jewelry appeared in my mind. I relayed this to Gail. "Your mom is showing me jewelry that she says is passed down to you from her. In particular, there's a special ring that she is talking about – something that was given to you. Do you understand this?"

Again, Gail could not validate this message but said, "My mother loved jewelry. I have to think about what ring she is referring to."

As I tuned back into what was being communicated from the spirit world, the next message was one of utmost importance for Gail, who was still mourning her mom's passing. "Your mom says, 'Please don't feel as if death separates people.' She wants you to know she's still with you, even though she's in a different plane of existence. She says she's discovered a lot of things since she's crossed. She is making me feel as if she's really expanded her ideas about who we are as spirits. It's important for her to pass this information along to you so that when it's your time to pass, you will not be afraid of dying. Your mom comes through with a great deal of reassurance about this.

"She also thanks you for the good job you did with her caretaking before her death. She shows me a wheelchair and says she had trouble climbing stairs."

"Yes, I did take care of her and she was in a wheelchair near the end so she couldn't climb stairs."

To lighten things up, Gail's mother brought through a humorous message. "I hate to ask this, Gail, but were you thinking of having cosmetic surgery?" I inquired.

Gail blushed and responded, "Well, yes, I was recently talking about having a Botox injection done. Why?"

"Your mom told me to tease you about that. She says, 'Honey, it's what inside that counts'," I laughed.

"She always used to say that," Gail said, joining in the laughter.

"She also wants to talk about your hair. Have you changed your hairstyle recently?"

"I just had it lightened. That's amazing!"

"Well, she says she likes it that way much better than when it was dark."

At this point, the reading took a turn towards Gail's future. "I am being shown that you will do some major redecorating and overseas travel in the near future. Anything planned?"

"Yes, as far as the decorating goes, that is. I am planning on moving next year. I would love to travel," Gail said with a smile.

"There will also be some sort of recognition for you in your career, a certificate or award given. Your mom is showing me that this will happen in the near future."

Aware that the session was drawing to a close, I asked Gail if she had any questions. She thought for a moment before responding.

"I always ask my mom to let me know she's around by sending me pennies that I will find in different places," she said. "To me, it gives me comfort that she is still around. You know—pennies from heaven. The other day I asked her to do this and at first I didn't find any. I was really down. Then I went to the grocery store and as I was checking out, I looked down and there was a penny by my feet. Is this really her doing that for me?"

"Yes, it is, but your mom is showing me a dime. You've heard of pennies from heaven but she will be sending you *dimes* from heaven soon," I clarified.

Gail's face lit up, "That would be neat and a perfect validation because Mom's birthday is on the tenth of the month. A dime is 10 pennies!"

"You'll find dimes in the next week or so in odd places. Watch and see. Those are from your mom. By the way, remember earlier in the session when I told you she was showing me the number 10 and you couldn't claim it? Well, you just did by saying her birthday was on the tenth of the month," I finished as the session ended.

After this session, Gail returned periodically for other readings that focused primarily on her life and career, although her mother did come through in several of these, as well. When I spoke with her recently about these sessions, she cheerfully related that she is a much more positive person as a result of our work together.

"When my mother died, I felt as if someone ripped me open, took everything out, put me back together and told me to go live my life again. 'Move on,' so to speak. It was extremely devastating for me. We were very close. I ate and slept very little when she was sick and prayed a lot. I thought she would survive her illness. I really didn't feel anything hit me hard until after Mom's funeral; then the grief came. I felt so depressed when she died. Carole, I believe you came into my life because my mother sent me to you through an acquaintance of mine–someone I barely knew who told me she felt compelled to tell me about you."

"After our sessions, I felt exhilarated because it's as if I'm talking directly to my mom. You've told me things that only my mom and I knew. By the way, I did receive a nomination in the mail for a teaching award shortly after our first reading. You told me Mom said there would be recognition for me in my career!"

Gail proceeded to talk about how our sessions helped her with the concept of death. "After that first reading, I started to under-stand that Mom really hadn't left me. I now relate to her through signs, feelings and my intuition. When I close my eyes at night, I sometimes see a large, white flash of light, especially when I ask to see it and when I'm stressed. I feel it's my mom because we've always shared a sort of telepathic communication. I also thank the angels for helping me with my life. In particular, our sessions have given me a closer connection with the angels. When I feel down, I listen to the session tapes, which definitely prove to me that Mom is still alive in spirit."

I asked Gail if she had found any dimes the week after our first reading. With excitement, she told me, "On the seventh day after the reading, I was feeling very disappointed because I hadn't yet found a dime. I had been sick most of the week and stayed in the house most of the time. That day, I decided to get gas and a cup of coffee at a local convenience store. When I walked to the door of the store, I felt a slight tap on the top of my head and for some reason, I happened to look down at the ground. There was a dime right by my feet! At the same time that I saw it, I heard my mother's voice say to me in my head, 'I left you plenty of dimes but you were in the house all week so other people got them. Now go and get yourself a cup of coffee.' It was the sign I'd been waiting for!" Gail said, exuberantly.

Gail shared further validation of her mother's dime communications that happened a few months after the reading. "A friend of mine, Rita, who also knew my mom, had blood screenings done that indicated she had cancer, so she went into the hospital for further testing. When she took off her jacket in her room, she reached into one of the pockets and pulled out a dime. She had no idea how it got there, as she never stored spare change in her pockets. Rita is a very neat person and has always kept her pockets clean. Well, she and I both believe it was a sign from my mom, because she was given a clean bill of health. She said my mom was her good luck angel and the dime was a sign from heaven."

A Chip off the Old Block

The following case contains compelling proof that a father's love for his only child stretches from heaven to earth. It also answers a question that I am commonly asked concerning loved ones' involvement in our lives after they pass. In this story, Tina receives startling validation that her father helps her run her own business, much as he did when he was on earth.

Tina came for a private session to make further contact with her father who had come through during a group session. Pleasant, warm and professional, she took many notes during the course of our hour together.

"I sense your dad is here but he's having some trouble reaching my mind," I began. "This feels like a recent crossing to me. He impresses to me that he crossed from ongoing heart trouble and difficulties with breathing. His condition went up and down but near the end he tells me he felt as if he was spiraling downhill. His mother welcomed him into spirit when he finally did cross."

Confused, Tina said, "His mother is still here."

"Well then, who is the female in his mother's generation? Was there someone who was like a mother to him, a godmother perhaps?"

"I don't know a lot about his mother's side of the family but I'll check."

"She is very nurturing towards your father and feels like a mother. This lady spent much time with him when he was younger and is one generation removed from him. Can you claim the name of Betty?"

Tina thought. "I seem to recall there was an Aunt Betty. I didn't know her."

"He says he's with her, his father and your grandfather, who passed many years ago. I know that because I see him standing far back from your dad. This man is wearing overalls and is very earthy. He was a hard worker by the looks of his hands."

"That's my grandfather. He always wore those."

"He acknowledges Joseph and also Mary. He sends his love."

"That's his brother and mother."

"What is the connection to Florida?"

"Both of them live there."

"There is an acknowledgement for a name in the family that begins with the letters N-A," I continued.

"That's my daughter, Nalene and my mom, Naomi. I also have

a friend named Nancy that Dad knew."

"Your dad had a very easy crossing. When he was ready, he just slipped out of his body. He says he actually went to the other side several times before he finally crossed. He connects with you with much tenderness, right through your heart. There's a feeling here with him needing to tell you to release any doubts about not expressing your feelings to him enough. He gives me the impression that you've felt as if this has left you with some unfinished business regarding his passing. I'm to tell you it's healed, as far as he's concerned."

Tina quietly took in all I was saying.

"He kids you about being a perfectionist. He says you're a chip off the old block– that he was like that, too. He tells me that the two of you are very similar, personality-wise. You're definitely dad's girl. He says he's extremely proud of you. I'm to tell you that the business you're running will soon expand and you'll need more space. You'll see that revenues will increase. I'm also to tell you that if you sign any contracts with large sums of money involved, check it out completely before doing it. Your dad likes to talk business," I said with a laugh.

"He always did," Tina acknowledged.

"What have you been doing recently with a website? He shows me a business logo with your initials on it."

Tina's mouth dropped open. "Oh, wow! I am currently in the process of creating a website for my business. The logo is on every piece of my sewing work!" (Tina told me that she owns a company that produces custom-made products with embroidery and cross-stitch.)

"Your dad shows me that your business is still growing and this coming year will be one in which you make more profits at trade shows and other venues where more people will be able to view your work. By the way, he tells me there's a lady two generations back from you who also did embroidery work that was very beautiful. This lady gave pieces of this work away to others, including infants' clothing. Do you know who that would be?"

"That's my mom's mother. She did a lot of hand embroidery."

"She says she helps you with your business of crafting things through inspiration."

"You've hit nails on the head with how proud my dad was of me and how business-minded he was. He was always very encouraging to me," Tina said.

"Your dad says there will be some major contracts coming with your work and the need to hire extra help. He tells you to be specific and clear about what you want to see happen in your business. He will help you from the other side just as he did when he was here."

"I couldn't have done any of this without my dad," Tina emoted.

"Who is Jim? Your dad wants to acknowledge him."

"Jim is his very best friend! He's been having a hard time with my dad's passing."

"Will you please tell him that your dad said hello? I am hoping he believes in mediumship so it will help him when you tell him his name came through today. And who is Paul? I keep hearing that name."

"That's my mom's maiden name, her last name. Incredible!"

"Your dad shows me some sort of business award. Do you understand this?"

"Yes. Last year, I received an award from the Rotary Club I belong to. I also want to say that last year when Dad passed, my husband and I had left for Florida on Friday and he died on Saturday. It was so quick," Tina said, choking back tears.

"Do you know that he wanted it that way?" I said. "You see, he didn't want you to fuss over him or worry. He wanted to quietly slip away. Remember earlier in this reading when I told you there was a message about feeling unresolved about his passing and for you to make peace with that? He wants you to remember him as he was in the good times. He says you've looked recently at the photograph you have of him—remember those days. He feels it when you look at this photo."

"Every day, I look at the picture hanging above my desk of all of us with him on his golf cart."

"You are helping your mom deal with the transition of his passing, he says. There is a significance with the month of March with your mom. I'm not sure what that is. By the way, it looks as if she'll be traveling soon to a warmer climate, which will help her arthritis."

By the time the reading ended, Tina had taken several pages of notes. She thanked me for connecting with her father, which she said helped her to feel his presence more than ever. Like many times before, I felt blessed to be a part of a loving reunion.

A month after the session, I connected with Tina by phone. During the course of our conversation, she offered several validations of the information that came through in the reading.

"The day after I met with you, my husband and I went out to dinner with my mom. That evening she announced to us that she was planning on taking a trip to Costa Rica with one of her friends in March. I was astounded because of what you'd just told me about her traveling to a warm climate and a connection to March. Also, I learned from my mom that Dad did have an aunt named Betty who he was very close to when he was a young boy; you said the woman who came to get him was like a mother. You also mentioned that Dad had been in and out of his body before he actually died and that is true; he was resuscitated a few months before. When you described him as being a perfectionist, I knew it was him coming through because he definitely was. At his memorial service, we played Frank Sinatra's *My Way*. That song suited him."

Tina shared how her father's passing initially affected her. "At first, I was completely shocked because when I saw him two days before, he was in good spirits and like the old dad I knew. He was talking and laughing. So when I received the news that he'd died, I couldn't believe it. In fact, when you told me during the reading that he planned when to cross over, it confirmed that he wanted me to remember him like the last time I saw him, and that's why he went when I was out of town. I am an only child and he and I had always been very close. I ran the full gamut of emotions, from sadness to bitterness and anger, asking why this had to happen.

But then I realized Dad would never have wanted to be in a nursing home. He would rather be free from his body.

"I believe when a person dies, the soul has exited and gone into the afterlife," Tina continued. "In my will, I stated my wishes to be cremated because I know the body is only a covering for the soul. My belief in the afterlife was solidified by my session with you. The reading gave me complete validation of my dad's continued existence. I know I will see him again someday. In the meantime, I talk to that picture in my office. I know he hears everything I say."

The Military Man

One of the most significant messages that spirits communicate to loved ones is that of forgiveness for unhealed situations or unspoken feelings that occurred before they crossed. When we do a life review after entering the spirit world, we are given the opportunity to work on whatever was left unfinished while on earth. We become aware of how we could have thought or acted differently to show a more loving attitude towards family and others. The next story is a shining example of a father's change of heart from spirit.

David, 42, came to see me one evening. I was impressed to begin the session with a short meditation to help him relax;. After a few minutes, it was time to begin.

"The name William comes through very strongly with you. Does this make sense?" I queried.

"My grandfather used to call my mom [his daughter] William sometimes. Her last name was Williamson," David answered.

"Wait, — now I'm being corrected by your relatives who are telling me to ask you about the name Bill instead."

"Yes!" David said. "Her nickname was always Bill."

"This is a validation from her as I see her standing behind you, one generation removed. There is another woman with her also, either a sister or sister-in-law. Your mom is holding a dog and wants you to know he is with her. I don't know if you asked her to take care of this dog or not but she wants to make sure you know he is with her. He's black and white, very cute."

David nodded in agreement. "Yes, he was."

"Your mom stands with a man beside her, same generation, who was very close to her. This feels like your dad. She talks about having a very rapid crossing, as if something ruptured. She was here one minute and gone the next. She wants you to know she's okay now. Sometimes when people leave us unexpectedly, the shock of grief is an even greater trauma."

David nodded again. "Yes, that is how she crossed. She had a sudden heart attack."

"She says to say hello to your brother and his children." I could feel the thoughts of these two loving parents blend as they both connected to their son. "There is a message for you to keep an eye on your health. Make sure you check your blood pressure regularly because there is a tendency on your dad's side to have circulatory problems since some of the males died young from that."

David agreed.

"Your dad shows me a watch that was passed on. It doesn't work. He says there's been talk of wanting to get it repaired."

"Yes, I have it."

The image of the watch deepened in my mind. "Hmm, it looks as if the dial on this watch is specialized, that it has some type of drawing on it that moves. He is using my frame of reference because I once gave my grandfather a watch with a moving railroad on it."

David's dad certainly seemed to want to talk about himself as the reading flowed forward. "There is a strong Irish energy with him. He says he was in the service and was very proud of it. He shows me that at his wake he was recognized for that with a plaque and a flag. The service was very much part of his identity. His personality was one of being the strong, silent type; he didn't let a lot get to him. He was the rock, the strong paternal figure, the tough guy. The two of you have similar eyes and facial features. He appears to be solidly built."

"Yeah, he was. He was in the Marines."

"He's with other males on the other side, two of whom are related to him—feels like a brother and his father, who were in the service also. And there are a couple of men on the other side who knew your dad from the service. One crossed in a similar way, from a heart ailment, around the same time. This was a buddy of his."

"Uh-huh," David confirmed. "I know exactly what friend that is."

"The name Richard is associated with this. Does that fit?"

"Dick. His real name would have been Richard. Years ago, they spent time together."

"There's a strong connection here with fishing, of loving to fish."

"That's my dad!" David concurred.

"He acknowledges Tom and says hello."

"That's my brother."

"Your dad tells me about a shoulder injury or pain he had, which feels like bursitis or something like it. This really gave him trouble."

"Yes, it did. Dad had a bad shoulder."

The next message came through my mind with a lot of emphasis from David's dad. "He has some regrets of not showing his feelings more when he was here and wants to tell you about the importance of expressing them. He was a doer, not a feeler. He didn't tell the kids he loved them. Don't you be afraid of doing this," I urged him.

Engrossed in the reading, David sat wide-eyed as I continued.

"There was a fear of his doing that because he thought he would appear weak but he knows the importance of doing this now. Your dad was very enthusiastic about football and says he made bets on it. There is also a strong connection to Atlantic City."

David grinned. "He and I always used to gamble."

This spirit is quite a character, I thought as the reading rolled on. Suddenly, numbers flashed in my mind. *Oh, no,* I thought. *He's going to have me give his son lottery numbers!*

"He liked double numbers, two's and four's, and he will

sometimes inspire you with certain numbers to play with the lottery."

"That sounds like him alright."

As I looked at David, I was suddenly impressed with the sight of his beard. I sensed that I was supposed to ask him about it. "Your dad wants to draw attention to your beard. Did you have that when he was alive? There is some significance to it."

"He hated it," David said with a sigh.

As the communication drew to a close, an important message came through for David to share with his brother. "You know, your dad would never have come to see someone like me. He didn't believe in this. In that way, you're very different from him because you're open to it. He now knows it's a good thing to see beyond what the rational mind can prove. He also speaks of forgiveness issues with your brother and mentions counseling. Has he done that?"

"Yes, my brother has."

"Your dad wants to facilitate forgiveness through you to your brother. Your dad had a controlling side, - let's be honest. But he's working through that now."

David frowned. "Well, I don't know if he was exactly controlling."

"Let's say that he had trouble seeing other people's viewpoints," I conceded. "He makes me feel as if he was rigid."

"Yes, yes, he was."

After the tape clicked off, David's dad still wanted to talk. This often happens once spirits get the knack of the process. I sensed he wanted to leave his son with a smile. "He wants to leave you with a happy ending to all of this; he jokes that he was very proud of his hairy chest and that all of the ladies liked to rub it. He was a flirt," I chuckled.

David laughed out loud. "Yep, that's so true!"

Six months later, David told me how much hearing from his parents in spirit had brought him peace in dealing with their deaths. "I've always been intrigued with finding out about the other side. Mom believed in spirit communication but as you said in the reading, my dad definitely didn't; he was raised as a strict Catholic. Honestly, I really didn't know if we went on after death—that is, until I had my reading with you. There's been a tremendous change in me since. I knew it was all real when you described my dad's personality, especially that he was a ladies' man! Plus my mom told you her nickname, Bill, and you described my dog that was with her.

"Dad had been sick for five years before he passed," David continued. "When he died, we considered it a blessing since he was no longer suffering. My brother had a hard time with his death because he could not handle seeing him so sick. He lost patience and moved out of my parents' house some time before Dad died. Because my dad was hard on my brother – I believe it was because they were so much alike – there was some unfinished emotional business between them when he died. When you said that Dad wanted to talk about forgiveness with my brother, it made an impact on me since I knew my brother hasn't really made peace with all of this. Since I've shared the details of our session with him, he wants to come and experience a session for himself.

"I've heard from Dad since he died. One night I was sleeping on my couch and woke up talking to him. It was as if he was standing right there. It was so real, I know it was him."

I asked David what he learned from his dad while he was alive. "He taught me to embrace life and make a better one for myself than he had had. Dad labored in the mills for a long while and didn't get to travel much. He was glad I got a career in sales where I get to see the country–something he always wanted to do. As you said in the reading, my dad enjoyed life and he taught me the same."

I Miss You So Much, Mom
People often come to see me because they are struggling with confusing, painful emotions in their attempts to deal with the death of someone close to them. Depression is a common condition that many individuals confront in their healing journey through grief. The next transcript involves a woman who suffered

from depression most of her life, only to have it compounded by the death of her mother whom she had cared for during an extended illness. This session shows how loved ones in spirit return this nurturing attitude to us in our time of need.

As soon as Julie entered my reading room, she began to cry; in fact, she cried throughout most of the session. Although I had no idea whom she wanted to connect with, it obviously was someone she loved very much. I centered myself and asked the angels to help me. Drawing in a deep breath, I began.

"Your grandmother on your maternal side comes through first. She impresses me with problems in her lungs, an arthritic condition and the loss of her memory before crossing."

"Yes, she passed when I was very young," Julie said.

"She says there is also a connection with people in your family with depression. There's a lady on your maternal side who was also depressed. This applies to you, too. She talks about the need for you to get counseling, take the right medicine like anti-depressants and get in touch with your spiritual identity. Have you been in therapy?"

Julie shook her head and whispered, "Yes, I have."

"Sometimes you're feeling better than other times but there have been long periods in which you've felt very down. She makes me feel as if there were several crossings that happened very close together. Your grandmother says you've felt very lonely, closed in and abandoned."

Tears streamed down Julie's face.

"She wants you to know she helps you with these feelings of alienation. There's been a recent crossing on your maternal side in the last year or so. Would this be your mom?"

Julie swallowed hard and nodded.

I reached for her hands and took them into mine. A minute passed while I mentally connected with Julie's mom. "There's an acknowledgement from her to you for being her caretaker. I sense there was an extended illness with her and you are very much depleted from giving her care. Your mother and grandmother want to say they are far more concerned about you than you need be about them. They're in spirit and at peace. They are concerned about your being able to carry on. Your mom shows me a hospital bed and talks about being in it for a long period of time; she is very happy about being out of it now. There was a sense of her being imprisoned in her body and she was very glad when she was out of it. That doesn't mean she wanted to leave you," I reassured Julie. "She didn't want to be a burden to you."

Julie sat with her head down, crying and listening as her mother spoke through me.

"Your mom says she's been with you since she crossed and has been communicating with you. Have you smelled a sweet scent, like flowers recently? She comes to you this way."

"It's funny, the other day I smelled flowers and didn't know where it came from," Julie remembered.

In my mind, a woman appeared beside Julie's mom. "There's a woman standing next to your mom who says she came to get her when she passed. This lady would have preceded her into spirit and feels like a sister of hers."

"Yes, her sister did go first."

"Your mom could see her before she crossed and wanted me to tell you that. She shows me a tube, a drainage tube that went into her abdomen. Lots of fluid had built up in her body."

"Yes, yes," Julie said, tearfully.

"She says hello to the younger male, the one in your generation who's still here—must be a brother. Your mom is very beautiful. She is not hollow anymore, she says. It was important for her to look good and she talks about you helping her when she was ill with her make-up and hair. She shows me a tube of red lipstick."

Julie's face brightened. "Yes!"

"She holds up an Avon book. Did she use this brand or sell it?"

Julie laughed. "She used to always look at the Avon book when she was sick."

"She says she was looking over your shoulder when you recently went through the photo albums. Some of these were older ones–black and white."

Julie looked at me in amazement.

"She says there are old films that will be put together on one disc."

"Yes, I'm waiting for my brother to give me what he has so I can combine them. But these are photos, not films."

"Wait and see about this," I suggested. "I'm sticking with this message because it might be with someone else in your family. She is really happy you're putting these together because they will help you to keep her memory in your heart."

Images of colorful cards came into my mind. "She's showing me greeting cards."

"Yes, she kept every card anyone sent her."

"Your mom was quite a collector. She had many different things around her, many knick-knacks like birds and animals."

"She liked to look at pretty things and kept many of these things around her," Julie replied.

"Your mom appears to me looking as she did when she crossed, but she also wants you to know she is starting to become young again in spirit. She says she can be 30 again, an age when she was in optimal health."

I intuited that suggested activities would help Julie heal the grief she felt from her mother's passing and the gray cloud of depression that had plagued her for so long. "All of the tools you can gather along the way are important for you to use now. A spiritual practice like yoga, with gentle stretching, would greatly help alleviate some of your stress, tension and depression. Please try this if you haven't because it will help you. Also, do something outdoors like gardening, walking in your bare feet and connecting with nature. You need the healing that this will bring to you."

"I've been doing that."

"Good, good. That means you've been following the advice that your spirit guides have been trying to get through to you. I know this has been relatively recent but you need to move forward. Your counseling is also helping. There is no timetable with this. It is very hard to lose a parent since the strongest bond that exists is the one between parent and child."

Just then I saw a music box through my inner eye. "She wants you to know that she sometimes communicates with you through music. She had a few things that played music –wind-ups – that brought her comfort near the end of her life. By the way, there's a message here about liking Lawrence Welk and big band music. Hmmm, we may be connecting that to your grandmother," I said with a chuckle.

"My mom loved music and we couldn't stop my grandmother from watching Lawrence Welk."

"Yes, I don't think she ever missed a show!" I laughed. "Your mom kids you about playing cards and says others in the family play, too."

"Yes, I play solitaire on the computer."

As the session came to a close, Julie's mother strongly impressed me to tell Julie to not contemplate joining her in spirit. "Please know you'll be with your mom again when it's your time to cross. She will come and get you but she says you're not to do that now," I said with emphasis. "You know what I'm saying."

Completely surprised that anyone would know this, Julie said, "I *have* thought about going over there. I have to know, though, is she mad at me?"

"Absolutely not. Stop doing that to yourself. It makes her sad when you hold feelings of guilt. She stresses that it is very important that you not isolate yourself. Don't shut people out. Reach out to others but seek the source of your spiritual strength within. The care that you gave to your mom when she was sick is the same care she is now returning to you."

Julie was obviously touched by this message. "Does she know how much I love her?" Julie asked, her voice breaking with emotion.

The final message from Julie's mom was simple but powerful. "She knows. After all, she says you tell her that all the time."

"Yes, yes, I do."

Before Julie got up to leave, she asked when it would be possible to come back and see me again.

"Please understand that you need time to heal and deal with your grief through therapy," I advised her. "In time, you can come for another session."

After she left, I knew Julie had much healing to do in the months ahead due to the enormity of grief and depression she had carried for many years. I felt blessed that I was able to be a part of her journey in some small way.

Five months later, I spoke with Julie about her progress. She sobbed throughout our conversation, especially when remembering her mother's passing.

"When my mom died, I missed her terribly and wanted so badly to connect with her. I had never seen a medium before and I didn't know if I believed in this sort of thing. I was raised Catholic but lost most of my faith many years ago due to painful losses in my life. I had a brutal childhood and grew up very poor. Then my mom got sick, my only brother turned against me and my fiancé left me. It was one loss after another and my faith in God was gone. After Mom died, my cousin recommended I go to you after she read about you in the newspaper. I hoped you could connect me with my mom.

"When I came for the reading, I was uncertain whether it would be real. During the session, my mind began to open to many of the things you said, which seemed to give me a reason to believe in the spirit world. This is mainly due to the fact that there is no way you could have known the things you told me. For example, I couldn't believe it when you mentioned about smelling flowers, and that it was Mom coming to me. It was confirmation that you were really talking to her since that had just happened to me. The other thing that really hit me was when you told me that my aunt, Mom's sister who had died before her, came to get her. This aunt had always been a protector for my mom and they were very close. It gave me great peace to know they were together again. You also told me she suffered from depression, which she definitely did. During the session, I felt as if you were reading from a book because you seemed to know things about her so well. It was like I could touch Mom again."

I asked Julie how she was coping with her depression.

"I am still struggling with that and my grief. My mom was my last true emotional bond in this world. Life seems so barren. When I took care of my mom when she was sick, I really learned who she was—a wonderful woman who never cried when she was diagnosed with cancer. I've gone to some grief support groups and therapy. Although I'm uncertain about my faith, our reading gave me hope. It's put a large question mark on the rational part of my brain that says this couldn't be true."

CHAPTER SIX

GENERATIONS

To infinite, ever present love, all is love, and there is no error,
no sin, sickness, nor death.
— Mary Baker Eddy

My training and experience has blessed me with the opportunity to communicate with thousands of spirits. In some readings, especially those in which the sitter has a large extended family who've crossed over, my small reading room becomes packed with their energetic presence. It can get confusing when several spirits, anxious to be recognized by loved ones who have come to the session, send me thoughts simultaneously. In these fascinating cases, I witness not only "family reunions" but meetings among family members who may have never known each other while alive. When this occurs, I explain to clients that their ancestors are not only related to them biologically but karmically; that is, they share both a genetic and spiritual purpose as relatives. Truth is, whether we knew them or not, ancestors are our teachers in many ways.

One of my friends and colleagues, Nick, is trained in helping people release generations of unfinished emotional karma within families. Several years ago, we presented a workshop together in which I delivered healing messages from participants' relatives in spirit and Nick facilitated sessions focusing on the release of unhealed family karma. I watched in amazement as, one by one, people faced and dealt with previously unresolved emotions like sorrow, anger and forgiveness concerning issues such as incest, alcoholism and infidelity. For the first time in some of the participants' lives, they were able to let go of deep-seated pain that had held them captive for most of their lives. By the end of the workshop, because of the intense healing that had taken place, the room was charged with an undeniable energy of freedom and relief. To me, the evening was a testament to the power that our lineage holds for us.

When clients hear from deceased relatives that they barely or never knew, they are often surprised. I've come to understand that these loved ones in spirit help us with our lives on earth through inspiration and, at the same time, learn through our experiences, which they might not have had when they were alive. For example, I've done sessions in which women in their thirties or forties hear from great-grandmothers and grandmothers who express admiration for their granddaughters' career accomplishments; they communicate about their granddaughters' abilities to experience life opportunities that they never had because of the prescribed role of women in earlier times.

Another example is when male clients hear from their grandfathers and great-grandfathers in spirit who frequently validate the family's male lineage by giving proof of both first names that were passed down and descriptions of family occupations. If a client or someone in his family is doing family genealogy, this will also be mentioned as proof that they are aware of this fact. Sometimes, spirits will assist in tracing the family tree by offering suggestions on where to find critical information. One of my male clients had numerous relatives come through with very specific messages; in fact, his session probably holds the record for the number of names received in one sitting—not to mention the amount of evidential material these talkative spirits delivered. Halfway through the session, I commented on how many people showed up to speak with him. He laughed, adding that he'd written 40 books about his family tree! Needless to say, I was exhausted by the close of the session.

Some clients hear from spirits who were not related to them biologically yet played a significant role in their lives. One such example comes to mind: I read for a woman whose godmother, a woman from her grandmother's generation, came through. I felt a strong heart bond between the two and told her so. My client could not recognize her even though I remained persistent in obtaining information that would help her identify the spirit. When she finally realized it was her godmother, she cried and admitted that she talked to her in her thoughts quite often, asking her for guidance. She also shared that this woman had been like a grandmother to her since her biological family was splintered by divorce during her childhood.

The sessions I am recounting in this chapter contain extraordinary proof that our ancestors continue to influence our lives long after their deaths. Some of the sitters in these sessions had no conscious knowledge of the existence of particular relatives who communicated with them; others enjoyed close, nurturing relationships with their loved ones. Some received and continue to receive physical after-death communications from these relatives. All have come to believe in the soul's survival after death.

The following story illustrates how loved ones from several generations act as guides who support and inspire family members on earth. It's also an example of how loved ones in spirit are guardians for future generations; and how they often give prophecy of the coming birth of a child. As a follow up to this intriguing session, the two women received remarkable validation from the family matriarch in spirit immediately after they left my reading room.

Little Green Apples

On a beautiful spring evening, Sally, 49, and her daughter, Sara, 20, came for a session. I joined hands with both women and said my prayer. Immediately, I sensed the presence of many spirits; a man stood on Sally's left, directly behind her.

"Your dad in spirit is bringing through the names Maria and Ann or Anna," I began.

"I think he's referring to his sister, Mary, and sister-in-law, Ann. They're both still alive," Sally said.

"Well, how is their health?" I asked, knowing that one of the most common reasons spirits acknowledge the living is due to some health concern they have at the time of the reading.

"Mary fell down the steps just a few weeks ago," Sally answered. "She is not doing well at all. Ann is not in good health, either. Could you possibly be hearing the name Hannah instead of Anna?"

"Well, yes, that does happen sometimes if names sound clairaudiently similar."

"That is my grandmother's name."

"Oh, I see. Yes, I believe the name is a double validation for both her and the aunt you recognized."

As the reading progressed, I sensed the presence of many family members and began to receive a host of names, which I repeated to the two women. I felt like a teacher taking attendance for this roomful of lively spirits.

"Paul is here. So is Elizabeth and Charles," I reported. "And Tom."

"Yes, yes. They're all relatives who died a long time ago," Sally said, turning to Sara. "You wouldn't know them, but I do."

I was pleased that Sally, unlike some clients, was familiar with her family tree; it made the reading flow much easier.

"It's funny," I said, "They are showing me that they're together having a family picnic in an outdoor setting—eating baked beans and hot dogs. They must have done this when they were alive. By the way, there's brown sugar in those baked beans."

Amused, Sally nodded in agreement.

"Is my great-grandmother coming through?" Sara piped up. "I really wanted to hear from her."

I closed my eyes to focus on the group of spirits. "There's a lady who says she passed from congestive heart failure or pneumonia. She is wearing a yellow dress, symbolizing joy and happiness, and a large-brimmed hat. Do you recall her wearing this hat?"

"Uh, I do," Sally responded. "I have pictures of her wearing it."

I was struck by the resemblance between Sara and her great-grandmother. "You look so much like her, especially when she was young. The shape of her face and her eyes are much like yours. Have you seen pictures of her?" I asked Sara.

"No, I haven't," Sara answered. "My mom says I'm a lot like her; that's why I wanted her to come through tonight. She died before I was born."

"Well, the two of you look so much alike," I said. "I also see that she did a lot of baking—she is showing me that she often wore an apron with things stuffed in the front pockets. She used a rolling pin to roll out dough."

"Yes, she made wonderful soft rolls–a favorite of mine," Sally said.

I could feel this spirit's personality. "She could be very loving yet stern, as I see her standing behind you with one hand on her hip. She was a bit of a disciplinarian."

"Oh, yes. That's true," Sally agreed.

"I see her surrounded by lacy things–Victorian tablecloths and hankies."

"Yes, she loved those types of things," Sally confirmed. "She always had a lace tablecloth on the dining room table."

I sensed this lady was holding an infant who had crossed a long time ago and shared this with the women.

"Yes, my uncle, her son, had a twin that died young."

An image of a faded marriage certificate flashed in my mind. I described this to Sally.

"I have that stored in a plastic bag at home," Sally said.

"There is a prayer book of hers, too," I added.

"Yes, I have that, as well."

Then the great-grandmother impressed me with a message that brought a smile grin to Sally's face. "She shows me a big apple tree. Do you remember this? She usually made an apple dish from these."

"Apple cake!" Sally remarked. "That's where my recipe comes from that everyone loves so much."

"She comes around you when you're making this cake, peeling the apples. She wants to talk about these fond family memories." Obviously, these two women shared a loving bond through baking this favorite recipe.

"I learned to cook from her."

"There is also a message here about cooking the apples to make applesauce," I continued.

"Yes, she did that once in a while, too."

Because spirits use my emotional and mental sensitivities to communicate, I often experience my own memories based on the thoughts being transmitted. "Wow," I said, "I'm starting to get hungry!"

The next message was intended for Sara. "She is a guide of sorts for you. That's why the two of you share similarities. She will come to you in your dreams and tell you things. She helps both you and your mother with setting healthy boundaries for yourselves in relationships. She tells me that you, Sara, will have a child someday–a little girl who is with her now in spirit. I see her so clearly with your great-grandmother who is taking care of her now."

After the reading, I chatted with the two women as we walked to my front door. The reading had gone well and everyone seemed pleased. Less than 15 minutes later, I received an astonishing phone call from them. When I answered the phone, Sally was breathless with excitement; she told me that a strange thing occurred when they got into their car.

"As soon as Sara and I opened the car doors, we were overcome with the smell of apples. I said, 'Oh my, Sara! Can you smell that?' We looked around for apple trees nearby but saw none. We thought perhaps the smell was coming from outside of the car; it wasn't. This lasted until we got home then began to slowly fade. I believe it was my grandmother!"

I listened in amazement. "Well, I guess she's letting you know she's around!" I said. "What a validation!"

Later, Sally informed me that Hannah often used Granny Smith apples when she baked. "They have a distinctive smell — pungent and sweet – unmistakable to me since I bake with them often. That's what we smelled that night and we smell the aroma from time to time in our house. I know it's a sign that my grandmother is around."

She related how her grandmother's death affected her. "At

first, I felt very lonely and empty. Since she died, she's never been out of my mind. I've felt her presence many times, especially when I'm going through a really rough time. Once I was going through a difficult time in a relationship. Then one day, I was standing at my kitchen sink; all of a sudden, I felt her behind me. A sense of peace and calm swept over me and I knew she was there for me."

Sally believes she is receptive to the other side because she grew up in a family that supported these beliefs. "Both my mother and grandmother had psychic abilities. My mother would tell me things that she had no way of knowing in advance. I know this has been passed onto Sara and me because I also know about things before they happen. Taking classes on healing and metaphysics led me to a belief in reincarnation. I know that when we die, we go on — only our bodies are buried."

I asked Sally what effect our session had on her life. Without hesitation, she answered, "It gave me the reassurance I'd been praying for. I needed to know that Gram was still with me. When you described her dress and her pose – standing behind me with her hand on her hip, wearing her apron with the pockets full – I knew it was her because I have pictures of her like that. And the signs she continues to send us have given us peace and healing."

The Family Tree

Relatives in spirit often indicate that they're aware of what's going on in a person's life by validating events or circumstances that have occurred since their death. They come through with insights on aspects of clients' lives (relationships, health, money or career, for example), and impress me with thoughts about what they've learned on earth as wisdom to be offered up to the sitter. This holds true whether or not the client was particularly close to the individual giving the message. In the following session, a man receives valuable perspectives about his career from an uncle who passed many years earlier.

Walter, a statuesque man with a gentle demeanor, came to receive intuitive guidance about his work. This is the extent of what I knew about Walter when he arrived at my door. Little did he know, he was about to have a family reunion in which his mother, father and another family mentor would offer him spiritual wisdom.

"Your parents are here," I began, as I perceived two spirits standing directly behind and on either side of Walter. "Your mother seems to be the stronger communicator of the two and wants to thank you for caretaking you did for her before she died. She offers much gratitude to you for doing this. She is happy to be young again and is showing me that she's in a garden, surrounded by flowers." (This is an example of how spirits show me where they spend time in the spirit world: by sending me an image of their home there. Interestingly, their surroundings in spirit frequently reflect their personalities while on earth.)

I continued to describe what I perceived. "I feel that your mom wants to say she's sorry for being a bit cranky prior to her crossing. She says it was because she didn't feel well. It's important that you know that's why she was this way sometimes. Her personality was basically loving and kind but the pain made her crabby."

Walter nodded in agreement.

"I am hearing about someone by the name of Flo. Who is that?"

"That's my aunt," Walter answered. "That would be Mom's sister-in-law. She's still alive."

"Your mom says there is a health concern around this lady. I am also aware of the names Margaret and Mary."

"That's my mother! Her name is Mary Margaret."

"She is talking about a long period of convalescence before passing. That's why she's so happy to be young again. In her beautiful spirit garden, she is soaking her feet in a fountain. She says she used to soak her feet to relieve soreness when she was alive. I feel your mom suffered from arthritis and osteoporosis."

"Yes, she did. She had severe arthritis and was in a lot of pain."

"She says she felt like a prisoner in her body before passing and that she is so glad to be free of that."

"Yes, yes, she did."

"She also points to her eyes for some reason. I feel as if she is suggesting that you get your eyes checked."

"Mom was always concerned about my eyesight because she was legally blind and didn't want me to go through that."

I saw a small dog sitting on the lady's lap. "Your mom must have owned a little dog – one that barked a lot."

"Oh, yeah, she did."

"She wants to acknowledge Betty and Rose."

Walter chuckled, "Betty is another sister-in-law of Mom's and Rose is her cousin."

"Your mom is emphatic about letting you know that she is at peace and in paradise. She says, 'I've come home.' Her main purpose in coming through today was to let you know where she is over there."

"Is my father coming through, too?"

I focused on the energy around Walter. "There is a man with the name of John. Who is he? He is standing on your father's side of the family."

"That is my dad's oldest brother."

"Okay," I continued, satisfied that the connection was beginning to form. "I also perceive a man who is saying he was a hard worker. He shows me his weathered hands. He passed from a stroke and suffered quite a bit of memory loss. Your dad was like you–a genuine and honest person."

Walter nodded. "That was Dad, alright."

I was aware of a large group of Walter's relatives in spirit, lined up behind him. I sensed that they were letting him know they were reunited. When I relayed this impression to Walter, he acknowledged that some of his mother's extended family had been separated for one reason or another for years. "Are you the one who has been doing the family genealogy?"

"Yes," Walter answered. "I've been dabbling in it lately."

"I'm being shown that you'll trace the family tree as far back as the late 1700s. Relatives on the other side will help you find the information you need."

Another message quickly formed in my mind. "Your mom gives me the message that you are considering a move."

"That's one of the things I was going to ask you about. I don't want to move because I want to remain close to my family here. I am a mentor, so to speak, for my 16-year-old niece. With me, family comes first, yet I was thinking about moving because of work."

"I don't feel it will be right away. You have karma to finish here with your family, especially your niece."

"Well, I quit my job a while ago to come home and take care of my physically disabled parents. Every door I try to walk through employment-wise seems to slam in my face. I have training in helping physically disabled people but can't seem to find work at the moment."

"You have strong healing abilities. I sense very strongly that you need to work in a field where you would use these abilities to help people. I could easily see you working with natural remedies, like homeopathic medicine and herbs. But things haven't jived yet for you to find the right job. They will come together for you in the next several years. Right now it's important for you to just stay in the moment and trust."

"I was offered a job by someone I know but it would have meant leaving my family here. I can't do that right now." I became aware of another spirit standing behind Walter. "There's a man here who says he works with you very strongly on a spiritual level and he appears to be dressed in a brown monk's habit. Have you ever been aware of him?"

Walter responded quickly, "I had two great-uncles who were Carmelite monks and they wore brown habits."

"This man helps you with personal integrity and your life's mission, part of which involves teaching and mentoring. Have you ever taught?"

Fascinated by the accuracy of the messages, Walter blurted out, "Yes! Carole, I taught for two years in the public schools. One of my great-uncles also taught."

"He helps you with this," I assured Walter. "This agreement was made before you were born."

Intrigued, Walter added, "I was named after him."

"He wants you to know that you may not always teach formally in a classroom but rather by the power of your own life, your own example. He also did this."

"Oh, yes, he certainly did."

The monk continued to impress me with advice for Walter regarding his spiritual purpose in life. "Your great-uncle talks of the value of service work, something he did. He helped many people when he was alive. There will be some volunteer work coming for you but there is also a need for you to nurture yourself. Don't get out of balance with give and take, as you have a tendency to always be taking care of others."

The session went on for a while longer with guidance being given for Walter to write down and clearly focus on his career aspirations. "You may not get what you want right away," I advised him, "but some openings are coming for you in the spring."

About a year later, Walter shared his insights about our session.

"I came to you seeking closure on my mom and dad's deaths and to see if they would offer me any messages about my career. After I took care of them for 11 years and after their deaths, I felt as if I needed to get out again among other people. My life had been consumed with their care. I hadn't worked in over a decade. My mother died four years before my dad and so I had no time to really grieve her passing; I had to immediately take care of him. I had no release, so to speak. When he died, I really wanted to work again."

Even though Walter had still not found employment in his chosen field, he remained hopeful of finding a job in which he could use his abilities to help people. "I still haven't found anything," he said, "but the session offered me the encouragement I needed to keep looking."

Walter then shared his feelings about his parents' deaths. "Their deaths were, in a sense, a blessing. They had been physically incapacitated and their health continued to deteriorate. I felt relieved that they were no longer suffering but I really felt as if a part of me died, too. I had no outlet like a job, at the time, to immerse myself in."

I asked Walter about his spiritual beliefs regarding life after death.

He answered, "I know that when people die, they really aren't dead. They just become a different form of energy. Death is nothing more than a continuation of life. We may not be able to see that until we die but I strongly believe we can communicate with those who've passed. People like you, who have been trained to do so, can give the rest of us verification. For example, you knew nothing about me yet you told me many facts about my family.

"I felt guilty that I hadn't done enough for my parents after they died," Walter confided. "The session helped me with that feeling when Mom came through and thanked me for taking care of her. It had been so hard for me since she complained a lot because she didn't feel well. I was accustomed to dealing with people's pain and deaths because of my former work in nursing homes and hospitals. But it's different when it's your own mother.

"Grief is something only the living feel because I believe our loved ones go on to a better place after death," he continued. "Even though I participate in organized religion, I am very open to metaphysics. I was first exposed to mediumship many years ago, believe in astrology and meditate often. Some people who are followers of mainstream religion are too close-minded to accept that we can talk to our deceased relatives — but not me."

On the subject of receiving signs from loved ones in spirit, Walter had this story to relate:

"For two or three weeks after my dad died, I had a hard time sleeping. Four nights in a row, I woke up between 3 and 4 a.m. to the sound of my mother's voice calling my name loudly and clearly several times. I haven't had this happen since and I have no idea what it meant. But I know I heard it. Maybe she was trying to tell me everything was going to be fine and that Dad was there with her."

A Grandmother's Wisdom

In addition to giving evidence of life after death, a substantial portion of my work involves counseling people from a spiritual perspective concerning their life challenges. As previously mentioned, loved ones in spirit will also offer their viewpoints and advice. It is important to remember that spirits can share only from the vantage point of their own accumulated spiritual understanding and life lessons. Yet, in my experience, those in spirit will do what they can to help ease our emotional pain. From the other side, loved ones are aware of our lives and often help us through prayer and inspiration to cope with tough times. In the following case, a grandmother helps her granddaughter with her unresolved feelings of grief and guilt after a friend dies.

Kitty, a soft-spoken, kind woman, attended one of my group programs about six months before she came for a private session. On the phone, she told me she needed some peace about an issue that had been bothering her for some time. That's all I knew before we began.

"A small-framed woman, very beautiful, who says she passed from a heart-related condition involving fluid in her chest, comes through for you. She has a small waist and wears a flowered dress. She's been helping you with self-healing recently. When she was here, a good portion of her life was consumed with taking care of others when they were sick, so it's natural for her to continue doing this. She feels like a grandmother to me."

Kitty's face softened as she remembered her grandmother. "Yes, that describes her," she said.

I sensed the presence of another spirit stepping into the reading. "There's a man who says he passed quickly and unexpectedly. There is a connection with the name Joseph. He impresses me that something was wrong with his stomach or that area of his body. He makes me feel as if other organs in his body were also involved. It feels like cancer to me. Does that make sense?"

Kitty nodded. "That's my grandfather who passed from cancer."

Another man suddenly appeared beside the first one. "A man

is here for you who is wearing shorts. He is balding slightly, although he has some of his hair on the sides. He says he liked to golf. The name James or Jim is being acknowledged."

"James is my husband's father and also his brother's name. This sounds like my father-in-law, Jim. He loved to golf."

"Will you please tell your husband his father said hello and he's happy his clubs were passed down in the family?"

"Yes, I will. We recently gave them to our daughter."

After these two spirits made an appearance, I again connected with Kitty's grandmother. "Your grandmother was an extremely nurturing woman, almost self-sacrificing. There is a message to you about being strong even though you're a very feminine, gentle woman and very much like her. For some reason, she says you need to release the past but keep hold of the good memories and to release any pain or guilt. Some writing you've been doing helps you with this."

"My dear, dear grandmother," Kitty emoted. "I miss her so much. It makes me think so much of the past and my good childhood memories. But I've been very sad over the death of an old friend, which was from an apparent suicide. I first met him when we were 18. I don't know how much of what I'm doing to cope with this is really helping me. It hurts."

"Your grandmother says this is a time of deep emotional clearing for you. You may feel her around your shoulders with a slight, tingling sensation. And speaking of shoulders, she is appearing to me wearing a white sweater around her shoulders."

Kitty's mood instantly lightened. "Yes, yes, she always had that sweater around her. But I was really hoping to hear from my friend today."

I explained how this process works and that I couldn't guarantee a spirit's presence in a reading. I sensed the reason this woman's friend was having difficulty coming through was because of the way he died; his heavy emotions apparently prevented solid communication.

"I can't make spirits come here. Your grandmother is the main communicator who is coming through for you today. She makes me feel as if the hardest part of dealing with your friend's death has been not being able to talk about it."

"Yes, I suffer. I have no closure because we didn't have the chance to say goodbye. I have no answers to anything about him."

"The feeling I get here is a strong connection between the two of you–a sort of soul mate relationship. Was there love? Yes, most definitely, I am hearing. 'Yes, I cared for you as much as I could. But I couldn't express it'."

"I always felt that he was carrying a lot inside and couldn't or wouldn't confide any of it," Kitty said. "He seemed to be running from something. He was very frightened."

"People come into our lives for many reasons. Sometimes it is short-term, sometimes longer. They help us with different lessons. We may not know exactly why until later. Believe it or not, you did touch this individual's life. You've wondered many times if you could have done something differently to reach him. You've been feeling guilty because you've felt as if you hadn't done enough. Please understand that what an individual does with his life is always his responsibility."

Kitty pulled a photo from her purse. "I have a picture that I brought for you to look at. Maybe it will help to connect with him through it."

Although I usually don't use photos or objects from a deceased person in sessions, I sensed in this case it might help the communication process. As I took the photo from Kitty and focused on it, I began to receive impressions.

"There was definite depression with this man. There were many heavy emotions that weren't being dealt with. I feel he had some financial problems that were very hard for him to handle. This led to depression. It feels as if there were a series of unfortunate events that happened to him. He had problems with the ups and downs of life. Some people adjust better to these things than others. Your friend had a lifelong chemical imbalance in his brain. As I connect with him, I feel as if I'm imprisoned within myself and there are walls around me. I feel as if this crossing was very quick. Was there an investigation into this?"

"I don't know. The financial problems had to do with his losing an executive position in his company," Kitty confirmed.

The photographic connection was working well. "As I intuit his emotions, I feel like I'm a failure. The truth is, he was intelligent and had a lot to offer but didn't believe that. I am being told his passing devastated his family. It is very important that his family know what led to his mindset so they can come to terms with this. They need to seek counseling because they are holding much guilt over his passing. Please tell them this."

"Yes, I will," Kitty said with resolve. "I am a good friend to his aunt."

"You helped him," I said emphatically. Your love has made a difference in his life. Continue to send him prayers. Please put this to rest."

As I neared the end of the session, I asked Kitty if she had any questions. "Yes, I do," she replied. "I've come to a juncture in my life where I don't know what my mission is. My girls are raised and I have a wonderful husband but I feel I'm not good enough sometimes. I am not a weak person but I sometimes feel unable to help myself, although I can easily help others. My friendship with this man was unresolved, the wound never really healed and then his death opened it up again. I must be able to go on with my life."

"Your grandmother again reminds you to draw on the strength within you. You have given a lot to others and will continue to do so. Your mission now is to return that love to yourself. You are a hugely compassionate person and can offer your heart through volunteer work–a hospice, nursing home, hospital or working with animals."

"Yes, I've thought of doing that and I want to. Do you believe we choose our circumstances in life before we come here?"

"Yes. We are constantly drawing circumstances to us to learn. Relationships, work— they are all karmic for us. By the way, that's also part of your mission now—that is, discovering your spiritual side."

"Since my friend's death, I've been more centered in my spirit."

"You can now look at the pain of his crossing and see it in the scope of spiritual growth for both of you. All souls are constantly evolving. He is getting the help he needs on the other side."

At the conclusion of this reading, Kitty seemed relieved and uplifted by the messages her grandmother had delivered. I hoped this would help in her spiritual journey of making closure with her friend's death.

Several months later, Kitty shared her experiences since our session. Throughout our conversation, I sensed the depth of her spiritual awareness, honesty and compassion.

"Since I last saw you, Carole, I've had some remarkable closure on my friend's death. I credit our session with that since at one point, you asked me if an investigation had been done into his death. I decided to check into that and was able to obtain a copy of the police report. Some things that were contained in it answered questions about how he died. It was definitely a suicide, although no one knows exactly why he did it. If it hadn't come through in our reading, I wouldn't have thought to get this information.

"I believe that life is a journey and that some of the things we encounter in it are by our choice. I've always been on a spiritual quest but my friend's suicide caused me to seek more answers. I believe we feel pain so we can grow spiritually. When we are done with our lessons here, we go back to our spiritual home. Since the passing of my grandparents and my friend, I look at life differently. I try to live it as if I am having a life review. For example, I ask myself what impact my actions will have on others. I've discovered that what's really important in life is not material but family, love and how we can help each other. I feel as if I live with one foot in the spirit world and one on earth now."

Kitty commented on the strength of the communication during the reading. "It was so good to hear from my grandmother when she came through. My best childhood memories are of her and my grandfather. I knew that if I had a private reading, she would be the one who would be there for me, and she was. You told me about a porch swing during the reading and I've since remembered that my great-grandmother, her mother, had a swing on her front porch that many people sat on. The session reinforced the close connection I still enjoy with my grandmother. I actually feel closer with my grandparents now than before they died. Even though I miss them terribly, I find it very comforting to know that when I cross over, I'll be with them again."

The Healing Heart

Some people have the unfortunate experience of suffering more than one traumatic loss in a relatively short period of time. When layers of grief compound with little or no time to recover, physical illness may occur because the body is a direct reflection of our thoughts and feelings. In the next story, a woman who is grieving the loss of a love relationship, her beloved pet and the passing of her grandmother, all within six months of one another, receives comforting confirmation that she is not alone. This session also shows how spirit loved ones use humor as a healing tool to lighten the heavy burden of grief.

When Sandy came for her appointment, she greeted me cheerfully and shook my hand. The warmth of her bubbly personality, refreshingly pleasant and open – almost childlike – immediately struck me. She settled comfortably in the rocking chair as I said my prayer.

As I focused on the energy around her, I sensed the presence of a robust older woman with rosy cheeks on Sandy's right side. "A strong female comes in for you. She looks like you. I'm unclear whether this is a mother or grandmother but she feels very motherly to me."

Sandy's face lit up. "That's my grandma! Mom is still here."

"Did she raise you? The feeling I get it with her is that of a mother."

"She was my guardian angel," Sandy said with pride.

"She says the angel statue you have in your home is from her. She impressed you to buy that."

"Yes, I do have one. Isn't that cool!"

A clairvoyant image of a round brooch with a lady's profile, or cameo, appeared in my mind. I described this to Sandy.

"I don't have a cameo but she gave me this several days before she went to the hospital," she said, grasping the necklace she had on. "It was a couple of days before she died."

"Yes, I see. She shows me a lady's profile but there's also a brooch."

"Hmm, I don't know of one."

"She passed from congestive heart failure."

"Yes, she did."

"There's a message here about you remodeling your home recently. I'm supposed to ask you about window treatments, or some kind of problem with them. Does this make sense?"

Sandy looked puzzled. "Well, I've been remodeling my home. In the last two weeks I finished some tile work but I'm not sure about window treatments."

I asked for clarification from Sandy's grandmother. "The feeling she gives me is some sort of problem with them."

"No, I haven't had any problems with that." Sandy's face remained blank for a minute and then she blurted out, "Oh, yes! *She* had a lot of trouble with new vertical blinds she had bought."

"Thank you," I said, relieved that Sandy was able to claim this evidentiary message. "Please understand this is just her way of giving you a message that I would have no way of knowing."

"That's for sure!" Sandy laughed.

"She says hello to your aunt and says she was with the person in your family who was in the hospital this past year."

"Oh! That was me! I was in the hospital!"

"You know she's always with you. She's been with you since the time you were very young, since the time you were a little baby."

"You're making me cry," Sandy said, reaching for a tissue. "She was my everything. I miss her so much. It's been so hard to go on without her but I'm doing alright, I guess."

"Who - close to her - would have broken a bone?"

"Another person I know who passed had a broken arm and she was a friend of my grandmother's."

"Your grandmother is bringing her through to let you know

this friend is with her. There is someone with the last name of Johnson who you know. I'm to tell you that this person, who has someone in the family who is ill, is being prayed for."

"I don't know anyone by that name."

"Yes, you do. This person has a loved one in spirit who is bringing this through for you to deliver."

A moment of silence followed until the name suddenly clicked with Sandy. "I do know a Chris Johnson and her father hasn't been well lately. That must be it."

"Okay. May I ask why your grandmother is showing me brightly colored flowers?"

"She loved flowers. I have pictures of all of her flowers set up around her ashes, which I have."

"Boy, is she full of love for you! She says she couldn't wait to come through today. There is a dog with her whose name ends with the letter Y. Did you ask her to take care of this dog? She gives me that feeling."

"Buffy! I had him for 17 years! Actually, I asked Buffy to take care of Grandma!"

"If you've wondered if you did the right thing with this dog, I'm to tell you yes."

"Oh, my God! I did question whether or not to put him down. I've had so many dreams about Gram since she passed but they're weird. Usually she's sick and I can't find her. When I do find her, it's too late."

"That's your fear coming through. You did all you could for her. She was ready to go and when she did, it was quick. Her family over there came to get her."

A strange yet familiar image came into my head. "Why is she showing me the *Wizard of Oz*? Is there someone over there by the name of Dorothy?"

"Grandma's got a sister, Dorothy, who passed."

I laughed out loud at how ingeniously spirits communicate. "I guess she thought I wasn't going to get the name right so she showed me the *Wizard of Oz* to make sure! I'm supposed to ask you about the cookies you used to dunk in milk to soften them."

"Uh, huh. She gave me the recipe and I made them once and I don't really know how to cook or bake. They came out as big as softballs! That was a standing joke with us."

We both laughed. "Your gram surely had a sense of humor because she is showing me that she used to store hankies or tissues in her bra," I said amusingly.

"Yeah, she did! She put them in her cleavage!"

The reading took a more serious turn when the topic of Sandy's health came up. After doing an aura scan, I sensed that emotional issues of grief and loss had caused her to have serious heart problems, to the degree of having surgery. "Your emotions are intricately linked with your body. It's impossible to separate the two. Look at what was going on in your life just prior to getting sick," I suggested.

"There were three things. I had a relationship break-up that was tough and my dog died, but the biggest thing that broke my heart was losing Gram. I also have a serious blood disorder. I've always wondered whether my grandmother also had this condition."

"It seems as if there's been a problem with the platelet count of your blood, which I'm being told is genetic. What you really did, subconsciously of course, was close your heart because of what happened. You were hit hard by all of the loss in your life with no time to recover. You must heal from all of this and then your physical body will respond. Release the past and pull all of your energy into the present. Stress is a major factor here, as well. It's important for you to set boundaries with your work so you don't become drained. Meditation, affirmations of self-love and guided imagery will help you heal. The most important thing for you to do now is nurture yourself."

"My job as a psychologist is demanding but I love it. I do a lot of speaking and teaching."

"Yes, I see. Your grandmother tells me she stands right behind you when you speak. She experiences the joy you feel when you do this."

Sandy's eyes lit up. "Does she? Wow! That's nice!"

"She says to say hello to Cindy."

"Cindy's my sister. I don't see her very often but I will remember."

In the last part of the session, guidance came through for Sandy's brother who had financial problems concerning a car. When she left my house that evening, Sandy smiled broadly and commented on how strongly the information about her grandmother had come through. "It's amazing," she said.

I felt satisfied in knowing she had received exactly what she needed to heal – namely, love – from heaven.

About 18 months later, I reconnected with Sandy by phone. I asked her how she was doing since we last saw one another.

"I'm feeling much, much better," she said. "My health is still not the best but I feel better able to cope with it. Part of that is due to the sense of emotional relief I felt after our reading, which gave me the reassurance that I'll be okay. I was dealing with so much grief at the time I saw you and our session was the first step in the right direction towards healing.

"My grandmother was like a mother to me because she raised me since my mom had me when she was very young. I spent every weekend at my grandparents' house and was really closer to them than my mother. My gram's unexpected death destroyed me because she was everything to me. She went into the hospital and died two days later. Although I was grateful to have been with her at the end, I suffered recurring dreams months after her passing. I was tormented by not knowing where she was, if she was okay and whether or not she had finished her mission here. After I came to see you, the dreams changed into my searching for her in different hospitals and not being able to find her. Lately, the dreams have changed again and are much more peaceful because they center on my childhood memories of her. In some, we are having discussions in which she answers me. She is no longer dead in my mind but alive. Imagine that!"

Sandy spoke candidly about her spiritual beliefs. "I was raised Methodist but at a young age rebelled against organized religion. For many years, I was afraid of death because I had no idea what happened to us after we die or where our souls go. I must admit I was skeptical when I came to see you on the recommendation of a friend. I needed to see for myself what would come through in the reading since I had never had one before. Some of the things you said were shocking because only my grandmother would know about them—her sister Dorothy's name was mentioned and my precious dog, Buffy, came through that day. I was really surprised when the message about the blinds came through. I had forgotten about her having trouble with those. I also couldn't believe that you knew about the problem with my blood platelet count! But the most amazing thing to me was when you mentioned the cookies I tried to bake. That was a joke between us for years that not many people knew about.

"I still miss my gram a lot but now I know I can still communicate with her, especially through my dreams. The reading has totally changed my fear of death. I now believe I'll be with my grandparents and Buffy again when I die. My grandmother taught me many things, such as kindness and empathy that I use in my work as a counselor. She's been my biggest inspiration and still is."

CHAPTER SEVEN

SOULMATES

I shall live beyond death, and I shall sing in your ears
Even after the vast sea-wave carries me back
to the vast sea-depth.
I shall sit at your board though without a body,
and I shall go with you to your fields, a spirit invisible.
I shall come to you at your fireside, a guest unseen.
Death changes nothing but the mask that covers our faces.
The woodsman shall be still a woodsman,
The ploughman, a ploughman,
and he who sang his song to the wind
shall sing it also to the moving spheres.
-Kahlil Gibran

Over the years, I've done many readings for people who've lost spouses or partners with whom they shared decades of life and love. Such a loss is devastating and is second only to the passing of a child in terms of the magnitude of grief and stress. The majority of clients I've seen in these cases have been women because they typically outlive men and are, as a rule, more open to seeking the counsel of a medium.

Two of the most common questions I'm asked by a surviving spouse during sessions are: "Is my beloved alright on the other side?" and "Is my beloved still around me?" I believe it's important to not simply give pat answers to such questions just to make clients feel better—anyone can do that. In order to give peace of mind and assurance to people that consciousness does go on after death, the evidence given during readings must be strong to support the survival of the soul after death. Besides offering proof of identity and other evidence, I pass along messages about how spirits give spouses signs to communicate their presence, such as blinking lights, ringing phones or other synchronicities. As I previously mentioned, some spirits will appear engaged in their favorite pastimes or in a particular environment they enjoyed on earth; this seems to give loved ones peace of mind that they are carrying on with life in the spirit world. I have witnessed people come into a session with emotional energy laden with grief then leave one hour later totally transformed by the information given. Love that is transmitted from beyond the grave is a powerful healing force in wiping away tears of loss and grief.

The death of a spouse or partner is a huge transition for most people and a time in which major adjustments must be made. Clients have told me that it is like starting an entirely new life. During this time of change, it is comforting to know that help is being offered by the very one who is being mourned. I can't tell you how many readings I've done in which a deceased spouse comes through and tells the surviving one that assistance is being given to help with a specific task! For example, Florence came for a session in which her husband of more than 50 years, who had recently died, spoke to her. After validating his identity, he told her that he was helping her handle (through inspiration) the couple's finances, including balancing the checkbook. He also said that he inspired her to seek out the services of a financial advisor so she could wisely invest their life savings. When I delivered this message to her, she admitted she had never dealt with the couple's finances before her husband's passing but was now forced to do so. However, she said she had recently gotten the idea to call an old friend who is an accountant who subsequently connected her with a good financial consultant. She also had been inspired to take a class at a local college in basic household financial management. I told her that her loving husband who was watching over her from spirit transmitted these ideas in order to ease her way after his death.

Nestled in the bonds of intimacy that soul mates share are cherished memories. During readings, spirits communicate these specific memories to establish their identity and to deepen the heart connection between themselves and sitters. Because memory is thought, I commonly receive these messages primarily through telepathy. People often cry and sometimes laugh in recognition when these come through. The bond of love is strengthened and grief is released. As for my part, I feel as if I'm sharing the precious stories of clients' lives with their loved ones by painting their memories back to life.

Spouses in spirit often give assurance that they will be reunited in spirit with the loved one left behind. Harmonious lives together on earth can continue in spirit if both parties choose. Many spirits who communicate to soul mates on earth emphasize the need for them to be happy and continue on with their lives because it is not yet their time to return to spirit. This includes messages about finding love again with another person. Although it may be difficult to understand, when we cross into spirit, we see a broader, more comprehensive perspective of life in which we realize the nature of our and loved ones' spiritual pathways and how relationships contribute to our growth. I believe it is from this understanding that spirits encourage loved ones to find joy and fulfillment with others. As strange as it sounds, I've delivered messages in which deceased spouses comment on how they are helping the surviving spouse find love again with another person. Interestingly, clients validate these messages by admitting that they asked for this "blessing" from their beloved in spirit.

All relationships teach us about ourselves by mirroring our soul connections with others. As I mentioned in Chapter Three, before we come into earthly existence, we consider the karmic lessons we need to learn in our next incarnation. Based on this awareness, we make agreements with others on a soul level to carry out these plans. Even though we may have no conscious awareness of what our karmic missions are, our souls store this knowledge and when the time comes, we meet and engage in relationships with those with whom we've made prior agree-ments. I've done readings for people who describe meeting their significant other and being magnetically drawn to him or her, instantly knowing this is the person they will marry. This is because the soul codes they've made long ago are activated by the recognition of a partner's codes. Relationships, both long and short-term, are a two-way street of learning for both people, teaching lessons that wouldn't be possible alone. Compassion, trust, nurturing, patience, harmony and cooperation are examples of soul qualities learned through close interaction with a partner. When these lessons are complete, at least for the time being, relationships transform or end. Physical togetherness may end but the lessons endure.

Each story in this chapter reveals an indestructible bond of love between two people that survived death. Despite obvious differences such as the nature and length of the relationship being mourned, each client in these sessions was profoundly affected, in a positive sense, by hearing from a a love in spirit.

Knock, Knock

Nancy, a petite, middle-aged woman, sat in my reading room as I explained the process of mediumship and nature of the spirit world. As I talked, I sensed this reading would be easy and strong; in other words, I wasn't going to have to pull teeth, as I sometimes have to, in order to receive communication from the other side.

I began by doing an aura assessment in which I sensed the energy and colors around Nancy. "Before you came here tonight, when I was meditating, Mother Mary was here with her blue healing light. She comes around you so much and is quite prominent in your energy field. You must pray to her a lot."

"I pray the rosary every day," Nancy said.

"Part of her message is that there is healing going on in your family now and because you're the matriarch, she comes to you." Although I wasn't sure what this message meant, I trusted it had meaning for her.

The distinctive scent of roses suddenly filled my mind as the room began to fill with Nancy's deceased relatives. "I'm getting a message that someone in spirit communicates with you by scent–particularly, roses. There is also someone in the family by that name. You really have a big family on the other side," I commented, as many spirits continued to line up behind her.

"Nana, my mother-in-law, is in spirit and she loved roses. Everyone thought she was my mother because we were so close. Rose is my sister-in-law and she's still alive."

"She (Nana) is a strong communicator and couldn't wait for you to get here. Her thoughts are very rapid as she comes through. She says she used to light votive candles for the family's healing and acknowledges St. Jude. She was very a religious woman. There is a nun with her who was very close to her."

Nancy looked perplexed then said, "She was in an orphanage with nuns but I'm not sure who this would be."

"Keep the message, as this is someone she's with. She says there have been several deaths in your family recently and you felt as if you hardly had time to recover."

"Yes, that's true."

The spirit of a man in Nancy's generation stepped in beside her. "This man comes through like a husband. Nana, his mother, was the one bringing him here." In my mind, I saw an image of the letter J. "By the way, where does the name starting with J fit in?"

"Nana's real name was Jenny, but we simply called her 'J'."

"She wants you to know her son, your husband, is with her in spirit. He had a heart condition that he calls a 'bad ticker.' Before he crossed, he was very weak but he's regained all of his strength in spirit. He had many tests with heart monitors and much blood work. There was also something going on in his throat."

"Yes, he had his larynx removed."

"He says he wishes he would have shown more emotion when he was here and said 'I love you' more often. He likes your glasses — they're different ones than when he was alive. He likes those."

Nancy laughed. "These *are* different. I'm glad he likes them!"

"George, a tall man with dark hair, is with him, as is a friend of his who died from stomach or liver cancer."

"I have an uncle by that name in spirit and I think I know which friend you mean."

"Your husband is concerned about your health in the chest

area. This feels like bronchitis to me. He sends healing to you at night for this. Also, a younger male in the family has his name and he's very proud of that."

"That's my grandson, Matthew. We call him Joey. You know, he tells my daughters and me that he can see his grandpa. Do you think he really can?"

"Yes, children are very open to the spirit world. This is common. You'll get signs from your husband that he's around. I feel he will ring the phone to let you know he's around."

"That's already happened. My one daughter gets all types of things that we think are spirit-related. The other day, she asked for Nana to come through and her old rocking chair rocked from side to side. In the last two days, all the lights in my house have been blinking."

"I sense your daughter is very mediumistic. Spirit will come to the family member who's most open. I'm to ask you about the watch that stopped running right after his death."

Nancy paused and thought about this. "I don't know, unless you mean the one my grandson had. I believe it stopped running for awhile."

"There's your validation."

The next message that came through was so uncanny that Nancy later told me it gave her chills. "Your husband was playful, a jokester. He comes to you and the family in this way, through a short type of thing, like a knock-knock joke."

"Wow!" Nancy cried out. "I can't believe you said that! Every day, my young grandson, Joey, will say to my daughter, 'Knock, knock.' After my daughter says 'Who's there?' He answers by saying, 'Pop-Pop.' I think Joey talks to him all the time."

"Yes, your husband plays with him. He also shows me a closet with a bare light bulb hanging in it. He says there are a few of his sport coats in there and that there's some type of phenomenon that goes on there, too."

"Joey's toys are stored in there. We haven't noticed anything yet."

"Hmmm, by the way, he shows me a specific toy of Joey's, a

push-toy that bubbles pop up inside. Sound familiar?"

"Yes, Joey still plays with that every day. My husband was very close to him, even though he was only nine months old when he died. Because he couldn't talk, my husband would make a sort of clicking noise to communicate with him. To this day, Joey makes that sound with his mouth, as if he is still talking to his grandpa."

"He loved this boy. Talk to him and tell him it's normal to see spirits so that when he gets older, he won't feel silly about it."

Nancy's husband continued to give validations to pass along. "He says there was a discussion or disagreement lately over buying this boy a tricycle or Hot Wheel car. Do you know about this?"

"Oh, my daughter's husband joked about buying Joey a motor-cycle and she told him no."

"He wants to tease you about this. I'm also supposed to tease you about losing keys."

Nancy laughed. "My daughters kid me about that. They said they were going to buy me a clapping device to find things with!"

By the end of the session, my reading room was electrified with vibrant energy from the spirit world. Nancy was pleased and amazed at how clear and specific the messages had been. I told her that she was fortunate to have a husband and mother-in-law who were strong communicators, proving they're very much alive in spirit.

About a year later, I spoke with Nancy about our session.

"When my husband died, I was in a state of shock. Even though he had been sick for three years, it was still a shock to lose him. My life at the time was fast paced because not only was I caring for him daily, I was also working in the real estate business he and I shared. When he passed, I felt a huge void that I didn't know how to fill. My work helped in this way because I've never been the sort of person to just sit around. I was relieved he wasn't suffering anymore yet I didn't want to let go of him after 49 years of marriage. I finally realized it was selfish to feel this way.

"Three years after his death, I'm still adjusting emotionally to being a widow. I've decided to not change anything in my house because all of my memories are here. I've lived here 40 years and he and I raised four children in this home, as well as working together in our business. Family was always important to us and my husband was my best friend. I have no desire to find anyone else to take his place."

I asked Nancy if our session had helped her deal with grief.

"Although I was raised to believe in heaven, I was skeptical about whether it was possible to talk with people who have died," she answered straightforwardly. "Years ago, I went to a fortune teller but had never seen a medium. The reading with you changed me into a believer as far as mediumship is concerned. I had a positive reaction to it because everything in it made sense. The things you told me were exactly as they had happened. When you mentioned about my new glasses and my husband liking them, it amazed me. Also, the message about the knock-knock jokes blew me away since it was a joke among our family that my grandson was talking to his granddad in spirit like that. And we think we know who the nun is that you mentioned; my mother-in-law had a close friend who died who was a nun."

At the end of our conversation, Nancy shared an intriguing incident that happened during her husband's funeral. "His funeral was on a dark and gloomy day in January. With *Taps* playing in the background, the casket was carried into the mausoleum as we stood watching. All of a sudden, a ray of light came out of the sky, shining directly on the casket. It was there for a minute and then left. I feel that it was him telling us he was fine in spirit," she said tearfully.

The 18th Hole

Some clients have never been exposed to spirit communication and do not know what to expect during a reading. Before I begin a session, I ask clients if this is their first reading. If so, I spend a few extra minutes assuring them that they won't be scared by the information given before I explain how the process works. Such was the case with Linda, a pretty, well-dressed woman in her forties who came for an appointment one evening. When she entered my reading room, I sensed she was sad and nervous. I advised her that I don't give "bad" messages to people, that my work is about healing. Polite and reserved, she listened as I explained how the spirit world communicates through mediumship. I barely finished my opening prayer when an insistent message began to come through in my mind.

"What is your connection to Florida? I sense it very strongly with you."

Immediately, Linda's eyes widened. "My fiancé, Michael, and I went there several times because his parents owned a place that we loved to visit."

"There's also a message about golfing. This links to him and I'm feeling that he's the one who's crossed. He really wanted to come here tonight for you. A man is standing here with golf clubs. He says you've golfed, too, and kids you about feeling that you weren't good enough to play with him. He says you did it to please him."

Linda listened intently but said nothing.

"This feels like a real soul mate connection and as I connect with him, I feel a tremendous amount of love that goes on despite his crossing. This is a heart-to-heart communication."

A tear trickled down Linda's face.

"He shows me the number three, meaning there is significance to it. What is that, please?"

A minute went by then Linda responded, "I can't think of what that is." Another minute passed and she gasped, "Oh, yes! He's referring to the date we were supposed to get married, September 3."

"Thank you. He makes me feel as if his crossing was unexpected and sudden. There's been no closure with you emotionally because of this. He impresses me with something being wrong with his heart, lungs and in the stomach area. It feels explosive. He impresses me with an impact in his head area. High cholesterol problems run in the males in his family. This passing feels relatively recent."

"It's been five months," Linda responded. "The head impact is probably because he was behind the wheel when he died from an apparent heart attack."

A clairvoyant image of a man standing on a bright, green golf course formed in my mind. "As I look at him, he is showing me that he is standing beside a flag at the 18th hole, as if he's saying he's finished the game. It's very symbolic, understand? He wants you to know he still thinks of you as his sweetheart. He wants to acknowledge the man with the name that starts with the letters J-A."

"Could that be Jason?" Linda said with uncertainty. "That's his son."

"The name fits if he got some of his father's golfing gear because that's also part of the message."

"Yes, he did get those things."

"Michael wants you to keep in contact with his family. That's important to him, even though you weren't married. He's come through to you in several dreams. He's had to go through a period of adjustment over there because he had such a rapid crossing. He communicates a concern about his mother and wants you to help her with his passing."

An image of a boat floating in a beautiful harbor flashed across my mind. "He comes through with many memories the two of you shared and says you loved to go sailing. There is a photo of the two of you on a boat."

"Yes. I look at our photos several times a day," Linda said with sadness.

"He says the two of you talked about moving to Florida."

"Yes, we did."

"He says he was looking forward to his retirement there. He encourages you to continue with your life and to please nurture yourself. In that regard, he shows me a spa. He gives me the feeling you've visited one of these lately."

"Yes. We also talked about getting a hot tub."

"Oh. By the way, there's a message here that there is a leak in that tub."

"But we never got one."

"Then who does?" I asked, convinced of the message's validity. Linda thought. "Our friend just had one that had a leak."

"Okay. There is also a message about engineering work. This man had a good, clear mind. He says he was in a business partnership with someone else in the family. There's a man who will be involved in this business if he isn't already."

"Yes, his sister is the family member and I do know of a man who's been working there. Michael was a steamfitter and often read blueprints."

"He gives me the feeling that he was very well liked by many people, many of whom attended his wake. He shows me that the two of you went to wine and cheese parties. You know," I said, "this man would have given you the world on a silver platter. He truly loved you." Another message popped into my head. "Hold on because someone by the name of John is being validated. Who is this?" I asked.

"That's my husband in spirit."

"Oh, I understand," I said, realizing the burden of grief Linda must be carrying from losing two men in her life. "You've felt jinxed, so to speak, because you've lost two men in your life. You've thought, *I fall in love with someone and boom! They're gone.* Hmmm, no wonder you've felt this."

"Yes and my husband died from heart problems, also."

"You must release the fear-based thought of being jinxed. You must go on."

The session continued for another 10 minutes before Linda said she wanted to ask a question. "Do our loved ones in spirit know how sad and devastated we are when they pass?"

"Yes, and they don't want us to be because they are really still alive," I responded. "The bond of love will always be there. That's why we do mediumship, to prove the continuity of life. When we go into spirit, we see the purpose of our lives and what our relationships meant."

"You mentioned earlier about dreams. I've not had any that I can remember and I haven't felt anything from anyone close to me in spirit. Why?" Linda asked.

"Give it time. An easy way to connect with a loved one is through a photo before going to sleep. I have a feeling he's come to you but you are not fully open to receiving this type of communication. Plus it may not happen right after someone crosses."

At the end of the session, Linda thanked me politely. She seemed pleased with the reading yet somewhat puzzled by some of the information. I knew that although everything didn't make sense to her right now, she would later understand the messages. I also realized that her heart was mourning over losing two men she loved dearly and that this, along with her anger at the seeming injustice of death, temporarily clouded her spiritual vision. I hoped that the reading shined light on her pathway to healing.

Six months later, I called Linda to check on her progress. Throughout our conversation, I had a hard time believing this was the same distraught woman who sat in my reading room with a dark cloud of grief over her head. Her voice vibrant and full of optimism, she talked about life since we last met.

"When I came to see you I was nervous and skeptical about this process. I didn't know what to expect and the only reason I came for a reading was because a friend of mine told me how much her reading with you had helped after her husband passed. Despite her recommendation, I had to experience it myself to believe it. Funny, as nervous as I was, as soon as I sat down for the session, I immediately felt at peace.

"About 13 years ago, my husband passed suddenly from a heart attack. My only son was 10 and I felt heartbroken, afraid and overwhelmed at the prospect of raising him alone, especially since things had been going so well for us up until that point. I had been active in my church for many years and attended services on a weekly basis. When my husband died, I began to turn away from the church because I felt I didn't get the emotional support that I needed from the members. Although I still believed in God, I was angry with Him for taking away my husband. I had no strong beliefs in the spirit world and didn't think about it much.

"When I met Michael and we fell in love, I was very happy for two years. Then he, like my husband, died suddenly. Again I was alone and abandoned. I felt as if I really knew what it meant to have a broken heart because the two of us never got to fulfill our plans. My anger with God increased. That's when my friend told me I needed to see you. After the reading, I not only felt like a different person but my closest friends told me they noticed a difference in me. I started to read books about healing grief and the spirit world, which have given me peace and a stronger belief in the afterlife. I know it was really Michael who came through in the reading because you had no idea who I was or why I came to see you, yet the details were so accurate. Who would have known that one day I played golf with him for fun, just to please him and he kidded me about my game? Or that he and I had a strong connection to Florida where his parents lived? I went into the reading a skeptic and came out a believer."

On the subject of her faith, Linda said, "I still pray to God to take the sadness away and to bring me happiness again. I haven't returned to church, though. Each night I kiss Michael's photo and talk to him. Even though I haven't had any dreams about him, I trust he's with me."

The Third-Grade Photograph

The following transcript shows how certain spirits need time to adjust on the other side before being able to communicate to loved ones. It is also notable because it provides startling confirmation about an old photograph that mysteriously appeared following the death of a client's long-time sweetheart.

Debbie, an attractive brunette with a warm, vivacious person-ality, came for a session at a bookstore where I was doing readings. When we met, she immediately announced that she was discouraged by two previous readings she had with other mediums in which her partner, Tom, did not come through; she admitted that she was ready to give up if my reading didn't convince her of his presence in spirit. I told her, as I do all clients, that I couldn't guarantee anything, only that I would do my best to interpret what comes through. Seemingly satisfied with this explanation, Debbie settled into her seat as I took her hands and said my prayer.

As the energy began to flow, I sensed an older woman on Debbie's left side holding a couple of young children. "Your father's mother is the first one through and she is holding two children. One was not fully formed, so this may be from a miscarriage. Do you know about these children?"

"My grandmother lost a little girl and my mother had a miscarriage when I was two," Debbie said.

"Your grandmother played the piano and really enjoyed music. She acknowledges she had breathing problems before she died."

"Yeah, this all makes sense to me."

Several other relatives in spirit – a cousin and his family – stepped into the reading to acknowledge their presence. After validating their identities, I delivered their messages of support to Debbie.

"You're to know that during the deep periods of grief you've been through recently, your family in spirit has been there for you. There's also a message here about some financial and legal concerns you've struggled with."

A large tear ran down Debbie's face. "Yeah, that's right."

"Please know you're being helped," I assured her. "They also want to talk to you about a change of residence."

"I moved two years ago. Recently, my parents have asked me to move to Florida to live with them."

"They are showing me a change of residence for you," I said with resolution. "This feels very positive, a new beginning. Spirit will help you with this. They are showing me boxes being packed and lots of furniture."

"Yes, I'm going through things right now because I'm considering opening a new business, an antique shop."

"Yes, that's a distinct possibility. Please release your doubts and fears about all of this."

A minute elapsed before I felt another spirit step into the reading. "This man who comes through stands right next to you and says he's been sending you signs that's he's around. He rings your phone sometimes."

"That just happened two days ago! My phone rang only once and no one was there. I thought it was Tom."

"He wants to talk to you today about his mother and the rest of his family about forgiveness. This is an important message from him."

Debbie stared at me and said emphatically, "I know, I know. His family has been trying to keep his mother and me apart. I'm not supposed to call her. It's a long story."

"He says it causes him pain that this is happening. He never wanted this."

As the reading continued, I was aware that a spirit guide was acting as a facilitator in the communication process because apparently Tom wasn't strong enough to come through on his own. I explained this to Debbie.

"He's having trouble reaching my mind so a guide is helping. This death feels recent to me."

"It's been almost nine months. I went to another medium who told me the same thing–he was weak. He didn't come through at all in that reading."

"Nine months is recent." I paused, waiting for more information to arrive.

"I'm to tell you that the photo you have of the two of you on the mantle is something you look at often. He wants you to remember him as he was then. Also, he is sorry for leaving the way he did, so unexpectedly. You felt much panic when this happened. He hovered around his body after he left it until his grandmother helped him through the tunnel of light. You've been under a tremendous amount of stress since he passed. I'm seeing you having difficulty sleeping. He stands behind you now with his hands on your shoulders, soothing you. I know this sounds crazy but he says that he sings you a lullaby sometimes. Did he sing when he was here?"

"Sometimes he did," Debbie answered, dabbing her eyes.

"He holds a small, thin book with drawings of cats in it that look like cartoons; not a cartoon strip but something like that.

There is significance to this. Is this something he gave you?"

"Cats were his favorite. I think I have something like that. Oh, yeah! I gave him a book exactly like that!"

"That's interesting because I see him with a cat in spirit."

"He was very close to a cat when he was growing up."

"This man is going through healing on the other side. He's in a spirit hospital. He says he's undergoing counseling over there, too, and is working with a man who also had an alcohol problem, a spirit counselor. His crossing was so quick he needed time to adjust. Did he, at some point in his life, have a substance abuse problem?"

"That's how we reconnected seven years ago. I had known him before and then we met again through a recovery program. We helped each other."

"I feel he has a lot of gratitude for that. It's like the 12-step program slogan that says to have an attitude of gratitude. He also wants to acknowledge a nurse, someone he knew, for helping him. Who is this, please?"

Debbie thought for a moment. "My friend, Paula, is a nurse and he knew her. I'm very close to her. She has psychic ability and has seen him around me many times."

"There's a man who is still alive, related to him, that has a heart problem because he points to his heart. He says this runs in the family."

"That might be his brother. Of course [my fiancé] Tom died from a heart problem."

"He wants to talk about some of his clothes. One is a brown jacket with a front zipper; the other is a leather jacket."

"I gave them to Paula's husband!"

"Do you have his wallet? He says you do, and there is a message about a small photograph of either you or him that he acknowledges." I waited for the image to become clearer in my mind, but it didn't. "I'm not sure what this means."

"Yes, I have the wallet. The day of the funeral I found a photo of myself – a very small one – from third-grade that Tom always kept on his refrigerator. It was face up on my bedroom floor, at the foot of my bed. I knew it was a sign from him. I also had his third-grade picture. So the small photo does have meaning to me."

"Thank you. I would also say that one of these pictures has writing on it."

"Yes, mine does!"

"I'm to tell you that you will be helping other people who have experienced loss or are afraid of death. This reading brings healing and closure but please know you are also meant to pass along what you have learned to help others. When these opportunities come, don't pass them by. Your fiancé was afraid of death and there was emotional suppression with him. That's why he needed to go through the counseling he is doing on the other side. Sometimes when people have heart problems, it's related to blockage of their emotions. You helped him with developing a different perspective and getting in touch with his emotions, he says."

Debbie listened carefully.

"He says he felt like an alien at times. There's a feeling here of being disconnected from others."

"Yes."

"The alcohol and drugs he used enabled him to feel more real. I also feel as if there was a chemical imbalance with him, even though he wasn't diagnosed with that."

"I believe that, too."

"He realized that when he crossed over. The spirit healers are also working with him with color." I felt the energy of the session begin to wind down. "He leaves you with the message that there are better days ahead. In the time ahead, you will connect with him through feelings and music. There'll be synchronicities with your turning on the radio and hearing songs that remind you of him."

"That's already happened. I knew it was him," Debbie said with a smile.

Debbie came to me for additional spiritual counseling sessions to help adjust to life without Tom, and she took my psychic development classes. We spoke recently.

"Tom's death from a massive heart attack was shocking because it was so sudden. I was downstairs taking a shower and heard a thump from the kitchen. My intuition must have been working because for some reason I sensed he had a heart attack. When I went upstairs to see what happened, he was on the floor. I called the paramedics and did CPR but I knew his spirit was gone by looking into his eyes. Later, the cardiologist told me he probably died before he hit the floor.

"After Tom died, I started to read books on healing grief. I had always believed in the spirit world but my study of it really began then. Prior to this, I didn't know much about it; so I bought metaphysical books that explained what happens to us when we die and what it's like on the other side. Shortly after, I had two readings that left me feeling frustrated. In one, the medium told me Tom just wasn't strong enough to come through. In the other, not enough evidence of Tom's identity was given for me to believe it was really him. It didn't feel real. I was about to give up on mediumship when I read in a flyer that you were giving readings at the bookstore. I jokingly told my friends that this was the last time I'd try this sort of thing–you know, three strikes, you're out! Of course, as you know, I was amazed at what came through that day. When I listened to the tape later, I knew it was Tom because only he would have known the things that came through, like about my third-grade photo I found the night of his funeral."

When asked what effect the reading had on her grief, Debbie said, "The reading changed my life. It led me to open up my spiritual belief more strongly that when we die, we'll be fine. I can honestly say that I have no fear of death now. I also know that relationships are eternal. I've been able to help others because of what I've been through by sharing my experiences with them. After a while, I knew I must go on with my life, that I had things to take care of — a purpose."

About her relationship with Tom, Debbie added: "I was meant to be with him when he died. We had known each other years before my marriage then we reconnected again when we both entered treatment for alcohol and substance abuse. We helped each other maintain sobriety. I am so glad that when Tom died, he left knowing that someone really loved him."

Debbie eventually moved to Florida to be with her parents. Although she had no plans at the time of our first reading, the message about her making a move to a different area of the country had been given over two years earlier. She is continuing her spiritual studies and is getting back into one of her passions which is filmmaking.

Please Don't Worry About Me

One of the most potent messages that spirits deliver to loved ones is to be at peace with their passing with the reassurance that they have returned "home" safely. Spirits will frequently impress me with this message during readings when the sitter has feelings of uncertainty or fear about their whereabouts. These comforting messages are similar to calling home to let family know we're safe when we are away on a vacation. Coupled with strong evidentiary information, these messages bring much needed healing to the grieving process.

The following transcript is taken from a session with Lisa, 55. As is typical, I knew nothing about her before we began.

"There is a man in your father's generation who stands behind you with his hands on your shoulders," I began. "He passed from problems with his heart, although he had other ailments. He says he's been helping you with feelings of being alone and abandoned lately."

Lisa quietly nodded.

"There's a message from him about your putting paperwork together recently and finalizing things, putting things in order. He says he's been helping you with that through inspiration. I'm seeing a dollar sign related to this, so this must relate to money and it feels as if it relates to insurance. You've contacted different people to help you with this. He shows me many figures and an impression of you going through your checkbook. I hope this makes sense to you."

"Yes, it does," Lisa said softly.

A clairvoyant image filled my mind. "He is showing me a particular piece of paper with a signature on it. I'm not sure what it is but it looks like it might be your husband's signature. So he's passed recently? It feels as if you are in a period of adjustment with this."

Lisa nodded again in acknowledgment.

"What is your connection with Maryland?"

"My husband and I went there several years in a row on vacation."

"He says you have one of these photos of the two of you on vacation somewhere by your desk." (Later, Lisa told me she had a photo of the two of them on vacation that she used in a collage at the funeral.) "He tells me he had more than one surgery in his stomach area and that tubes were inserted there. There was scarring with this. As I connect with him, I feel he had a weight loss and some of the major internal organs, like the liver, were affected by illness. There was a jaundice condition with him and distension in his stomach. This has a cancer feel to it. He says he felt really sick. The drugs you gave him at the end, like morphine, helped. He wants you to know he just floated up when he left."

"Yes, I understand that. He died from pancreatic cancer that spread to his liver. Oh, I'm so glad the drugs helped."

"He wants to thank people for praying for him before he died. It did help him for a time because he says he went into remission. And it helped him with his transition into spirit. Please don't think it didn't work; it did but he stresses that it was his time to cross. He says he was out of his body before he actually passed so I don't know if there was a coma with him but it feels like it. On the other side, he went into a spirit hospital to rest for a while. The older female—feels like a mother – came to get him. "

"Yes, he was in a coma for two days. His mother has died. He always said she was waiting for him!"

"When he was in the coma, he went to the other side because he says it made it easier for him. He says, 'You thought I was gone then. You kept checking my heart and pulse, but I wasn't quite ready'."

Lisa's eyes clouded with tears.

"Since he's crossed, he's been with you and gives you signs."

Lisa started to say something about her radio when I stopped her "Don't tell me, let me give you more evidential information first. He says he moves things on your table, so pay attention to this. Also, there's a message about moving books."

"Oh no! I'm missing one. I just recently looked for it!"

"It's his way of being playful, letting you know he's around. He wants to tell you it was hard for him towards the end because he couldn't talk but playing music in his room when he was sick really helped him."

"We played country music for him. Even though he couldn't talk, I saw a lot in his expressions."

"Your husband was quite a character and could be a jokester at times. His personality was outgoing with a big smile and he was very well liked. By the way, Charles says hello and so does Bill."

"Charles is his father and Bill is my dad."

"It's very important for you to be surrounded by your friends during this time of transition. Let yourself be nurtured. I'm seeing you going out with girlfriends on a shopping trip and there will be some traveling coming, both weekend and extended."

Lisa gasped. "I'm going with friends on a shopping trip tomorrow!"

"You're to buy yourself something," I said emphatically. "That's coming from your husband and he wants you to think of what you buy as being from him. He says he was with you when you recently bought shoes."

Lisa broke into a big smile. "It gives me comfort to know he's around."

"He gives a message about your being safe, in particularly about changing or fixing locks. He urges you to do this."

"One of my locks just broke. Okay, I'll get it fixed."

"There was a poem or tribute that was written especially for him and he talks of you wanting to frame this."

"Yes, I wrote his eulogy."

"Part of that was funny, wasn't it? He says he wanted you to put those things in there because they suited him to a tee."

"Yes!"

"What is your connection with Virginia? He is impressing me with that."

"We got married there!"

Lisa's husband talked about his new life in spirit. "I'm to tell you he had a hard time detaching from eating after he died. He says he loved to do that and he loved rigatoni and all types of pasta."

Lisa's mouth dropped open. "I can't believe it! That's what he always liked!"

I explained that when we cross into spirit, it's like being born again in that we have to adjust to being in pure spirit form again and release physical attachments.

"He says he has no regrets about his life. He lived it to the fullest."

"I asked him that one time and he did tell me he had none," Lisa said. "He said he was at peace with everything."

"He is robust again in spirit because he was kind of hollow-looking when he crossed. That's important for you to know. He says he didn't want chemotherapy. It would have prolonged things when he was ready to go. You knew that."

"Yes, I know. We persuaded him to try it but he really didn't want it."

"He's fine! He says not to worry about him at all. He wants you to go on with your life and date again when you're ready. Don't worry about hurting him by doing that. Sometimes when people lose a spouse, they feel guilty about dating someone else. He's saying, 'Don't'."

At the session's end, Lisa asked questions. "How do I get a closer connection with my spirit guides?"

"Meditate every day. You have a female guide working with you to help you with your spiritual mission. There is also a child guide who comes around you."

"When we cross over, do we come back until we get it right?"

"Yeah, we do," I laughed. "Your husband will be over there for awhile. You'll see him when you cross. When the time is right for us to come back to earth, we reincarnate. In parting he wants to tell Denise hello. Who would that be?"

"She's a friend of mine."

As Lisa prepared to leave, I commented on the number of clear messages she had just received from her love in spirit and how I hoped this had helped her.

"I needed that. I really, really did," she said softly.

"The reading with you made me realize that there really is eternal life and I am so grateful for that," Lisa said six months after our session. "Before John died, I wasn't convinced about life after death. I was raised in the Pentecostal branch of Christianity and there was much talk of heaven but I wasn't a strong believer. I hadn't been to church in years before John died and I was unsure of what I believed spiritually."

Lisa spoke about her feelings following her husband's passing. "I felt completely lost. We had been together nearly every day for 32 years in a good marriage. Over the years, I had been on medication to control depression that deepened after he died. I really didn't want to eat much at that time. When I came for the reading soon after his death, I was finalizing a lot of John's paperwork from his military service for his death certificate, which you validated in the reading. I didn't know what to expect during the reading; I had seen a psychic years ago but I hadn't put much stock in what she said. I was open to all of this but still unsure. Afterwards, I felt so relieved, as if the weight of the world had been lifted off my shoulders."

I asked her what messages given during the reading stood out in her mind. Without hesitating she replied, "When you told me he was thanking me for the eulogy I spent time writing and that part of it was funny. That was true. I *did* put funny things in it. The message made me feel good that he liked what I wrote about him. I also remember that you said I had checked his pulse to see if he had died and that he had actually gone over there beforehand in the coma. This was all true and no one else really knew that. And the pasta he ate! He loved to cook and that was his favorite. When

I heard this, I knew it was John."

In parting, Lisa said, "When I returned to my work as a nurse [after the reading], one of my friends told me how different I looked. She commented on how the lines on my face had disappeared. I feel at peace now with the realization that I can talk with John in spirit because he is always with me. His death raised curiosity in me, which was enough to go on a spiritual quest to find the answers. Thank you for that."

CHAPTER EIGHT

OTHER COMMUNICATIONS

Is death the last sleep? No — it is the last and final awakening.
Sir Walter Scott

Each reading I do is automatically tailored to the sitter's needs by Spirit and is a combination of many factors, special in its own way. As you have seen, some contain facts so specific that they provide irrefutable evidence of life beyond death. Others are primarily emotional in nature and address the dynamics of family and inter-personal relationships. Still others reveal what is beneficial to surviving family members' healing by giving guidance and direction in regard to various modalities of healing. Most bring all of these themes together with the end result of peace, comfort and healing. Such experiences generally have a profound impact on people's lives, often changing them forever.

The transcripts in this chapter represent a cross-section of many readings I've done, and I've selected them because each is unique regarding the particular circumstances surrounding the passing, the nature of the relationships involved or the specific information revealed. In its own way, each case illustrates how those in spirit communicate their continued presence in loved ones' lives from beyond the veil of death.

Can You Forgive Her?
The following story reveals how a man who took his life delivers spiritual wisdom about forgiveness to his sister. It is a striking example of the regret that those who pass from suicide feel in spirit and a powerful reminder of how such a tragedy in life can become our strength, if we choose.

Roz, a slender, earthy woman in her early fifties, attended one of my group programs in which her brother, Tim, who had committed suicide, validated his presence with several strong evidentiary messages. As I engaged in the reading with her, I sensed that she could benefit from a private session that would hopefully help her gain emotional closure with her brother's traumatic passing. She readily agreed and came to my home the following week.

Roz settled comfortably in the rocking chair in my reading room as I took her hands in mine and recited my opening prayer. As the session began, I was immediately impressed that I needed to address some challenging issues that she and other family members had about Tim's death.

"You've been doing a lot of healing work – especially with other members of your family – since your brother's crossing several years ago. He wants to talk about another female in his generation who is still alive. I get the feeling this is a girlfriend or wife."

Roz lowered her eyes and said, "His wife."

"Do you still have contact with her?"

"No, I don't. They were divorced when he died."

"Okay. This makes sense to me now. The reason he is talking about her is to tell you that there is healing that needs to be done between her and you. He says there will be contact between the two of you in the future."

Roz looked at me incredulously but said nothing. I proceeded with the reading. "You are not a person who holds animosity but your brother talks of the need to forgive this person. It feels to me as if there was some blame that this break-up caused his suicide. I feel there has been bitterness—bad vibes, definitely. He urges you to please begin to deal with these feelings. Your brother is doing counseling on the other side and he has come to his ex-wife with forgiveness. Don't hold bad feelings towards her."

Roz was silent as the reading went on. "As I connect with Tim, I feel he was a sensitive individual; he took others' emotions on and stuffed his own. That runs in your family, especially with the males. By the way, I sense a man who always wore a white tee shirt around you who passed from a heart condition. This was sudden and it feels as if his heart exploded. Is your dad in spirit?"

"Yes and he did die from heart problems. It was a sudden, massive heart attack."

"He and your brother are together over there." I refocused and again connected with Tim's emotions, which certainly seemed to be important for him to convey to his sister so she could understand how he felt prior to taking his own life.

"He says he felt abandoned and like a failure when the divorce took place. He wants to communicate these things so you understand how he felt at the time."

"I think I understand," Roz said with hesitation. "Yes, he felt alone; his kids were growing up and his wife didn't want anything more to do with him."

"I also feel there was a depression with him–undiagnosed. It would not have been his nature to ask for help. He talks about seeing now – because of all the healing he's done in the spirit world – what he could have done to stay here and work things out. He says out of everyone in the family that you were the closest to him. He's thanking you for the love you gave him—and still give him."

"Yes, we were very close," Roz said in a soft voice.

"Your brother talks about hunting and shows me a rifle. He acknowledges a man around his age who went hunting with him. The name starts with the letters D-A."

"Oh, that's his best friend, Dave!"

"He is also giving me the name of Joseph. Who would that be?" Roz looked uncertain. "I have no idea. I can't place him."

"File it," I said, as I continued. "There is a message here about a dog, a Springer spaniel to be exact. Where does that fit in?"

Roz thought for a moment. "Oh, his brother-in-law has one. He and Tim were close."

"He says to say hello to him. There is also a message about getting a new truck."

"My other vehicle is not in good shape; we were talking about getting a new one but I don't think we're going to do it."

"Well, wait and see, he says. You may be surprised." Suddenly a strong clairvoyant image flashed in my mind. "Why is he showing me a dirt road that is in an isolated area? He also shows me a tree he liked to sit under."

"I believe that's his friend Dave's place where Tim went to visit every day. That's where the tree is that he always sat under."

"He died very quickly, without any suffering. He simply blacked out from the gunshot. [In the message program Roz attended, Tim showed me the gun he used to shoot himself in the head.] Again he emphasizes that he can see now what he could have done differently. He also makes me feel as if some of his depression was also caused by not feeling well physically. I feel he had problems standing up straight and he is showing me a cane he used."

"Yes, he did."

"He is out of that pain now because he is whole again."

A few other messages came through about other members of Roz's family before Tim resumed sending me thoughts about how he felt in life. "Your brother held back a lot. He was not the most outgoing person. One of the things he had to deal with on the other side was what happened in his marriage. He invested a lot of himself in it and when it ended, he felt he let the family down. He simply couldn't live up to the expectations, even though they were really self-imposed. His wife was very demanding. It was emotionally abusive for your brother. "

Roz nodded adamantly. "That is so true."

"You've done much healing on your own. You will now be taking that to another level when you work on deeper levels of forgiveness towards her. He's had to deal with this in spirit, he says. He wants to thank you for taking care of his kids, even though he is still parenting from spirit. You've been like a mother to them. The oldest boy has a tendency to be similar to him, you know. He is very sensitive. By the way, he will be moving soon. Please suggest to him to get counseling so he can deal with his dad's death," I advised her.

"I will. My mother and I have gone to a local support group for survivors of suicide. Luke [Tim's son] has decided to move to Canada. I am still a bit upset with Tim for doing what he did, although I hold no bad feelings towards him."

"Well, he says that there are regrets about doing what he did. He is able to see from his vantage point in spirit that he could have made different choices. He urges you to make the choice to work on forgiving his ex-wife."

"Are you suggesting that I need to do that in person?"

"You can do it on a soul level if that is easier."

"That will be a tough one. For some time after Tim's death, the thought of her enraged me. We all felt as if she was the one who pushed the button that caused Tim's death. We know that right before he died he put in many calls to her."

"Maybe so but no one can ever make us take our own life," I explained. "We are not that powerful, you see. I understand what you are saying but it is part of your spiritual growth to understand that there may be catalysts in something like this, yet no one else can make a decision like that but us. You will come to terms with this—it won't be overnight."

"Yes, but she abused him terribly," Roz protested.

"Ah, but he allowed it. We are not victims," I said firmly. "Tim says to also keep an eye on your other brothers because there is a family predisposition to depression. One of them has also thought about doing what he did."

"Okay, I will. There was a time in my life when I talked about suicide, too," Roz admitted. "I told Tim and he helped me through it."

I asked Roz if she had any questions. After a moment, she said, "I don't know if this can even be answered—did he plan to do this?"

I mentally sent this question to Tim and awaited a response. "He had thought about it before but the actual act was done spur of the moment. It wasn't planned per se. There was no note left behind. He makes me feel as if he was overwhelmed by his emotions. He says this is hard for him to talk about because he doesn't want to reconnect with those feelings, yet he knows he needs to for himself and you."

"I didn't think it was planned," Roz said. "I think he was trying to talk with his wife and threatened to do it. She probably said to go ahead. They had gone to counseling together, but from what I could see, it was always about bashing Tim. She didn't take any responsibility for anything."

"There was a lot of dysfunction in that relationship," I said. "And there is a feeling I get of men in your family who drank too much. That runs in your family. And yes, there was emotional abuse going on."

"I know."

"Tim says he sends you signs he's around by flashing the lights."

"That hasn't happened but the light in his old bedroom came on the other night by itself. Is that what he means?"

"No, the lights will *flash*," I said, staying with the message I heard. "Watch and see."

Near the end of the session, Roz said, "There is something I want to ask that has bothered me for a long time. My older sister, who I've not always agreed with, told my mom that she has been communicating with Tim since he died, and that he told her he never felt loved by the family. Do you think that is true?"

"Your brother was a very sensitive person who had some problems with his thinking. He didn't love himself enough and had low self-esteem. I told you earlier that there would be some healing in the family because of this death. It is a remarkable chance for the family and this is what your brother wants–to come together with new understanding."

"When my mom called me and told me Tim had died, I was in total disbelief," Roz said when I spoke with her shortly after our session. "In fact, I said something really stupid like 'You're kidding.' Awhile before he took his life, he had said to me that he was going to do it and I kidded him that he wasn't going anywhere without taking me with him. I just couldn't believe he had really gone through with it. At first I felt as if I should have taken him more seriously but I knew there was really no way I could have stopped him. For months I was in extreme sadness. I also worried whether he had suffered in dying because no one found him for about 12 hours afterwards. I was upset with Tim because he didn't open up to me about everything he had been feeling, although I did realize he was in much emotional and physical pain [from hip replacement surgery] before he died. As I was driving to my mom's house on the day he died, I heard Tim's voice in my head: 'Roz, you were right. I shouldn't have done it.' I knew it was him coming to me to let me know he was still around me. This incident helped me to change my view of death, which I had always feared."

Roz talked honestly about her spiritual beliefs concerning life after death. "I was raised Lutheran but hated attending church because I didn't like getting up early and dressing to go. I believed we go on after death but I was always afraid of the uncertainty of it all. The communications I've gotten from Tim have helped me to not fear death anymore. Also, nowadays, more and more is being revealed through books and TV about the other side. As far as reincarnation goes, I am not really sure whether we come back here or not. I want to talk with you further about that sometime."

Later on the night of our session, Roz received an amazing validation that her brother had given during the reading about flashing lights. "When I went home that night, I walked into my living room and glanced at Tim's picture that sits on my mantle. At that moment, the lights that are on either side of it blinked two or three times. I couldn't believe it! And later, the small light in my microwave oven flashed when I opened the door. I checked the bulb but it was fine. So what he said he would do, he did. I also placed the name of Joseph that you gave me. He was a good friend of Tim's that had done car repairs for the family."

I asked Roz how hearing from her brother in spirit has helped her. "After our session, I felt a sense of peace that I hadn't in a long time. The reading gave me proof that Tim is alright; the description of his personality and what he was feeling were very accurate. I really needed to hear about the respect and affection he had for me because it's given me great peace. After I left, I told Tim, 'If you want me to forgive your ex-wife, I'll try to do that for you'."

It's Never Too Late For Love

The following transcript is taken from a phone reading I did for Betsy who desired to connect with her first true love who crossed many years ago at the hands of a relative. Of course, I knew none of this when I initially connected with her. During the session, she heard from several unexpected spirits, including a man who had been a father figure to Betsy and a woman she had cared for during a long illness. This session is impressive for two reasons: it illustrates how people to whom we have shown kindness and love toward remember us in spirit; secondly, how loved ones who have died in a tragic way urge us to move beyond the circumstances of their passing for our spiritual growth.

When I do sessions by phone, I follow the same procedure as with in-person readings. I meditate and pray to clear my mind and strengthen the link with the spirit world. The thoughts I receive from spirit beings are not limited to time or space, making the communication just as clear as when the sitter is in the same room. This is similar to praying for someone who lives many miles away.

At two o'clock sharp, my phone rang; I greeted Betsy and explained the process of spirit communication. While saying my prayer, I became aware of a man standing directly behind Betsy's left side.

"A man who feels like a father is coming through and standing directly behind you. He says he was in the service. Is your dad in spirit?"

"Yes, but I didn't know him," Betsy said.

"Well, this man certainly feels like a father to me. And there is another man who stands right beside him. Was there a man who crossed who was like a father to you?"

"Yes. And he was in the service."

"Okay. Both fathers are here for you today. Your stepfather was very forthright, the kind of man who liked to claim his territory, so to speak. Do you remember him wearing white tee shirts a lot?"

"Yes, all the time," Betsy said with a laugh. "And that's exactly right as far as his personality goes."

"He says he used to march in parades in a uniform and felt a duty to his country. He gives me the feeling that he was a staunch male, a real man."

"Yes, he was a policeman so he wore a uniform a lot."

I paused to listen to a message this spirit was giving me for Betsy. "He says that there's been a problem with the women in your family with depression; that's on your mom's side. By the way, there's a strong Irish ancestry on that side, too."

"Yes, that's true."

"You have suffered from depression. I'm to tell you that the up and down feeling you've had will be leveling out and to take small steps in walking through a condition that involves fears or phobias. This also involves grief because of recent crossings, some of which happened close together."

"Yes."

I sensed the presence of an older woman step in. "There's a lady here who had a long illness who wants to thank you for taking care of her. She wants to let you know she's at peace now after struggling for so long. She says you drove her places like doctor's appointments and she talks of your good heart. Please understand that these little things we do for one another do matter. We may not realize it at the time but these things make a difference for someone else."

"Oh, yes, she was a very dear friend of mine. She was sick for a long time and I did give her rides."

"Would you please tell her family she said hello and that she is aware of the child that is coming into the family."

"Oh, wow! That's amazing! Yes, there is a child coming to them!"

Several of Betsy's relatives came through next – including two children of her uncle's who had passed as infants. Anxiously, she asked if I could connect with a man close to her who had crossed when he was 18 years old.

"Let me try to open the link. Please think of him right now and send him love. We'll see if he comes through."

I closed my eyes to focus. An impression of two spirits formed in my mind. "Hold on, because your stepdad is bringing through a younger male, someone close to your age. Let me connect with him."

A few moments passed as I listened for a message. "You've thought a lot about this man and that's what brings him through today. It's almost like a soul mate connection that the two of you have. He says you spent a lot of time together and that you were going steady."

"Yes," Betsy said.

"His personality is one of being outgoing, kind of like a daredevil. Does that make sense?"

"Yes, he was."

"He talks of being careless and it is somehow connected to his crossing, which was sudden. There was also some underage drinking with him. He says everyone was shocked by his death. He makes me feel as if there was a sudden impact to his head."

I paused, waiting to hear more. For some reason, this spirit did not want to talk about the details of his death. "He says that the two of you had gone steady and had talked about marriage."

"Yes, we did," Betsy said, her voice strained with sadness.

"You spent a lot of time together and went swimming. He wants to acknowledge a female in his age group who is still here, like a sister. If you still have contact with her, please tell her he said hello."

"Yes, I will tell his sister that! I hope he knows that I still love him."

"Yes, he does. I am supposed to ask you about going to a picnic together."

"Hmmm, yes, we did go to an amusement park once."

"The name of Jim is somehow connected to you or him. Who is that?"

Betsy was silent for a moment. "I don't know anyone by that

name."

"Just file it then. You will think of it." A clairvoyant image of initials carved in a tree with a heart surrounding them appeared in my mind. I described what I saw.

"Yes! He carved our initials in a tree!" Betsy said excitedly. "I wanted to ask you if he will incarnate when I'm here. Will our paths ever cross again?"

"It's hard to say because it depends on his purpose. Our souls always choose to come back at the proper time. You were devastated and shocked when he crossed but rest assured you will see him again. He shows me a photo of the two of you that you look at from time to time. He wants you to know he's been happy for you as far as your other romantic relationships are concerned. He says you've often compared him to others."

"Definitely. When I have dreams of him, is he really there with me?"

"Sometimes. But he is also symbolic of the perfect love for you."

"That's nice to hear, especially since he died in a violent way. You see, my uncle murdered him. You said there was an impact to his head. I know that he fell to the pavement after being shot, even though he was shot in the chest."

I was shocked by the information Betsy disclosed, even though I have heard many disturbing things come out in sessions. Nonetheless, I continued transmitting what I perceived. "Yes, and his neck was broken in the fall," I told her. "He wants you to know he holds no animosity towards you for what happened and doesn't want you to either. It's taken you a long time to forgive."

"Oh, yeah," Betsy sighed. "I don't think I've done that yet. Has he forgiven my uncle for what he did?"

"Yes. Your friend says that you think about what would have happened if he had lived. *Would we have married? Would we have had children?* He wants you to focus on the good times instead of these regrets. That is why he came through with memories of happier times. He also wants to make sure you know how much he cares for you."

"I am happy as long as he knows I felt the same. Did my uncle make it to the other side?"

"He is with someone who passed from cancer. Who was alcoholic on that side? I get a strong impression about this."

"Whoa! My dad and my grandmother were. My grandfather, my uncle's father, died from cancer and had the same first name."

"Your uncle also had this problem of alcoholism, along with a violent temper that got worse when he drank. He could pop off at any minute."

"Yes, he was like that."

"Please try to move beyond all of this."

"I will."

As the session ended, I detected a sense of relief on Betsy's part. Apparently she had been carrying grief for many years over losing the love of her life who was murdered by her own uncle–a bitter, angry man whom she needed to forgive in order to move on. One thing was clear: she had a strong spiritual support team of loved ones willing to help.

Betsy and I had other phone sessions after this initial one. Because she suffers from agoraphobia (fear of open spaces), she was unable to see me in person. I recently spoke with her about that first session, which took place nine months earlier.

"For years I was angry at God for taking Jack from me. He was my first true love. Since he died, I've never been able to recapture the feeling I shared with him. We had been good friends since we met in elementary school with not a day going by that we weren't together. He lived two doors down from me and we would do many things with each other—go to the zoo, ride the bus into the city and listen to records. The feelings I had about his death were anger and guilt, which stemmed from my uncle being the one who killed him and because I felt I should have treated him better when he was alive. My uncle was an alcoholic who was disabled and very angry. At his trial for the murder, I felt terribly torn between my love for Jack and maintaining loyalty to my family. My uncle got off with 15 years probation since the jail had no provisions to house handicapped people.

"I believed in God when I was a young girl but I couldn't understand why He would take Jack when he was so young. Plus all of our future plans for getting married and having a family were gone. I stayed angry until my first daughter was born—that gave me proof that God is really good. I then pushed a lot of my anger down, which turned into panic attacks and depression. I am able to leave the house now but only for short periods of time."

When I asked Betsy if our session had helped heal her years of grief over losing Jack, she responded, "I thank you from the bottom of my heart because I now feel as if he's not really gone. The reading uplifted me; I feel much lighter. I definitely feel more at peace with his death. I do believe there are no accidents and his passing was meant to be. Ninety percent of my anger is healed as a result of our session. Some things you told me that I couldn't place were later confirmed, like the name Jim, who I remembered was his best friend at the time. Other things that stand out in my mind are when you mentioned we went swimming, which was a favorite activity, and the tree carving of our initials, which is still there. I recently made plans to show my daughter that tree. I now feel Jack is so close to me sometimes that I can reach out and touch him."

The Red Rose

The following reading helped to provide peace and closure for a woman who lost her best friend of many years. It's a good example of how months of depression and grief can be alleviated by spirit communication and how the bond of friendship survives death.

Devon, a quiet, neatly dressed woman of 42, sat across from me. As I looked into her doe-like eyes, I felt a burden of sadness and depression surrounding her. Although spirit communication was choppy throughout this session (some are not as smooth as others), she nonetheless heard from someone very special: a man she had missed immensely.

When the reading began, Devon's mother was the first to come through, identifying herself by the illness she passed from, which involved blood work and other medical tests.

"Someone in the family had a blood transfusion," I said.

Devon was silent as she thought. "Hmm, I'm not sure."

"Your mom tells me about a strong connection with the month of May. What would that be? It's most likely a birthday for someone close."

"That's when my birthday is."

Soon I sensed the presence of another spirit being ushered in by Devon's mother. "There is a man by the name of George coming through. He wants to say hello. Do you recognize him?"

Devon began to tear up as she answered softly, "Yes. He was my friend."

"Is this who you wanted to hear from tonight? He gives me that feeling. He feels your thoughts, as those in spirit do, and says you summoned him here. Who is Robert or Bob, please?"

"I'm not sure."

"George makes me feel as if there was a strong heart connection between you two. That bond survives death, please understand this," I assured her. "He is a guardian for you in many ways because of this. He wants you to let the younger males know – younger than him, that is – that he's still with them and alright."

"I'm not sure who that would be," Devon answered.

I was getting frustrated since nothing seemed to connect. I could tell this reading would not be an easy one insofar as obtaining validation; Devon seemed unable to claim much of what was being said.

"George tells me you've had some recent dreams about him," I continued.

"Yes, I sure have," she said, perking up.

The next image in my head made absolutely no sense (not unusual when spirits are communicating). Nonetheless, I described it to Devon exactly as I saw it.

"George shows me a turtle. What could this mean?"

"I have no idea, unless it's because he used to tease me that I'm slow," she giggled.

"He says he didn't know what to expect when he crossed. It's different than he anticipated."

Devon listened intently.

Next, I felt a mild sensation of restriction around my heart. "This man says he had heart and lung problems and that's how he died. He was on oxygen at the end of his life."

"Yes, he was. When he passed, was it frightening or peaceful for him?"

I awaited George's response.

"Peaceful, but he gives me the feeling that there was some disorientation. Again, it had to do with his mental state of not knowing what was waiting for him on the other side. He may not have verbalized this to you but he sure wants to talk about it now. He says that he wasn't the most open-minded person when he was alive but he's doing that now. He wasn't the most talkative person; even now, it's like pulling teeth to get anything out of him. He's not sure how to reach my mind."

A minute passed before a name popped into my consciousness. "Who is Tom? He is acknowledging him."

Devon looked confused. "I don't know a Tom. Oh, wait! Yes, I do. Tom's a friend of George's."

"Okay, he now gives me the impression that he was involved in a business. He says he spent a lot of time on this business and regrets not spending it on relationships. He is emphasizing this message to you. He wanted more time here to do that but his time to pass had come. If he has any regrets, this is it. Now, he is saying the name of Richard."

"That's one of his sons!"

"One of the boys lives out of state."

"Oh, yes, one does."

Just then, I connected the dots about the younger male who George mentioned. "Remember the younger males he wanted to acknowledge?" I reminded Devon. "They would be his sons. He also says that one of his sons is moving soon. Do you know about that?"

Devon nodded.

I paused to listen to what George would say next. The thought of a cucumber salad with sour cream dressing entered my mind, so I relayed this to Devon.

"That was one of his special dishes," she laughed.

Then I was onto the next impression: someone painting. I relayed this to Devon.

"I painted rooms in his house when he was alive," she confirmed.

As the reading progressed, George seemed to get the hang of talking with me; the information was stronger and clearer. "There is a connection with Florida."

"Oh, my God!" Devon said and began to cry. "I'm sorry for breaking down. George and I always went on vacation to Florida. One of his sons lives there, too."

I handed Devon a tissue and paused while she took a moment to calm down. The message about Florida was obviously emotional for her.

"What is the connection with a wallet?" I asked. "Do you have his wallet and did you recently go through it?"

Devon's eyes grew large. "Yes, I just went through it the other day!"

I explained to her that this type of message is often communicated to provide confirmation that loved ones in spirit are aware of what we are doing.

"Strange, he is showing me a large unit in your home – an air conditioner or furnace – that you just had serviced recently.

"Yes, I did. Oh, my goodness! I can't believe it!"

"He mentions the name Paul. Who would that be?"

"Paul is handling his estate right now."

"He makes me feel that everything will go smoothly with the estate." A minute elapsed, then: "He wants you to know he is with you when you are driving, Devon."

She acknowledged the message.

As we wrapped up the session, Devon, now smiling, thanked me. "You don't know how good you've made me feel."

"Well, good," I said, grateful that the reading, although difficult at first, had helped her. "But don't thank me. Thank

George. He's the one who came through with everything. I'm part of the process, that's all. Now that we've got the man talking, he doesn't want to stop!"

We both laughed and I happily noticed that Devon's mood had lightened. George's parting message was touching; I saw a beautiful, red rose.

"He is handing you a red rose as a symbol of unconditional love. He wants you to have it."

Devon's eyes misted. "That's interesting because I put a single, red rose on his casket when he died."

"He's returning it to you now. The circle of love is never ending."

When I spoke with Devon about 18 months later, she shared how the reading had both reinforced her spiritual beliefs about death and alleviated her depression over losing George. She also offered validation on some of the evidential information that she had not claimed earlier.

"When George died, I was devastated. He was my best friend. After my mother died earlier, I moved in with George and his family. Through the years, we became very close. With him gone, I felt totally alone and wanted to die, also. I felt like someone had ripped my heart out. I was still feeling low when I came to see you about five months after his death.

"On the way home after the reading, I cried but they were happy tears. For the first time, I was at peace with his death. The information you gave made me feel as if he was still with me. Some of the details were so specific that only he would be aware of them—like the furnace repair. That really blew my mind because just two weeks earlier, the family had called someone to look at it. It was a blessing, too, because the repairman said it would have started a fire if it hadn't been fixed.

"Remember George gave me a message about watching over me when I'm driving? Well, I had been in a car accident shortly before our reading and it could have been much worse than it was. I feel that he *was* guarding me. You also mentioned him being involved in a business and spending much time there; he was a chiropractor for many years and worked for himself."

Speaking candidly about her beliefs regarding life after death, Devon continued. "I've always believed the spirit goes on and that we will come back to live other lives. In fact, I believe George and I knew each other before this lifetime. When he was alive, he told me he felt this way, too. It gives me comfort to know that I will see him again and that we will be together."

Live Life to the Fullest

After crossing over, we retain our earthly personalities until we become aware of our higher, divine identity. While the personality is still intact, a spirit being can use it as a teaching tool for surviving loved ones. The following transcript demonstrates how effective this "power of example" can be.

When I met Rachel, 24, I was awed by the tenderness, beauty and wisdom of her soul, which was far advanced beyond her age. She and a group of friends had attended my "Bridges of Love" mediumship seminar a few months before. The audience for the seminar had been large so I had no awareness of her being there or whether she had received a message that evening. I held her hands, said my prayer and zeroed in.

"Your grandmother from your mom's side comes through very strongly for you. She was actually here before you came today. She is stressing how happy she is in spirit and wants you to tell your mom and aunt that. And who would Nancy be, please?"

"That's my mom," Rachel answered.

"She shows me a ruby, so there must be a connection with the month of July, a birthday. The names Betty and Harry are being recognized. Do you know them?"

"July is when my grandmother was born. I don't know Betty or Harry. I'll have to ask my mom."

A young woman appeared next to Rachel's grandmother. "Jennie says hello to you. She is not suffering now. She's laughing and smiling. I have a sense that the short time she was here, she made a real difference in people's lives. This crossing feels like a cancer to me."

Rachel sat straight up in her chair. "Yes, she had cancer."

"She says she's over that now. This is a lady who didn't hold onto the bad times or resentments and she is not holding onto that illness either. She says there was a remission when she got better, then sick again. She was very weak at the end but she now chooses to not identify with all of that. She'd rather focus on her strengths and the good times she had."

"Yes, she was like that."

"She acknowledges a woman here who was either a very close friend or a sister. Did she have a sister?"

"Yes, I am her sister."

"She really wants to acknowledge this relationship. She's with a small, light-colored dog. It's a purebred. He brought her much joy."

"She had a Pomeranian. My dad has one, too."

This spirit's thoughts were clear and pure, like a ray of sunshine– warm and soothing. "Her personality is one of someone who always looks on the bright side. She'll come to you when you need cheering up. Please remember her as she was. She says she's become young again in spirit."

Rachel nodded and Jennie continued to impress me with her thoughts. "She says there is a split within your family and healing needs to happen. It feels like a separation. Are your parents separated?"

"Yes."

"She talks of forgiveness with that. She says, 'Live and let live'. She talks of the importance of this and urges you to release any resentment about this. She emphasizes to tell your father she loves him, so it feels as if there may not have been closure with him before she crossed."

Rachel was clearly absorbed in the reading, listening to every word.

"She gives validation of a birthday in the family around this time. Jennie is showing me a bracelet with various colored gemstones. She says that you or someone in the family has a bracelet like this. The stones represent family members' birthdays.

Do you have a birthstone bracelet like this?"

"Hmm, I'm not sure. I'll have to think about that. The birthday around this time is my mom's."

"There's a message here about your schooling. She shows me a certificate coming to you. I see it right above your head."

"Yes, I've been looking into getting certified to teach yoga."

"She talks about you pursuing your dreams. Your spiritual side is opening up now and so are your psychic abilities. Jennie encourages you to trust more, especially where decision-making is concerned, in the coming year. Teaching is part of your purpose, as is working with children. She'll be helping you with this from spirit. Loved ones help us with these things because from their perspective, they can see our life's mission. They can then guide us down that particular pathway. Over the next year, you'll notice some wake-up calls as far as spiritual growth is concerned. You will be drawn to holistic health, aromatherapy and homeopathy and offer these services to people and children."

At this point, I was impressed to deliver other intuitive guidance. "Your spirit guides are advising you to heal grief from the past by working with the power of your breath, which brings in divine healing and light. This will help to clear your heart of the sadness and move forward. They are also suggesting that you practice yoga, which works with the body's energy meridians and helps to release karma."

Rachel sat quietly as the reading continued.

"Your sister says someone close to you has been depressed and is being treated for that now. Do you know who this is?"

"Yeah. That's my mom and she is being treated."

"Jennie says your mom will go to Florida and the sunlight will help her. She also makes me feel as if there is another connection with her to that area."

"She and I went there and she also went by herself."

"Are you involved in a relationship? Jennie wants to say hello to the man with you whose name starts with the letter D."

"That's my husband, Dan!"

"She sends her love and is happy that the two of you are

together. She also sends love to the younger male who plays baseball."

"Her son!"

"Your sister had a boundless enthusiasm about her and even kept this mood during her illness. She wants to thank you for helping her with that. There is also a huge thank-you to you for driving her places when she was sick. She says she is grateful for all the experiences she had when she was here. She compressed much living into a short lifespan. You know, it was her time to cross because she had come in for certain lessons that were finished before she did cross. One of them was to accomplish healing between her and your mom. Another was to learn to live life to its fullest."

As the session drew to a close, Rachel was mesmerized by her sister's communication.

"I feel her philosophy was to live each day as if it were your last. She wants to leave you with that message," I said. "She is drawing back now."

Rachel hugged me after the session. As I would discover less than two years later, this wouldn't be the last time she'd hear from her sister.

I met with Rachel several times the following year because she was a student in my mediumship development classes. Since her sister's passing, she had embarked on a deep spiritual quest to further her understanding of both the afterlife and her own life's mission. She shared some of her insights:

"Before Jennie died, I was open to the possibility of the other side but since I hadn't lost anyone close to me, I really didn't know much about spirit communication. I had unusual experiences when I was younger, like the night of my grandfather's funeral when I saw him sitting in a chair at the foot of my bed. I guess I didn't think much of it at the time but I now see that it was his way of letting us know he was still there. When I had the private session with you, I saw spirit communication in a different light. The reading helped me to open and see my spiritual pathway more clearly. The specific details that came through from Jennie were very healing. The description of her personality was exactly the way she was. On many occasions, she would tell me to live life to its fullest. Throughout her illness and despite three transplants, she never complained. Her outlook on life has taught me to view life differently. I now realize that any of us can pass at any time so it's best not to worry about the little things in life that don't matter.

"I was heartbroken when Jenny died, yet I loved her enough to let her go. I realized it was selfish to expect her to stay here in so much pain. The night she died, I meditated in the hospital. In the stillness of my mind, I talked to her and said, 'I don't want you to stay here and be sick. We'll all be okay so it's alright for you to leave.' She had told me a month or so before she passed that she was tired of being sick so I knew it wouldn't be long. There's not a day that goes by that I question her decision to be at peace."

Rachel has had many signs that her sister is around her in spirit. "I can feel Jennie around me all the time. She's rung my phone many times to let me know she's there. Also, I talk to her when I am having a bad day and I sense her answering me through my feelings. These things are very comforting. My belief in life after death has deepened because I know she is definitely with me, keeping me strong, just as she did when she was here."

Two interesting notes to this follow-up: Rachel confirmed the names and identities of two people in her extended family who came through in the session and the existence of a the birthstone necklace that had belonged to her grandmother. After checking with her mother, Rachel learned that Betty was her grandfather's sister-in-law who had passed just one week prior to the reading and Harry was her great uncle. She had no conscious knowledge of either one. In addition, Rachel looked through jewelry of her late grandmother's and discovered a necklace with birthstones of family members. (Apparently, I misinterpreted what Jennie showed me as being a bracelet, although the description was accurate.)

PART THREE
LIVING BEYOND GRIEF

CHAPTER NINE

SPIRIT SPEAKS TO US: UNDERSTANDING AFTER-DEATH COMMUNICATION

I believe that imagination is stronger than knowledge, that myth is more potent than history.
I believe that dreams are more powerful than facts , that hope always triumphs over experience, that laughter is the only cure for grief. And I believe that love is stronger than death.
- From the movie *The Crow*

A number of my clients have experienced contact with deceased relatives and other spirits through physical phenomena that occurred in their homes, vehicles, yards and workplaces. Many others connect with the spirit world through dreams. The common thread that runs through this chapter's spirit stories is that they all happened without assistance from a medium. During the question and answer portion of my group mediumship seminars, people often share their personal experiences. I never cease to be amazed at how the spiritual and physical worlds blend to produce astounding, often unexplainable signs and synchronicities.

The term "after-death communication" or "ADC" – first coined by Bill and Judy Guggenheim in *Hello from Heaven* (Bantam Books, 1997) – is defined as a spiritual experience that takes place when a person is contacted directly and spontaneously by a family member or friend who has died. One of the best books written on this increasingly researched topic, *Hello From Heaven* contains hundreds of stories of people who've experienced remarkable signs from loved ones that validate their continued consciousness after death.

From what I've observed in my work, the essence of the message being communicated by these manipulations or "calling cards" is "Hello! I'm here!" or "Pay attention to this!" These messages frequently bring comfort to relatives of the communicating spirits because they give evidence of life after death. In many readings, spirits impress me to tell loved ones that it is indeed they who are producing these occurrences. For example, a spirit may give validation that he is communicating with his wife by ringing the phone or doorbell. Some spirits will place or move objects in loved ones' homes to grab their attention. Others give messages about the appearance of specific birds or animals in relatives' yards. The timing of these communications sometimes coincides with events like birthdays or anniversaries of the recipients or the spirits. I know of one family that receives validation from their son through various means on the date of his passing every year.

Spiritually speaking, what purpose does an ADC serve? After hearing many of these stories, I believe loved ones in spirit want us to know they survived death and that they are still with us. This brings peace of mind and facilitates healing from grief. ADC's are heavenly signs that we are not alone and proof of a higher plane of existence than the earthly one—giving us hope, comfort and reassurance. The synchronicity of these messages reinforces our connection to the spirit world, which is always part of our consciousness whether or not we are aware of it. In addition, ADC's serve as wake-up calls about life issues and challenges we face, such as illness and financial or emotional difficulties. Frequently unexplainable by physical laws, they remind us that not everything is definable by science as we presently know it, although more research is currently being done on the subject of ADC and mediumship.

My work reveals that the most fundamental tool in healing grief is awareness of the continuity of life after death. Much like having a reading with a medium, ADC's powerfully reinforce life after death by creating an undeniable link (because they are visual or auditory) between the spiritual and physical worlds. Spirit beings are continually around us and, as you've seen through the stories in this book, are quite persistent in their attempts to contact us. ADC's assist in this process. To help you better understand how this happens, I've organized this type of communication into categories according to the particular "vehicle" that spirits use to convey their presence.

Electricity

Spirits can manipulate lights and electrical equipment to get our attention. I've talked with numerous people who have had these experiences happen in their homes, offices and cars. Interestingly, many of these episodes occur when they are thinking of or having a conversation about a deceased relative. Lights may dim, flash or go off completely. Computers, stoves, toasters, TVs and radios may temporarily malfunction, even though they were previously in good working order. They may turn off and on or make strange noises.

Adele, grieving over the unexpected loss of her husband, told me that the hallway light next to their bedroom flickered consistently not long after his passing. Despite checking the bulb and its tightness in the socket, she could find no reason for this to happen. She believed it was his way, among other signs he gave her, of bringing comfort.

The lights in my reading room occasionally flicker when I do private sessions. I once did a reading for a woman whose grandmother came through and in which the lights and the tape recorder in my reading room went out for a few minutes then came back on. We both laughed as I thanked the grandmother for allowing the session to continue being taped.

I've received correspondence from clients who are discouraged to find that part of the cassette tape from their session did not record. This has happened on two different recorders with high quality recording tapes. What is interesting about this phenomenon is that portions of the tape record, while others don't. Nowadays, I advise clients to take notes as back-up to the tapes. I have no explanation for this occurrence other than electro-magnetic interference of spirits' energy.

I once did a demonstration of mediumship for a group in a pub setting on a Sunday when the business was closed. Halfway through the two-hour program, the video game beside the bar spontaneously started to play, emitting loud, electronic beeping sounds. We were initially startled then amused because it was an obvious confirmation of the message I was delivering at that moment. I resumed giving messages only to have my assistant's travel alarm clock on a nearby table buzz. I joked that the group must have some particularly noisy relatives who wanted to party that day!

Some spirits like to use the TV set as a focal point to reach loved ones. Shortly after her husband's death, Lisa (whose story appears in the Soulmates chapter) woke up at two a.m. with an overwhelming sense of sadness and despair. In the morning, she shared her experience with her sister, Linda, who had been staying with her and sleeping on the living room couch. Linda asked Lisa what time she had awoken. When Lisa told her, Linda gasped and said it was the same time that she happened to look over at the TV (which was off) and saw what appeared to be Lisa's late husband's face floating on the screen. She added that Lisa's cat sat quietly and stared at the apparition, apparently captivated. Lisa felt it was her husband's way of letting her know he was still around in the midst of her depression over his passing.

Another woman's late husband used a type of Morse code through the TV to communicate with her. She was working at a desk in the room where he had always watched TV when she heard a strange clicking noise coming from the set, which was turned off. She unplugged the set. The clicking continued for another five minutes then quit. She believes it was her husband's way of comforting her in a quiet moment.

How is it possible for spirits to make use of electricity? Although the exact mechanics are unclear, I believe it's because spirits are thought-forms without physical matter and substan-tially electrical in nature. Because thought is energy, it can affect other forms of energy such as electricity. If spirits direct enough focused thought energy to making lights flash, for example, it could produce those results. TV sets, in particularly, seem to provide a strong conduit for spirits' energy to be projected upon. Further research is needed to determine the precise means of how this is possible.

Telephones

Another common way for spirits to communicate is through the phone. In these types of ADC's, a deceased loved one's voice may be heard, the line may be silent, or a voice imprint is left on an answering machine. Several years ago a lovely, older German woman came for a reading in which her late husband said that he "calls" her telephone answering machine. I asked her if this had happened and she said no. She later told me that two days after the reading, she returned home to see her answering machine message light flashing. When she tried to retrieve it, an eerie sound like none she'd ever heard was on the tape. She believed it was her husband calling her as promised in the reading.

One day I received two astounding phone calls from Barb and Nora, both clients. Barb wanted to know if it was possible for a person to call her own house. She explained that she had received a call with no one on the other end of the line and the caller ID feature registered her own number. I told her I had never heard of such a thing happening. Barb added that she had been especially down that day, thinking about her husband who had recently died. A few hours later, I was surprised to receive another call from Nora (also a widow) in which she asked me the same question, as a similar thing happened to her that morning. I shared Barb's experience with Nora and although I wasn't absolutely sure, I told her I didn't think it was a normal occurrence. Since there are no coincidences, I attribute these phone calls to spirit messages that, for some reason, occurred simultaneously. (During the course of writing this section, I received two anonymous calls on my desk phone. When I answered each one, there was static in the background and no one on the line. In the days before and since I've written this section, I haven't had any such calls. A clever spirit certainly had a sense of humor!)

Moving Objects

One night while watching *White Noise*, a movie about a man who receives spirit communication through his TV, Ginny, heard a loud crash in her hallway. When she ran to investigate, she discovered that a painting of herself that had hung for years undisturbed above the staircase had inexplicably fallen and come out of its frame. Shaken by the experience, Ginny called me to see if I could provide insight about who in the spirit world might be trying to contact her. During the session, her mother – a strong, controlling woman – came through and admitted that she had moved the painting to make Ginny aware that she was helping her with her troubled marriage to a man who was alcoholic. It was definitely not a coincidence that Ginny had received this message when she was watching a movie about after-death communication; it was the best time for her mother to get her attention.

Another example of spirits manipulating objects involves Sara who inherited her grandmother's favorite gold necklace, which had a chain that was considerably tangled and knotted when she received it. She and her mother tried without success to unknot it. Several days later, when Sara picked it up to give it another try, it was mysteriously untangled. She has no explanation other than her grandmother in spirit wanted her to enjoy what had been her favorite piece of jewelry.

Spirits are capable of moving just about any object imaginable to announce their presence including keys, rugs, dishes, furniture and books. I've also heard of things reappearing that were seemingly lost. A client shared with me that she searched in vain for a charm of her late husband's favorite football team in his dresser where he always kept it. A few months later, she happened to be looking in the dresser for another item and found the charm — as if it suddenly materialized.

At one of my programs, a woman asked if I had any impressions about why angel statues in her home were always being rearranged. I strongly felt it was her beloved grandmother trying to get her attention. Another woman questioned why the sliding door on her van mysteriously opened by itself on several occasions when she was preparing to leave the garage. When I tuned in, her rambunctious grandmother who had loved to travel came through and clearly identified herself as the culprit.

Scents

Probably the most common way for spirits to reach us is through scent. Many people have shared stories with me about smelling a particular scent that they associated with a deceased relative or friend. Flowers, especially roses, are the most frequent. After-shave and perfume come next, followed by cigarette or cigar smoke. Not by coincidence, our sense of smell is closely tied to our memory of people, places and events and can activate these codes in our brains. I believe this association is how and why spirits can communicate with us effectively by using scent. An interesting observation I've made is that spirits are capable of producing scent through telepathy; in other words, they impress a scent – such as lilacs or a certain brand of perfume – on our minds. The best way I know how to describe this experience is that it is like remembering what something smells like even if the memory is from years ago.

I once did a program in which a woman talked about her deceased daughter who comes to her periodically through the smell of cigarette smoke. When her daughter (a smoker) died suddenly from a heart attack, her mother raised her two young children. On the days they graduated from high school, the woman (a nonsmoker) smelled the distinctive odor of cigarette smoke in her house.

Many years ago, I lived in an apartment that was haunted. Besides producing other strange manifestations, the ghost that resided in this old building somehow manufactured the smell of tobacco and alcohol, which permeated my living room. The smell would last for a few minutes then dissipate. When a large cloud of ectoplasm (spirit matter that looks like smoke) emerged from my bathroom wall one evening, I knew it was time to move! I've discovered that in the case of hauntings, it's best to set boundaries with the invading spirits by verbally telling them they don't belong in your space and strongly suggesting they move on to the other side by seeking the white light. It's also helpful to cleanse the energy of the dwelling by burning white sage and visualizing healing white light permeating the entire structure.

The familiar scent of a loved one can be comforting to people in grief. I read for a man who had just lost his wife of many years. When she came through, she told him it was okay that he sometimes held her clothing and pillow, with the scent of her perfume on it, to his face for comfort. He was astonished that I knew about this private act of remembrance.

When certain spirits come through, they talk about producing scents so that loved ones will recognize them. Some spirits use scent as their calling card to let others (who may have never known them personally) realize they are around. In my mediumship training, one of my teachers, Patricia, had been a personal secretary to the famous medium Arthur Ford. He came to her many times after his death to give her information about the spirit world and other metaphysical subjects. In addition to cracking the so-called Houdini code (before his death, Houdini placed a paper with writing on it in a safe that only his wife knew about), Arthur was notorious for smoking big, smelly cigars. Every now and then, Patricia's students would detect the unmistakable stench of cigar smoke when Arthur decided to make his presence known. It became a joke when I was in training that we'd better be good because Arthur was watching us!

Nature

One of the most fascinating ways that spirit beings communicate is through nature, including the repeated appearance of certain birds, animals and insects. I have given many readings in which spirits deliver messages about a particular species of bird coming close to the house or being in the yard of loved ones as a messenger from heaven. For example, a woman's father came through in her session and said that he would send bright red, male cardinals to her yard. The woman readily acknowledged that these beautiful birds regularly flutter against her front window. She knew it was a sign from her dad, as he'd always loved cardinals.

In my first book, I wrote about the appearance of butterflies in my life during the time I was writing that manuscript. As a result of that experience, I decided to use a butterfly as a symbol for my work, especially since it connotes transformation, freedom and the spiritual evolution of the soul. I've met others who have had similar experiences with butterflies. Alice, a good friend of mine, told me about an encounter she had last summer. She and her sister were at a cemetery doing genealogical research two weeks after Alice's friend, Jen, had died unexpectedly from unknown causes. The night before, Alice asked Jen to send her a sign (specifically through the appearance of the butterfly) that she had made it safely to the other side. While Alice was standing by the car the next day at the cemetery, a butterfly landed on her shorts and clung to the fabric. She allowed the pretty insect to climb onto her finger and said, "Thanks for letting me know you made it, Jen." It then flew away.

The appearance of flowers that grow out of season or in unexpected places can also be messages from loved ones in spirit. A client told me that as late as October, she noticed the lilac bush in her yard had a large bloom on it. She believed it was a sign that her late husband was watching over her, as she had an extremely difficult time adjusting to his passing.

Last summer, I visited my mother's grave for the first time in two years. I noticed that in the middle of the dirt, directly below the headstone, a single, yellow buttercup was growing. It was larger than any buttercup I'd seen and was the only one around; the surrounding plots had none. Seeing this happy, little flower was greatly significant because when I was a child, I used to pick buttercups and give them to my mom. To me, it was a symbol of our bond of love.

Carla's brother died tragically in a car accident. After her reading, she told me that he came to her when she was especially missing him through a monarch butterfly that hung around her porch. Its appearance gave her great comfort and made her realize that her brother lives on in spirit.

Other Signs

Spirits can come to us in just about any way imaginable. One woman shared with me that her late grandmother communicated with her by causing her computer to print out heart-shaped letters. Another told me on the day of the sale of her house that she and her late partner had shared, his favorite song came on the radio on the way to the real estate closing. And a man shared with me that he has felt "hugs" from his deceased parents — a warm embrace much like a blanket — both when he was lying in bed and standing in his kitchen.

Spirits frequently convey messages through sound and music. Song lyrics are especially useful in getting our attention. This happened to Doris, whose late husband sent her a powerful message one day when she heard three consecutive songs on the radio that reminded her of him. Another time while running errands, she left the radio on at home. When she returned, the song she had played at his funeral – a tribute of sorts – was on the radio, filling the house with fond remembrance.

Paula had a mysterious incident with her doorbell. Friends of hers and her late husband's were visiting one evening when the porch doorbell rang. When Paula went to the door, no one was there or on the sidewalk. She simply concluded that her husband was announcing his presence to his friends that evening.

Amy, another client, told me about an interesting device: an electronic voice recorder with a built-in "white noise" that spirit voices can be recorded upon. This device can be placed in a room where ADC's have occurred and left running to see what sounds it might detect. Amy, who has experienced strange occurrences in her house, has recorded unexplainable voices that sound as if they're emanating from inside a tunnel. "They're hollow sounding and really eerie," she said. "I have no idea who they're from but they are plainly not the voices of any of us living in the house."

Synchronicities

When two seemingly unrelated occurrences happen at the same time, it is defined as a coincidence. Spiritually and metaphysically speaking, when the union of these two occurrences creates meaning or holds a particular significance for us, it is a synchronicity. Because all souls are united in the universal consciousness of God, it is possible to receive messages from other planes of existence because we, as divine beings, are one with all dimensions. That is, we are in constant communication with the spirit world; it is simply a matter of tuning into its consciousness or frequency, so to speak, to be aware of it. Consider radio and TV waves that are continually being broadcast. Until we turn on our radio or TV set to receive the programming, we don't hear or see it. Synchronicity in receiving messages from loved ones is much the same in that we must first notice them in order for them to have meaning for us. When we do, the element of diving timing (higher awareness versus rational thinking) is involved; our souls open to the correct frequency, making us receptive to this type of guidance. Synchronicity often operates through our subconscious mind, which functions independently of our rational, conscious mind. If we allow it (and don't dismiss them as mere coincidences), our conscious mind can then translate these experiences and decipher their deeper meaning, which can be tools for spiritual growth.

Have you ever thought of someone you haven't seen in a while then soon afterwards hear from or encounter this individual? Did the exchange prove meaningful or helpful to you or the other person in some way? This is an example of synchronicity; your thoughts coincide with the physical presence of that person. Because the spirit world is comprised primarily of thought, it is possible that our thoughts in the physical realm can intersect it. Taking into account the unity and limitlessness of the universe, we are, in actuality, one with all consciousness and can readily communicate with other planes of existence besides the one we live on.

In fact, most ADC's could not take place without understanding synchronicity. If one's belief system does not allow for the possibility of communication except by known physical laws, a meaningful communication from nonphysical reality cannot take place. For those who do believe, synchronicity opens the door for them to touch the hearts and minds of those in spirit.

For example, imagine you are driving to your mother's house one afternoon and you begin thinking about your dad who is in spirit. Fond memories of your childhood, favorite activities and family get-togethers fill your mind as you drive. You feel your heart expand with the remembrance of your dad's love for you, and you for him. You pull up to a stoplight and notice the license plate of the car ahead of you, which just happens to spell out your dad's first name. A smile instantly lights your face as you realize this is a special gift from your dad–a magical moment suspended in time.

An intense desire to hear from loved ones in spirit can be answered by a synchronistic event, which can help immensely in letting go and coming to peace with their passing. I was missing my mother last year, right before Mother's Day. One evening around that time, I read my emails, one of which contained a photo my dad had taken of flowers he put on my mother's grave. I noticed that nestled in the beautiful flower arrangement was a large, artificial blue butterfly–the same shade as the one I use as a logo on my business cards. I asked Dad if he had chosen that specific butterfly to add to the arrangement. Turns out, he'd asked the flower shop to put a butterfly in it and had made no special request about its color. To me, it was a distinct message from my mom letting me know she was with me.

Dream Contact

In group sessions, I frequently ask if anyone has had dreams of loved ones in spirit; usually, at least half the audience raises their hands. During sleep, we are especially receptive to messages from spirit and our intuition because our rational brain is temporarily resting. It's the easiest and most efficient way for loved ones to connect with us because of our lack of resistance to and judgment of the experience. When we sleep, a part of our being called the astral body temporarily disengages (although it remains attached) from our physical body and travels to the astral world. There, we can work on stresses and challenges (often of an emotional nature) that we face in daily life. While in the astral world, we can also visit with those who reside there, such as deceased loved ones, pets and spirit guides. Although we may not remember these visits, we nonetheless travel there every night. Before waking, the astral body reconnects and realigns itself with the physical body. Normally, we remain unaware that we've traveled the equivalent of great distances and visited with others while we were asleep, unless this information is transferred into our long-term memory where we can retrieve it upon waking.

In dreams where we encounter departed loved ones, it is possible and quite likely that nothing is directly communicated except the deceased person's presence. Concerned that there must be an important or urgent meaning to the dream, people who have had dream contacts say, "Dad didn't say anything to me in my dream! He just stood there looking at me. The funny thing was, he looked like I remember him as a kid – not at all like he looked when he died from cancer. What was he trying to tell me?" My response is, "He's telling you he's still around and to not worry about him because he's at peace. He's survived death and he's no longer sick. He wants you to know he's still with you in spirit." That's a profound message in itself, without need of words.

Many people who have had these types of dreams question whether they were having actual visitations or merely remembering loved ones as they were in life. Generally, if the dream *felt* real, then chances are it was a visitation. In fact, many people admit that the one striking quality of the dream was that it felt as if the person was really there with them.

Less than a year after my mother died, I had a dream in which my father's mother who died in 1978 came to see me. She clearly appeared but said nothing. In the dream, I said to her through telepathy, "Grandma! Grandma! It's really you after all of these years!" I had never dreamt of her before then and couldn't imagine why she would come to me now, even though we'd been close. When I woke, tears were streaming down my face. I felt as if she was still in the room because her presence was so palpable. An overwhelming sense of love from the dream stayed with me the rest of the day. Soon after, I became concerned that my grandmother had come as a sign that someone else in the family was going to pass, since Mom's mother and father had appeared to me shortly before her death. Frantic, I called my friend Wendy (also a medium) to ask for her interpretation of my dream. I also shared my fear about another family member dying. She immediately assured me that my grandmother had simply come to let me know she loved me. When I hung up, I breathed a sigh of relief and said a silent prayer of thanks for the visit.

Loved ones also communicate information to the dreamer about other family members and friends. People have told me of having dreams in which a deceased relative gave them prophecy of births, deaths, health conditions and other important information. This type of dream contact usually comes to the individual in the family who is the most open to receiving it; these are often people who are aware of or have developed their intuition. I believe the transmission of information about future events is meant to help people cope with or prepare for major life changes.

Joyce, who attended a group program, asked why her husband dreamt of receiving a phone call from his deceased father in which he clearly gave information about the health of living family members. I explained to her that the phone was a symbolic way for her father-in-law to come through and deliver messages to his son because spirits will make use of the most effective and identifiable imagery to reach us. In this case, the phone call symbolized a direct link between the spirit world and earth.

Dream contacts can also serve as warnings about possible dangers that may be encountered by the living. Chris, who is highly intuitive, consistently receives dreams about her daughter, Missy, (living) from her deceased grandmother, to whom she was very close. According to Chris, the dream messages are often of a protective nature, such as the one in which she was warned about the potential hazards of Missy going swimming on a particular day. Chris always heeds these messages of concern from her grandmother and trusts that they are meant to protect her and her daughter.

Dreams influence healing during grief by providing a connecting link to loved ones who show people firsthand that they are alive and well in spirit, as well as giving them reassurance to go on with their lives. Dottie, who was overwhelmed with grief after the passing of her partner, Bob, who died unexpectedly from a heart attack, told me about a dream she had about a year after his passing. In the dream, she found herself sitting with Bob and two other men she didn't recognize in a beautiful, wooded setting at a picnic table. At some point in the dream, Dottie felt as if she didn't want to ever leave Bob or the serenity of this peaceful place. All of a sudden, the two men began repeatedly asking Bob what Dottie was doing there and admonishing him that she didn't belong with them. She woke with the strong realization that she must go on with her life because it was definitely not her time to pass.

Inspiration

In addition to physical signs and dreams, spirit beings come to us through inspiration. In their desire to help us, loved ones will impress their thoughts on ours. This form of contact is often subtle and feels as if it originates from our own thoughts, yet it is actually loved ones and spirit guides reaching out to us. Inspirational thoughts are loving in nature and usually offer guidance and direction for our life issues or challenges. Ideas or solutions to problems that come to us suddenly, like a light bulb turning on, are frequently heavenly messages meant to lead us down the right pathway that may be temporarily obscured from our sight by our own ego.

I've done readings in which spirits will impart to sitters that they inspired someone on earth to give a particular gift that was really from them. This can be anything from flowers for a surviving spouse to toys for grandchildren from a departed grandparent. People validate these messages by confirming they did indeed receive the item mentioned. Although some people may find it hard to believe, it is nonetheless true that loved ones in spirit are around us constantly and want us to know that. In this sense, they act as spiritual guides who give us a larger perspective than we are able to see on our own. Loved ones are capable of giving guidance from only their level of spiritual consciousness and knowledge. In this way, they differ from other spirit guides and angels, who often have a more elevated perspective. Please note this doesn't mean their inspiration is superior but different in the sense that spirit guides provide a more universal perspective from their familiarity with our divine life mission and purpose.

At times, loved ones will inspire us to help others by sharing with them how we've healed from the tragic events of their passing. The following story is an illustration of this:

Michelle came for a reading in which she wanted to know who murdered her only son, David, (24 at the time of his death) seven years ago. Despite being unable to connect with him directly, I intuited that Michelle was being urged by her son through inspiration to help other people – particularly parents who had lost children to violence – by sharing with them the tragedy of his death. I also felt that his absence from the reading was a strong sign that he'd moved on from the unfortunate circumstances of his passing and wanted his mother to do the same thing.

"Your son is not here but I am being given the strong impression by your spirit guides that he wants you to work with others who have lost children through violent crimes. I am being shown that you need to contact organizations that help parents who have gone through what you've experienced with your son's murder. You could really help them by sharing your story and how you've coped with enormous grief from this tragedy. Please consider it," I advised her.

I could tell this was not what Michelle wanted to hear. Disappointed that her son hadn't come through, she replied, "I've been to three other mediums and my son never comes through. I just don't understand why! Does he not want to talk to me anymore? Why won't he say who killed him? Why won't he come through?" she asked desperately.

"I don't know why for sure," I answered. "I feel it's because he's moved on from the trauma of the way he died and wants you to do the same by helping others. Your son is free in spirit and certainly wouldn't want you to stay stuck, now would he?"

A moment of silence passed before Michelle spoke.

"I'm already doing what you said. I had gotten the idea to speak to small groups about David's death. It's funny but sometimes when I'm talking, it's not coming from me. I don't know where the words are coming from but I know it's not from me."

I felt strongly that David was helping his mother by inspiring her with what to say. I assured her of this. "He wants you and others to know that his death wasn't in vain. He is helping you to help others heal from tragedy. His thoughts are his gift to you to help others."

I sensed that Michelle still didn't grasp the depth of the connection she shared with her son in spirit. Just before she left, I told her that she was doing exactly what she needed to be doing to help both David and her. She seemed to accept this, although she admitted she was still upset that he hadn't communicated in the reading. I explained to her that sometimes the karma of an unresolved murder must be worked out in ways that we don't understand. Our task is to move forward spiritually as best we can by practicing forgiveness. If we don't, we remain stuck in a quagmire of anger, resentment and blame. We are here on earth to learn from our experiences, both good and bad. Miraculously, the power of love heals all wounds.

CHAPTER TEN

LETTING GO AND MOVING ON: TOOLS FOR HEALING GRIEF

Only in the agony of parting do we look into the depths of love.
-George Eliot

From the minute I saw her as a pup, I knew Emma – a red, short-haired, miniature dachshund – and I were meant for one another. Precious and tiny at six weeks of age, she could easily fit into my palm. As she grew, our relationship became like mother and child, with Emma routinely sleeping in my bed, sitting on my lap and shoulders and wearing sweaters on her small body. When she was about seven years old, this happy picture suddenly changed when Emma was diagnosed with a serious and chronic breathing condition similar to cystic fibrosis. At first, the illness was kept under control by daily doses of oral steroids and antibiotics. After several years, the pills lost their effect and the vet recommended that the steroids be given by injection. Determined to do anything to keep Emma alive and breathing comfortably, I complied.

For the next five years, I took her to the vet's office at least once a month, sometimes more often. The injections worked for a short time then Emma's breathing would again become labored. Each time I went, the vet gently reminded me that Emma's medication would eventually harm her body in other ways such as damaging her kidneys or liver. It soon became evident that she could not live comfortably with a reasonable quality of life regardless of the medication. I knew the time was fast approaching to let her go, yet I remained in denial of the facts because I did not want to deal with her death. I could see that she wasn't getting better but I hung on in hopes that by some miracle, she would be well again.

Shortly after the Christmas holidays, I knew something had to be done soon. The shots were no longer working and Emma was struggling to breathe. Often, I was up at night with her as she wheezed and gasped. The vet told me there was nothing else that could be done. *This can't be happening,* I thought. It was hard to imagine my life without her. Yet I realized I must face the facts. With much resignation, I made the painful decision to end her life with euthanasia and set up the appointment.

In the next week or so, I changed my mind a few times when I thought I saw some improvement in her condition. *Maybe I can try a different medicine that will work*, I thought optimistically. I rolled the possibility around in my mind, forgetting that I had enough drugs prescribed for her in my house to open my own pharmacy. *I haven't done enough to help her,* a guilty-sounding voice in my head nagged. Two days before the appointment, Emma had a near fatal choking attack while eating and fell over in the kitchen, gasping. After this ordeal, which she thankfully survived, there was not a shadow of a doubt in my mind that my original decision was the right one.

From the time I made the appointment, I began to grieve. For more than 12 years, Emma and I had shared a loving companionship that was as deep and fulfilling as any. *How could I ever get over losing her?* I wondered. *Who will take care of her on the other side?* I frantically called on my spirit guides and my mother to help her cross over when the time came so she wouldn't be disoriented in making the transition. My mind was filled with the anguish of losing her and she wasn't even gone yet. I felt helpless and weak. Then I became angry. As illogical as it sounds, I was angry at anyone in my past who had ever hurt me in any way. *Life is unfair! Why does this have to happen to me when there are others who deserve to hurt?* I railed. *I hate so and so for hurting me.* That lasted for two days or so until a bleak, penetrating sadness replaced the anger on the day of the appointment.

After our final goodbyes, Emma peacefully and painlessly slipped away on the vet's table, resting on her favorite blanket with prints of bright, yellow ducklings on it. When I returned home, I could not bear to look at her food bowl, the chew bones she had so dearly loved that lay on the floor or the small plush toys she had enjoyed in better days. I felt enormously guilty for ending her life. The emotional pain was searing. My chest felt extremely tight; my heart ached with grief. I cried for three days off and on. Physically, I felt heavy and tired. Each night I prayed and asked for Emma to come back to me in my dreams. When that didn't happen immediately, I became sullen and disappointed. I resigned myself to the fact that she was gone.

In an effort to feel close to her every night, I framed a photo of Emma and set it on my nightstand. Having her image nearby soothed the rawness of my grief over losing her. I gathered items of hers – a small tee shirt, a plush hotdog and her current dog license – and put them together with photos to make an altar in her memory. The activity brought me relief and comfort.

In the next several weeks, a turning point occurred when I had a striking and vivid dream of Emma in which she appeared to be healthy, robust and young again. Her previously dull, red coat was bright and shiny. *Emma! You've come back!* I was overwhelmed with joy at our reunion. As I bent down to pick her up as I had always done, she suddenly began to shake off a thick layer of mud that was caked on her. Then I woke up. I could still feel her presence with me. I lay awake for over an hour in the darkness, going over details of the dream. I realized the mud was symbolic of all of the medication Emma had been on the last five years. Through the action of her shaking the mud off and by her healthy appearance, she was showing me that she was now free and whole again in spirit. My grief began to subside.

In the weeks since Emma's passing, I have gradually come to accept her death. Because of the dream, I know she lives on. My perspective has shifted away from loss towards gratitude with the realization that I enjoyed 12 years with an unconditionally loving companion. I give thanks for all I learned from her, not the least of which was compassion. Despite her death, she will forever remain in my heart.

I am sharing this personal story of loss and healing because it is still very poignant and fresh in my mind. Even if you can't identify with the circumstance of losing a pet, you have undoubtedly experienced some of these same feelings when you have lost someone you've loved.

An Individual Process

Grief is a natural human reaction to loss and a result of our having loved someone or something. No two people experience it in the same way. The time it takes to grieve is unique for each individual and is affected by factors such as the closeness of the relationship with the deceased, social/emotional support systems and spiritual beliefs. If you have lost a loved one, including a beloved pet, there is certainly no wrong or right way for you to grieve. I encourage you to do whatever feels most comfortable and helps your heart to heal during this difficult time. Crying, talking about your loved one to family or friends, and reliving cherished memories are natural ways to express your grief and overcome sorrow.

It is normal to experience a full range of emotions during grief—sadness, fear, anger, guilt, abandonment and loneliness. The intensity of these emotions often fluctuates following the death of a loved one; in other words, we deal with loss better at some times than others. We've all heard someone say that they have "good" days and "bad" days while in grief. Most people go through initial stages of shock and denial when someone close to them dies. Some become immersed in depression, which makes it difficult to move beyond grief. Depending on the circumstances and the person, it may take weeks, months or years to come to the final stage of acceptance of a loved one's death.

Grief can also create physical symptoms, such as sleep distur- bances (too little or too much), changes in appetite, fatigue, lethargy and muscle aches. Some people describe a hollow ache in their chest or a constant, dull headache. When I was grieving over Emma, I slept more than usual. At times, I felt dizzy and weak. I also suffered a back injury that nearly incapacitated me for several days. Physical symptoms of grief usually subside in a relatively short period of time compared to the emotional ones that frequently linger much longer.

It's vital to realize that the length of time we spend grieving for others is not a measure of the amount of love we had (or have) for them. Releasing the pain of loved ones' deaths does not mean we are also letting go of them. No matter how many years pass from the time of death, our hearts recall the love and relationships that we shared with them. When you are grieving, don't compare yourself to others as far as the length of time it takes. Know that your process is right for you by trusting that each tear you shed is part of your healing. Do not feel awkward or apologize for your feelings, because this is a form of denial that will hinder you in your progress. Allow yourself to experience *all* of your feelings.

Because the grieving period following a loved one's passing is confusing and emotionally overwhelming, we need support from family and friends. In the event that this isn't enough, we can choose to see a psychotherapist or join a grief support group. Grief is definitely not the time to be alone; we feel better and heal more quickly when we are connected to others who understand and help nurture us. We need the comforting reassurance of a shoulder to cry on, a hug or a hand to hold. If our loss is unexpected and devastating, like a murder, accident or suicide, we may temporarily require help with basic things like meal preparation, household chores and running errands. The important thing to remember is to reach out for the company of others. Friends and family who genuinely love us give us the time and space we need to heal.

Our Spiritual Beliefs Affect How We Grieve

Death causes us to question the purpose and meaning of life. As we turn inward to cope with feelings of grief, we look to our spiritual beliefs to give us peace of mind and emotional comfort. These beliefs directly determine how easily we come to terms with death and how smoothly we move through grief. For example, if we believe that our soul lives on after death, we're likely to move through grief more easily than if we believe that death is the final end of our being. Likewise, if we believe that God is compassionate, loving and forgiving as opposed to punishing, we are more apt to understand that our loved one is safe and at peace in spirit. In my career, I've not encountered a single person who isn't in some way affected spiritually when confronted with the loss of a loved one. The death of someone close to us reminds us that earth is our temporary home and someday we, too, will make the transition back into spirit. Death can also serve as a wake-up call for us to reflect on our lives and make needed changes, such as taking necessary steps to forgive, release the past or appreciate all of our relationships—including the one we shared with the deceased. It can likewise be a catalyst in expanding our awareness of our divine mission. I've had the rewarding experience of seeing many people's grief transform into peace and acceptance through their willingness to open up their spiritual vision by coming for a reading.

The unpredictability and certainty of death is a fervent reminder that all we truly have is the present moment—not the past or the future. At the close of my group mediumship programs, I frequently suggest that people honor the here and now of their lives and let go of all worries. I also recommend that it's a good idea to improve the quality of our relationships today. Even though it is possible to communicate with the spirit world, why wait until loved ones pass to tell them how we feel?

The Importance of Feelings

I consistently see people display a gamut of emotions during the process of grieving over a loved one's passing into spirit. If these feelings are submerged and not expressed openly during the grieving process, we remain trapped in the pain of loss and cannot properly heal. Because recognizing and expressing feelings is so crucial during the grieving process, it is helpful to examine each separately. (These are arranged in no particular order. Since each person's grieving process is unique, some or all of these emotions may be experienced.)

Sadness

A common reaction to death is sadness resulting from loss. We replay memories of our loved one's life and how it intermingled with and touched ours. If we are grieving an especially close relationship like a parent, spouse or child, we feel as if a part of us has died with the person. We grieve for what was, and perhaps what could have been, should that person have lived. We feel let down, tired or emotionally drained, as if the life has been drawn out of us, too. Physically, our heart feels heavy and our chest may ache.

These feelings can continue indefinitely and come up at the most unexpected times, even occurring long after we've moved through most of our grief. People, places and events can trigger a reoccurrence of sadness at any time. Typically, people re-experience sadness during a holiday season and on special occasions related to their loved ones, like birthdays, anniversaries or family gatherings. Often these feelings are bittersweet. About a year after my mother passed, I was watching TV at Christmastime (also the time of my birthday) and a commercial came on advertising a specially designed cake pan. A young boy, about five years old, sat at the kitchen table while his mother mixed a cake in the pan. Immediately, my mind went back to all of the cakes my mother baked for our family–a favorite pastime of hers. When I was still living at home, every birthday was celebrated with one of her homemade cakes. Although I'd been fine emotionally before I saw the commercial, a wave of sadness suddenly swept over me. In five seconds flat, I was back in my childhood re-experiencing the love my mother expressed through her baking. When the commercial was over, I managed to pull my thoughts back to the present moment—somewhat surprised at my reaction, yet grateful for the recollection of cherished memories.

Familiar places that we shared or visited with loved ones can also trigger sadness. Many clients who grieve loved ones that they've lived with have told me that they are unable to spend large amounts of time at home after the passing. Some won't return to familiar vacation or recreational spots because of associated memories. On the contrary, some people receive emotional comfort from staying in the same house or leaving their loved one's room and belongings relatively untouched long after their passing. They gain comfort and solace from the stability of their loved one's material possessions. In my experience, this happens most often when a person is grieving the loss of a child who passes at a relatively young age. Such was the case with Diana and Bill, who felt that by keeping their daughter Ariel's (who passed from cancer) room exactly as it had been before her passing, they could keep her memory alive. Diana spent many hours in Ariel's room, touching her stuffed animal collection, gazing at photographs on her mirror and going through the clothes in her closet. These activities brought her comfort by making her feel closer to her daughter.

It is normal and healthy to feel sadness when we grieve but not to the extent that it becomes depression, which makes us feel useless and hopeless. Feeling "down" is a normal reaction to loss but experiencing lows to the point of not wanting to go on with life is not. A primary indication of depression is loss of interest in life's usual activities, including disruptions in sleeping and eating habits and rejection of family and social connections. A person may also feel extreme fatigue and isolation. It is imperative to seek help immediately by contacting a mental health clinic in your phone directory, through the recommendation of your family physician or by personal referral from a friend if you or a family member is depressed.

Fear

The opposite of love is not hate; it is fear. It is the basis and root cause of all painful emotions, in addition to being the number one enemy of peace, forgiveness and ultimately, all spiritual healing. In the case of death, fear is frequently generated from a person's ignorance of what happens when we die and from religious conditioning that presents God in a vengeful or punishing light. Fear causes people to lack faith in the supreme power of God's ever-present love for us. As a result, people remain stuck in grief, refusing to see the light of healing and hope that is buried beneath the heavy wall of fear they have constructed.

People may also fear the uncertainty of their life without a loved one and the fate of their loved one after death. Both of these are healed through knowledge of and belief in the continuity of life, despite the illusion of death. When healing fear, we must come to a reckoning that no matter what, we will go on with our life, survive the pain of our loss, and grow spiritually from having experienced it. This does not mean that we will ever fully recover from the passing of a loved one; certainly we will never be the same; rather, it means that we trust in the healing power of love–the strongest force in the universe.

I've seen clients who can't bear to face the future after losing someone. Once they work through their initial layers of grief, however, they are able to move beyond their fear and face life with renewed confidence. I've also seen how death serves to enhance their spiritual growth, enabling them to grow in ways that would not have been otherwise possible.

The soul's true essence is love, which survives death. Fear is alleviated through understanding that we, as divine beings, don't die, we merely shed our physical body when it's time to return to spirit. Nor do we face judgment by anyone other than ourselves. We are always given the opportunity in spirit to heal and continue our growth in various ways.

Fear is an illusion that becomes stronger the longer we focus on it. Since we possess free will, we can choose to believe whatever we want, although we are always responsible for the consequences. What we spend time thinking about often becomes more real in one way or another. Focusing on love is the most potent antidote to fear.

Anger and Guilt

I have included these two emotions in one section because they are frequently experienced simultaneously and are related to one another. They occur when we feel cheated, caught off guard, frustrated or helpless in the event of a loved one's death. The normal reaction to these circumstances is anger and guilt. Women, in particularly, have a difficult time with anger because they are often taught it is not socially acceptable to express it. Unfortunately, this tendency to submerge anger leads to an increased risk of depression. Because of cultural conditioning, many women feel guilty for being angry and therefore have to work through both feelings at the same time. Although challenging, it is a necessity to do so in order to move ahead. Supportive discussion and therapy groups that encourage women to freely express their emotions are extremely helpful in these instances.

Some people are angry at the unpredictability of death and feel robbed of precious time with a loved one. Frustration stems from the inability to prevent death from occurring in the first place. In other cases, anger is directed at the one who died and circumstances surrounding the passing. This is especially true in the event of suicidal or accidental deaths. For example, several families I've done readings for harbored anger towards their children who died from drug overdoses. Angry at the helplessness they felt in the face of drug addiction and their children's repeated refusals to seek help, they struggled with the process of forgiving themselves for believing they could have done something to prevent the death. In the face of such tragic circumstances, they had to meet the challenge of forgiving their children for being sick with an addiction. It's completely normal to be angry in circumstances where we feel out of control. Yet rarely, despite our best efforts and intentions, can we control another's passing. It is erroneous, even egotistical, to believe we have enough power to do so. This does not mean that we sit by and uncaringly do nothing in the event of someone's suffering. What it means is that we work through feelings of anger that arise from feeling helpless, thus allowing our hearts to heal. Understanding the mindset and emotions of a loved one who died from suicide or addiction enables us to transcend anger and forgive.

However irrational it may be, guilt originates from our sense of wrongdoing in regard to the circumstances of another's passing or due to the nature of the relationship we shared. In the first case, we may feel as if we didn't make enough effort to prevent the passing from occurring. Again, this is common with, but not limited to, unexpected or tragic passings.

Gloria, 56, came for a reading in which she desired to connect with her daughter who died in a car accident several years ago. When her daughter, Gail, came through, she communicated to her mother about releasing guilt for not being able to prevent the accident. Gloria cried as she admitted that she felt guilty for not keeping Gail at her house longer after visiting on the evening of the accident so that on the way home, she wouldn't have encountered the truck that slammed into her car, killing her instantly. Although she knew it was irrational, Gloria felt as if she should or could have done something to prevent the accident. During the reading, it was clear that Gloria desperately needed to hear Gail tell her to relinquish the long-held guilt that prevented her from healing. Afterwards, she felt at peace knowing she didn't have to carry this burden any longer because she realized she was not at all responsible for her daughter's passing.

As you've seen, loved ones in spirit can facilitate forgiveness for unfinished emotional business in a relationship. An example of this is a person who didn't have the chance to make amends after an estrangement or argument with a loved one who passes. Wracked by guilt, clients who have come for readings in these circumstances express immense relief when their loved one communicates forgiveness from beyond the veil of death. Months, sometimes years, of anger and guilt dissolve in minutes. Lifting the heavy burden of guilt enables both parties to move on with their lives.

Abandonment and Loneliness

If we fail to understand that we are still connected through the bond of love after death, we experience abandonment and loneliness. The life we once knew has suddenly disintegrated, leaving us feeling isolated and vulnerable. It's as if a promise of peace, safety and serenity has been broken. We feel useless and disconnected from our purpose in life. In my readings with Annie (see Chapter Two), she felt as if her husband, Jim, had deserted her and her daughter Amie when he died. Because they had been together since childhood, she always assumed they would grow old together. Although she repeatedly spoke about her love for Jim and her best intentions for his journey in spirit, Annie admitted feeling a deep sense of abandonment when faced with the prospects of going on without him. For a long while, she could not see the light at the end of the tunnel. In one reading during a particularly rough time for Annie, she asked Jim (through me) if they would be together after she died. He assured her they would but that it was not yet her time to cross. After several readings and regular counseling, she began to comprehend that Jim was still with her in spirit through the indestructible bond of love.

With understanding and acceptance of the eternity of our spirit, we heal feelings of abandonment. If we not only believe but also *know* in our minds and hearts that consciousness continues after physical death, there is no reason to feel separation or loneliness. Although we may miss being together with a loved one physically, the thoughts, feelings and memories of our relationship assuredly survive death and are sometimes our only comfort. After sessions, I make a point of telling clients that they can connect with loved ones in spirit by thinking of them and by sending love and good intentions for their continued happiness. I've also suggested that they keep photos and cherished objects nearby since these strengthen the shared heart bond. As you've seen in Part Two, spirit beings make reference to specific photos, objects or pieces of clothing that were theirs on earth and how a loved one on earth recently looked at, held or wore these things. In my experience, spirits sense our continued connection with these items because of the love associated with them and understand that it's a tangible way for us to affirm our love for them.

In healing loneliness, it's necessary to establish and maintain supportive, nurturing family ties and friendships. For those who survive a sudden or unexpected passing of a loved one, it is vitally important. People who've experienced this have told me that if it were not for others' support, they would have collapsed under the immense strain of shock and grief. I've also heard people complain that they receive support from family and friends immediately after a loved one's passing but not in the following months. Love, friendship, and support are indispensable, especially during grief. I've recommended to many people that they join grief support groups (organized through local grief or mental health organizations) to ease loneliness. (See the resource section of this book.) The unity and support of these groups facilitate profound healing by providing opportunities to interact with others who share common circumstances.

Volunteering is another way of staying connected to community and a sense of purpose. When we help others, we have less time to dwell on feeling disconnected. There is a slogan that 12-step organizations use: "In order to keep it (love, peace, healing), we must give it away." This can also be applied in the case of healing grief since any activity that we do to help others ultimately helps us.

What Can I do to Feel Better?

Unfortunately, there is no magical wand that will instantly cure grief. The bottom line to healing is finding peace with your feelings of loss and growing spiritually from the awareness of your life purpose. With this in mind, I've found that certain activities can greatly assist in this process by re-establishing connections with your personal (the relationship you shared with your loved one) and your spiritual (the relationship you have with your Higher Self or God) identities. I've divided these activities into categories of "Doing" and "Being." These exercises will help you during the grieving process, especially with the exploration of your feelings.

Doing

Writing a letter to loved ones in spirit can be invaluable in clarifying and expressing feelings about your relationship with them.

This helps to make closure by putting your feelings in words, thereby making them real. The letter can address any aspect of your relationship and be any length, as long as it puts you in touch with your feelings. When I teach workshops on healing grief, I suggest that participants bring photos of loved ones to whom they'll be writing. Because it is visible and tangible, a photo promotes a more complete connection with those in spirit. Before and during your writing, look into the eyes of the person in the photo and see if you can make a soul connection. Imagine that you are speaking to this person for as long as you need to.

Before beginning, ask yourself, *If this person were here right now, what would I say to him? What are my deepest feelings about the relationship we shared? What important lessons did I learn?* The more specific you are in expressing your feelings, the better. Also, keep in mind that if you are writing your letter to someone with whom you had a painful relationship, you will need to get in touch with unresolved feelings like anger, guilt or remorse. This may take several attempts. Don't judge yourself for feeling what you do and remember, no one but you will read your letter.

When you are finished, you can either save the letter or destroy it. It can be placed with other items of your loved one's memorabilia if you want. If the relationship you are addressing has been a difficult or painful one, you may want to burn your letter as a symbolic gesture of releasing the past and embracing forgiveness.

Another way that photos can be used is in the creation of montages. Popularly used at funeral homes and memorial services, these displays capture precious moments in time with loved ones. They can also be hung at home or placed on altars. In some cases, a photo is all a person has to remember the deceased. Even so, it can be a valuable healing tool.

Laura came for a reading in which she sought contact with a friend from many years ago who had recently died. The relationship was unresolved due to lack of closure after an argument. I tried unsuccessfully to connect with this friend. Laura pulled a photo from an envelope in her purse and told me it was the only one she had of this man whom she hadn't seen in years. I suggested she use the photo to send love and healing to her friend in spirit since he would certainly receive it on a soul level. At the same time, she would assure her own peace of mind by releasing the pain she had carried for many years. She left the session feeling much lighter knowing that she could finally take action to heal the open wounds of the past.

Constructing altars for loved ones is a good way to keep memories alive through physical objects. This simply entails gathering specific items that were special to loved ones and arranging them in an area of your home or on the gravesite. Next to where my mother is buried are the graves of two young people who both died in their late teens. One day while visiting my mom's grave, I was surprised to see that an array of items had been placed by their headstones, including teddy bears, magnets and various stones with inscriptions on them. Obviously this young man and woman are loved very much.

Although it may seem strange, after my mother died I saved a bottle of her face cream and placed it next to an old, metal music box that I inherited from her. More than once, it's brought me comfort to look at it and remember her using it.

An altar is a way to honor those who have touched our hearts and lives. Recently I read in my local newspaper about a woman who designs "care bears" from items like blankets, quilts and bathrobes of deceased loved ones. The surviving loved ones who receive these stuffed bears cherish them because they are directly connected to those in spirit.

Rituals — customs, ceremonies or traditions that help to commemorate loved ones – are other activities that help in healing grief. A funeral is a familiar example of a ritual. Likewise, people who choose to be cremated sometimes leave specific requests for a particular ceremony to be performed in the dispersal of their remains. Linda conducted a ceremony in her late husband's memory when she released his ashes in their annual vacation spot while his favorite song was playing. One family I knew hung an ornament on their Christmas tree each year with their deceased son's name on it as part of their remembrance of him. Sue made her mother's favorite recipe of stuffed cabbage every year on her mother's birthday. Tom's family leaves the chair empty that his grandfather sat in at the table during holiday dinners each year in his memory. Rituals bring us comfort because they give us a sense of stability and comfort through their familiarity. Creation of your own ritual will help you to remember and honor the life of a loved one.

If you are the one who is giving comfort to others who are grieving, take action and offer to do something for them that will help in day-to day living. Preparation of a meal, tending to a garden, running errands or cleaning house are chores that often get neglected when people are grieving. Many people simply need someone to listen to them talk about a departed loved one, which helps release the pain of loss. Don't ever say, "If you need anything, call me," because most people in grief will never pick up the phone to do so. You must be the one to reach out. Your time and talents will help to ease someone's passage in ways you may not even imagine.

Being

Prayer and meditation are indispensable tools in connecting with the divine consciousness that resides within you. In my experience, people who pray and meditate have a much easier time dealing with grief than those who don't. These inner tools provide a sense of peace because they remind us of our inherent connectedness to God and all of life, despite the illusion of loss through death. Becoming aware of and listening to the voice within gives us reassurance that a larger reality than we are consciously aware of exists beyond the physical one. We can gain immeasurable solace from the realization that we are not alone during times of grief — or ever, for that matter.

Besides opening up to love, prayer is the most potent form of healing we can engage in. To pray is to concentrate our thoughts on the highest and best intent for others and ourselves, regardless of what we want or believe to be true or right. In some cases, that may mean we have to let go of our preconceived notions about the situation we're praying about. To do this, we must trust that the best outcome will occur, no matter what it is. *Thy will be done* means exactly that. We release expectations about the time and way the prayer may manifest. Prayer puts us in touch with the healing power of God through the unity of all creation, of which we are part. If you have recently lost a loved one, I suggest that you pray daily for their continued happiness in spirit. Pray to give thanks for the love you've shared and the spiritual gifts you've received from the relationship. This helps make the transition to the spirit world much easier and accelerates our passage through grief.

A simple prayer that I use every day and before I do readings is:

"Infinite Divine Spirit,
Use me as a channel of light, love and healing;
Make me an instrument of your peace today;
I give thanks for the multitude of blessings in my life
    and for the guidance, direction and healing that I receive from your
hands. Amen.

Meditation opens the gateway to the higher reality of our inner guidance and intuition. To do it, we must still the rational mind (the part that is involved in normal waking consciousness) and tune into our inner senses. Meditation restores and maintains harmony in our spiritual, emotional and physical bodies. In addition, it reduces stress, which is a chief reason people get ill. In the grieving process, it can alleviate stress and reduce anxiety by helping us to focus on the present moment instead of the past or future.

Meditation is actually a simple process that many people unintentionally complicate by trying to engage in rigid disciplines that sabotage the desired results. They become intimidated by the idea of having to meditate in special poses or for extraordinarily long lengths of time. I've discovered that keeping meditation as simple as possible is the best approach. When I teach mediumship development, I lead students in short, guided meditations that are usually no longer than 15 minutes. We begin by stating our intent for doing the meditation. For instance, in one exercise, students set out to meet a spirit guide who is working with them; in another, they write a question that they'd like insight about in their lives. Next, I lead the group in calming their minds by having them turn their attention inward, away from the outside world. This is done by simple relaxation techniques such as focusing on the breath, tuning into the chakras (energy centers in the body) or by imagining a wave of soothing light cascading from the head down. Then students mentally "go" to where the meditation is being led. Several minutes later, I slowly guide them back into normal awareness. Afterwards, we write about and discuss our individual experiences. Over the years, I've had great success with teaching this method of meditation that has provided spiritual insight and practical direction for many of my students.

To start your own practice of meditation, choose a time of day or night that you can regularly dedicate to get quiet and go within. It's helpful to do meditation at a consistent time every day so that on a subconscious level you will learn to relax into the process. Choose a place in your home in which you won't be distracted or interrupted and that is conducive to relaxation. Don't make it so comfortable, however, that you fall asleep when meditating. Your goal is to remain alert, yet relaxed and receptive for about 15 minutes.

In the beginning, you may find it best to try shorter periods of time where you are simply focusing on your breath. This helps you keep your thoughts in the present moment and disregard left-brain mind chatter. You can also repeat a word, phrase or sentence silently to still your thoughts. For example, say "Peace is with me now," "I am one with God" or simply "love." If you want, set a specific intent for your meditation by writing it in a journal. After meditation, write down your experiences. Remember, do not diminish the value of your inner journey by feeling as if you are merely imagining what occurs during meditation. Inner experiences, no matter how subtle they may seem, are just as real and valid as outer ones in the physical world. Spirit often comes to us in soft yet perceivable ways that we learn to recognize through repetition and trust.

The two mediations that follow are designed to help you reconnect with loved ones in spirit and with self-healing. Practicing each with an open mind and heart will enable you to reach deep states of relaxation and spiritual insight that are necessary for optimal healing.

Rainbow Bridge Meditation

Begin by imagining a soft, white cloud of light encompassing your entire body. Feel the warmth, safety and security of this light as it pulsates from your head to your feet. Imagine it is cleansing you of all worries, fear and pain. Standing within this light, you become aware of a gentle touch on your shoulder. You turn to greet a radiant, angelic being whose aura shimmers with gold. As your eyes meet hers, you are filled with the realization that this angel has known you all of your life and even before you were born. She slowly reaches out and touches you softly in the heart area. You instantly feel lighter, completely refreshed and free of any painful emotions that have weighed you down. Your mind is free and clear from doubt and fear. Silently, you gladly accept this gift of healing by giving thanks.

The angel has come to accompany you in your healing journey and reaches for your hand as you begin to walk towards a magnificent bridge that comes into view. It glows with a full spectrum of colors that are indescribably breathtaking. There are no colors on earth that equal their vibrancy. Brilliant shades of red, orange, yellow, green, blue and violet emanate from its arch. The angel whispers to you that this is the Rainbow Bridge that connects you to the spirit world where your loved ones reside. As you draw nearer to it, you become aware that you can easily float across it and arrive quickly and safely on the other side where there is a beautiful summer garden for you to enjoy.

You step onto the bridge and feel as if you are being carried from beneath by a strong but gentle force. One of the colors emanating from the bridge surrounds you as you float across. Notice this color and breathe it in. Feel its healing vibration and send it to any areas of your body where there is discomfort or pain. As you continue on your journey across the bridge, you share with the angel any difficult or challenging situations that you are experiencing in life. Now see these through the compassionate eyes of the angel who offers her wisdom about viewing problems as areas of your spiritual growth.

On the other side of the bridge, you step into a lush sanctuary alive with green grass and various brightly colored flowers. Birds are singing sweetly from the tall trees that shade this special place. An air of absolute serenity exists here. Breathe deeply, allowing your inner senses to adjust. Suddenly, you become aware of the presence of loved ones you have known on earth sharing this space with you. They step forward to welcome you to their spirit home. It is a joyful time of reunion as you embrace and walk with them through the garden. Spend a few moments with these kindred spirits, sharing memories and remembering their love.

If there were things left unsaid or there are unresolved feelings between you and your loved ones, take time to communicate these now. Realize that you are touching with one another heart to heart, where all healing begins and ends. Now listen with your inner ear for a special message that they bring to you. Open your heart to receive it.

The angel takes your hand again and leads you and your loved ones back to the bridge. As you turn to them, they tell you there is really no reason to say goodbye since you can return to see them at any time. You are filled with the realization that they have been with you all along and that death has not taken them from you. They are still with you through the bond of love and as close to you as your breath. This feeling gives you great peace as you step onto the bridge to return home to earth.

Slowly float back across the Rainbow Bridge on the wings of the angel. Open your eyes, take a refreshing breath and give thanks for all you have experienced.

Journey to the Temple of Healing

Start by imagining a white column of light that pours down from above your crown and surrounds your body. This light contains everything you could possibly need for your healing and is here for your highest and best good. Breathe in this light and imagine it permeating every organ, tissue and cell of your being.

Slowly and gently, you begin to drift higher and higher in this column of light. Feeling lighter and lighter, you find yourself standing on a gold-paved road with a beautiful, towering temple at the end of it. It is a perfect summer day with a bright, blue sky filled with fluffy, white clouds. You are filled with anticipation and excitement as you walk towards this temple that glistens in the sunlight. There are seven steps, each one a different color, leading to the door of the building. The steps – red, orange, yellow, green, blue, indigo and violet – represent levels of your divine consciousness. Slowly ascend them, noting how each one feels as you rest on it for a moment.

When you reach the top, the door to the temple swings wide open and a kind-hearted man emerges who introduces himself as the temple guardian. He tells you that there are absolutely no limitations in this temple. All things are possible as long as you open your heart and mind to receive them. As you step inside, you are immediately aware of a calm and soothing atmosphere. The man leads you through the stately temple halls into a quiet inner sanctuary where an inviting pool of clear, cool water with special healing qualities bubbles from a natural spring. Drink deeply from the water and feel its refreshing effects in your body.

The guardian ushers you into a room where a comfortable healing table stands in front of an altar. Spirit healers appear from behind a billowy, ethereal curtain to assist you in climbing onto the table where you will receive your healing. Take a moment now to make your requests for specific concerns or issues you may have.

Feel the healers gently touch your head, heart and feet as they channel life-force energy. Notice a wave of invigorating, tingling energy move through your body as it cleanses you of pain, emotional distress and fear. Your energy centers are filled with frequencies of divine light that dispels all negativity. Things that were troubling you automatically dissipate in the power of this light and the love it brings you. Perhaps you become aware of colors that enfold you or angels that come to assist. Simply notice them and open yourself to receive this healing. Give thanks for all you have received as you bask in the glow of feeling loved unconditionally.

Your mind slowly starts to drift back to full awareness. Gently rise from the table and return through the temple to the column of light. Bring your attention back to your body by gently stretching. Move your fingers, legs and toes. Claim and affirm your healing.

Remembering Who You Are

Long ago, you chose to come to earth to remember your true identity as a divine being through the individual expression of your soul. Life offers no guarantees and few certainties, except that we will all return someday to our home in the spirit world. In walking your spiritual pathway, remember that you are never alone because of the loving connection you have with your spirit guides and those who have gone home to the spirit world before you. One day, you will rejoin them with the realization that the illusion of death is temporary and that only love is real. Dying is our awakening to the truth of the splendor and eternity of our soul.

Understand that you create your own life, good or bad, by your thoughts and actions. Accept that you are not a victim of circumstances in life but are in charge of your own destiny and happiness. Honor your individuality by refusing to become ensnared in the trap of conformity and others' belief systems. Stand proudly in your individuality but with the strength of belief in the unity of all people. Your courage and conviction will inspire and encourage others who are seeking the light within.

Trust that your intuition – the quiet voice of wisdom within you – is the compass that guides you on your spiritual journey and consistently directs you towards self-realization. When we embrace our own internal guidance, we are less likely to meet with obstacles that block our progress.

At all times, strive to get in touch with the power of God's love that lives inside of you and use it to make the world better. You have come into life with certain talents, which are expressions of God's light and love as they manifest uniquely in you. Use these gifts to serve others and uplift the planet. Seize the moment to make a positive difference when the opportunity is presented. When you give freely, you are blessed tenfold. Help others to see how their spiritual lights can be used to serve mankind. By lending the comfort and reassurance you've gained in your spiritual journey, you will help to alleviate others' suffering. Love honestly and openly, making each day a new beginning to see divine potential made real through you. May God speed your healing and fill you with love.

RESOURCES

Healing Grief - Groups and Organizations

National Mental Health Association
2001 N. Beauregard St., 12th Floor, Alexandria, VA 22311
800-969-6642; 800-784-2433 to reach a 24-hour crisis center in your area.
http://www.nmha.org

Hospice Foundation of America
1621 Connecticut Ave., NW, Suite 300, Washington, DC 20009
This organization exists to help those who cope personally or professionally with terminal illness, death and the process of grief and bereavement. To locate a hospice in your local area, check the Yellow Pages under "hospice." Call the Hospice Foundation at 800-854-3402.
http://www.hospicefoundation.org

The Compassionate Friends
P.O. Box 3696, Oak Brook, IL 60522-3696.
This national non-profit, self-help, support organization offers friendship, understanding and hope to bereaved parents, grand-parents and siblings. It has local chapters in most states.
877-969-0010
http://www.compassionatefriends.org

American Foundation for Suicide Prevention
120 Wall St., 22nd Floor, New York, NY 10005
To order a listing of support groups in your area: International Headquarters: 888-333-AFSP
http://www.afsp.org

The Association for Pet Loss and Bereavement
P.O. Box 106, Brooklyn, NY 11230
APLB is a nonprofit association of concerned people who are

experienced and knowledgeable in the area of pet loss.
718-382-0690
http://www.aplb.org

Online Sites for Grief Support

Goodgriefresources.com
This website offers one of the most complete collections of grief support resources in one location.

Centeringcorp.com
A web-based support organization that is dedicated to providing education and resources for the bereaved, Centeringcorp offers books for children and adults, videos, cards and workshops for caregivers and families.

Griefnet.org
This site is an Internet community dealing with grief, death and major loss.

Mediumship and Spiritualism

Lilydale Assembly
5 Melrose Park, P.O. Box 248, Lilydale, NY 14752
A community dedicated to the religion of spiritualism, Lilydale offers programs, workshops and healing services to the public.
716-595-8721
http://www.lilydaleassembly.org

National Spiritualist Association of Churches
NSAC is the largest organization for the science, philosophy and religion of modern spiritualism in the world.
General office: NSAC, P.O. Box 217, Lilydale, NY 14752
716-595-2000
http://www.nsac.org

The Association for Research and Enlightenment, Inc. (A.R.E.)
Edgar Cayce, the great healer and seer, founded this nonprofit
organization to research and explore transpersonal subjects.
215 67th St., Virginia Beach, VA 23451
800-333-4499 (U.S.) Int: 757-428-3588
http://www.are-cayce.com

Research on Mediumship and After-Death Experiences

VERITAS
This research program of the department of psychology of the
University of Arizona was created to test the hypothesis that the
consciousness of a person survives physical death.
520-318-0014
http://www.veritas.arizona.edu/

The American Society for Psychical Research, Inc.
Located in New York City, ASPR is the oldest psychical research
organization in the United States.
5 W. 73rd St., New York, NY 10023
212-799-5050
http://www.aspr.com

Surivalafterdeath.org
Dedicated to providing free and easy access to material on
survival after death, this website also offers information on
psychical research.

Recommended Books

*The Afterlife Experiments: Breakthrough Scientific Evidence of Life After
Death* by Gary E.R. Schwartz with William L. Simon. New York:
Simon and Schuster, 2002.

Dare to Be Yourself by Alan Cohen. New York: Ballantine Books,
1994.

Edgar Cayce on Reincarnation by Noel Langley. Virginia Beach, VA: The Association for Research and Enlightenment, 1989.

The Etheric Double: The Health Aura of Man by A.E. Powell. Wheaton, IL: Theosophical Publishing House, 1969.

Extension of Life: Arthur Ford Speaks by Patricia Hayes and Marshall Smith. Roswell, GA: Dimensional Brotherhood Publishing House, 1986.

Journey of Souls: Case Studies of Life Between Lives by Michael Newton, PhD. St. Paul, MN: Llewellyn Publications, 1994.

Many Lives, Many Masters by Brian L. Weiss, MD. New York: Simon and Schuster, 1988.

Spirit Guides by Iris Belhayes with Enid. San Diego, CA: ACS Publications, 1986.

 **Carole J. Obley** is an acclaimed spiritual medium who has delivered thousands of messages from the spirit world to people seeking confirmation of life after death and healing from grief. She has been featured in newspaper articles and speaks on radio and TV. In addition to maintaining a private practice near Pittsburgh, Pa., she travels nationally to present seminars and workshops on mediumship and spiritual development. She may be contacted through her website, **www.soulvisions.net**.

B O O K S

O books
O is a symbol of the world, of oneness and unity. In
different cultures it also means the "eye", symbolizing
knowledge and insight, and in Old English it means "place
of love or home". O books explores the many paths of
understanding which different traditions have developed
down the ages, particularly those today that express
respect for the planet and all of life.

For more information on the full list of over 300 titles
please visit our website
www.O-books.net

SOME RECENT O BOOKS

Advanced Psychic Development

Becky Walsh

Serious as well as popular opinion of psychics and mediums is changing. No longer only gypsy fortune tellers or remote mystics, they are now part of mainstream culture. Here is the guide book for this new generation.

In learning to unlock and use our innate intuitive ability we can become better partners, parents, friends and work colleagues. We become better communicators, and better listeners- both verbal and non-verbal. Expanding psychic ability isn't just about becoming a psychic, whatever that means; it's about reaching your potential, getting in-tune with yourself and being the best person you can be.

There are many psychic development books on the market, but the vast majority are aimed at beginners. This is the psychics' bible, whether you want to tap your intuitive potential for everyday use or whether you are already a professional. The skills detailed in it can transfer to any relationship, any situation. These are not party tricks, they are life skills.

With Advanced Psychic Development, *Becky Walsh has crafted a tutorial for glimpsing 'oneness' from which anyone on a journey of self-discovery might benefit. Punctuated with delightful anecdotes of 'lives-in-progress' and the real-world challenges we all face, this book is a reminder that each of us has the choice to either honour or repress our most authentic human emotions — and that the antidote to fear is always love. Both reflective and practical, it serves as the best friend you may have always wanted, inviting you to 'look in the rear-view mirror' when you most wish to see the truth: 'happiness' is a question of perspective, 'lack' is nothing more than a belief, and — at the quantum level of our existence — everything is energy.*
Max Eames, Psychotherapist and author of *Wealth Mechanic*

978 1 84694 062 0
£9.99

The Art of Being Psychic

June-Elleni Laine

Psychic ability still remains a bit of a mystery to most, and yet we all have the potential to tap into the under-utilized areas of the brain in order to gain access to a world of creativity. Contacting the "creative source" and thinking outside the box of our own limitations in the style of artists as diverse as Da Vinci and Mozart up to Einstein and George Lucas of today, doesn't come easily. However, with the right tools, and a clear sense of purpose, we can develop our ability, learning to enter altered states at will, to produce art that exceeds our normal expectations.

This book shares the enjoyment of psychic art and removes the "Myst" from "Mystic", leaving the "I.C." moments. It offers a new perspective on self-awareness that has the power to liberate the artist within us all. Balancing intuition and logic, right and left-brain thinking, mind, body and spirit, will inevitably strengthen our connection to a source capable of producing much more than anything we already know.

A brilliant book for anyone wishing to develop their intuition, creativity and psychic ability. It is truly wonderful, one of the best books on psychic development that I have read. Fascinating and thought provoking exercises abound and open one up to an awareness of the right/left brain functions and how to balance them. Readers are shown how to access their creative right brain and so tap into their intuitive knowledge and psychic ability, this in turn opens the door to spirit communication. June-Elleni uses examples of her own spiritual awakening to encourage readers to explore their own potential. I have no hesitation in recommending this book, a must for every bookshelf.
Suzanna McInerney - former President, College of Psychic Studies, London

1 905047 54 1
£12.99

Christy's Journey

Peter Jenkins Watson

Christy's Journey introduces readers to reincarnation through the real life story of Christy, who under hypnosis discovers twelve past lives, both male and female, from ancient Rome to Britain, France, Italy, Africa, and America, spending time between lives on the Other Side. The story was transcribed from the recordings of her hypnosis regression sessions with the author.

Her journey begins as a teenage harpist entertaining King Edward I of England. She travels with minstrels but finally settles down as a farmer's wife. Christy's other females were: the leader of a coven, a French missionary, a happy middle-class mother, and a rich but lonely American housewife. Her male lives were: an Italian teenager killed in a brawl, a French boy who died of the plague, an African boy murdered in a raid on his village, a stillborn fetus, a deaf baby who died in his cot, and an army conscript who committed suicide. Finally, 2,000 years ago, a successful sculptor in ancient Rome provides the climax of her life journey.

These stories are vividly described. The author's reflections take Christy's experience to a deep level of understanding, suggestive of reincarnation.

978 1 84694 082 8
£9.99

Gods, Guides and Guardian Angels

Richard Lawrence with **Mark Bennett**

Life. Death. What it means to be human.
Be amazed and inspired by answers to some of the biggest questions you could
ever ask...

Do we live forever?

What's it like on the "other side"?

Can we communicate with the deceased?

Do "Gods" really exist?

Who are the Ascended Masters?

Have guides changed the course of history?

Could a guardian angel save your life?

*In this fascinating book, Gods, Guides and Guardian Angels, author Richard
Lawrence takes us on a joyful and insightful ride into the world of the afterlife,
the reality that there are indeed other intelligences that abound in the Universe,
and the poignant Karmic message that the essence of who we are does go on long
after our physical life has ended on Earth. To be assured that we are not alone in
this awesome personal journey is both comforting... and most certainly,
inspiring..* **Lynne D. Kitei**, M.D., bestselling author of *The Phoenix Lights*

978 1 84694 051 4
£9.99

The Good Remembering

Llyn Roberts

Introduction by NY Times bestselling author **John Perkins**

Through the ages, spiritual teachers, healers and shamans have pointed us towards a world beyond this one; a world of powerful, loving energies, and beings of light. Their voices speak to us, and if we are prepared to listen, they will change our lives and the future of our planet. This inspired rendering of the collective wisdom of these voices draws on native traditions from around the world, offering a message from our ancestors of high caliber inspiration, a beacon lighting the path through changing times.

From the foreword:
These are exciting times to be alive! While it may seem that the world is heading into a state of chaos, a more accurate description would be evolution. Times of evolution, like the birth of a child, are exciting, if not exhilarating. And these are exciting times.

Through my journeys on the human path I have come across many books and sources of information claiming to help lift the veils of illusion and enlighten those who take their message to heart. Some channels and sources of trans-mission seem to convey their message with a touch of static or ego sifting. I have found Llyn's message to be a clear transmission, and although it is important for readers to discern for themselves the relevance of the message, you will find that every word was carefully chosen by the author for relevance, clarity and compassion.
So prepare to lift the veils of illusion as you turn these pages, and as you do, you will learn that you play an essential role in the unfolding of the universe.
Dr Brian Luke Seaward, Ph.D., author of *Stressed is Desserts Spelled Backwards* and other titles, founder of "Inspirations Unlimited" and "The Paramount Wellness Institute" in Boulder, Co.

978 184694 038 5
£7.99

More Adventures in Eternity

Gordon Phinn

Gordon Phinn's first book *Eternal Life* won him a dedicated worldwide following. Adventures in Eternity describes the author's unique explorations and the unfolding of his higher self as his guide's teachings release Gordon from being a grateful disciple to a self-initiated explorer and all-round multi-level shapeshifter through astral plane training. The author is a spiritual counsellor and past-life regression therapist who discovers he can communicate with beings of all statures from ascended masters to 'dead' relatives, as well as revisiting his own past lives and future selves. Our human journey into the unseen dimensions of the planet is mapped with the exploratory joy of the disciple unleashed from the staid solemnities and stale pieties of religion; with delicious irreverence our destiny is unveiled. This book appeals to all those who are intrigued by out-of-body astral travel and near death experiences who want to know more.

A great contribution to the advancement of human Consciousness. It's a treasure trove of afterlife knowledge packaged in a marvellous series of firsthand retrieval and exploration accounts of his, and of some of the many non-physical Helpers and Guides of his acquaintance. Such a rich level of close-up details within these accounts gives readers much deeper insight and understanding into our existence beyond physical reality, and into the activities of our afterlife's inhabitants. I find Gordon's interaction with Higher Self to be very revealing of the nature of our role and purpose within Consciousness. In reading this fascinating and entertaining book readers will come to more clearly understand from a "big-C" Consciousness perspective who and what we human beings truly are.
Bruce Moen, author of *Afterlife Knowledge Guidebook*

978 1 84694 081 1
£11.99

Soul Companions

Karen Sawyer

As our world rapidly moves towards ever greater spiritual, environmental and political challenges there is an urgent need for us to listen to the voices of respected healers, seers, visionaries and shamans whose wisdom, insights and leadership will inspire and guide us to make our planet a healthier, more peaceful and equitable place to live. For over two years, the author met and entered into profound dialogue with such remarkable people.

This unique and important work brings together over 40 of the conversations that took place, revealing that there are many dimensions of existence overlapping and permeating the world as we know it. Every one of us has spirit helpers that can guide, heal and inspire us on our journey through life.

This outstanding and intimate collection includes conversations with renowned teachers Sandra Ingerman, The Barefoot Doctor, R.J Stewart, Robert Moss, Simon Buxton, Denise Linn, Leo Rutherford, William Bloom, Philip Carr-Gomm and Llyn Roberts.

Join Karen Sawyer as she also talks with Elena Avilla, the 'Curandera' or curer from Mexico - Uncle Angaangaq, an Eskimo-Kalaallit Elder from Greenland - Icelandic Druid Jörmundur Ingi - Sami shaman Ailo Gaup from Norway - Rabbi Gershon Winkler, Aboriginal Jewish shaman - Tiokasin Ghosthorse, a member of the Cheyenne River Lakota Nation of South Dakota - Egyptian Sufi, Master Ali Rafea - Andras Corban Arthen, 'Cunningman' of the Glenshire witches in Scotland and many, many more.

This treasure trove of spiritual wisdom will inspire you in your own quest for spirit guide contact with practical 'how to' advice. Learn how to recognise the signs and talk with the spirit beings guiding your life.

Soul Companions is a stunning book. It assembles an amazing collection of interviews with some of the finest and most unusual people from the worlds of alternative thinking and teaching. For anyone interested in the future of human growth and development this is an absolute 'must read'.
John Matthews author of *Walkers Between Worlds*

978 1 84694 060 6
£14.99